*Pocket*

# LON

AA

Published by The Automobile Association,
Fanum House, Basingstoke, Hampshire RG21 2EA

**Editor:** Robert Baker

**Maps:** prepared by the Cartographic Department of the Automobile Association.
Tube Map © London Transport

**Filmsetting by:** Servis Filmsetting Ltd, Manchester

**Printed and bound by:** Grosvenor Press (Portsmouth) Ltd

The contents of this publication are believed correct at the time of printing. Nevertheless the Publishers cannot accept responsibility for errors or omissions, or for changes in details given.

First published 1987
Second edition 1992

**ISBN 0 7490 454 4**

Published by The Automobile Association, Fanum House, Basingstoke, Hampshire RG21 2EA

# Contents

| | |
|---|---|
| inside front cover | **Abbreviations and Symbols** |
| | English, French, German, Italian and Spanish |
| 4 | **About This Book** |
| 5 | **Useful information** |
| 6 | Tourist Information |
| 10 | Accommodation in London |
| 14 | Entertainment |
| 18 | London's Transport |
| 21 | British Rail |
| 22 | Airports |
| 28 | Sightseeing Tours |
| 31 | Shopping in London, Markets |
| 39 | Sport |
| 44 | Pageantry, Ceremonies and Events |
| 55 | **Driving and Parking in London** |
| 68 | **Exhibition Centres** |
| 70 | **Wembley Complex** |
| 75 | **Gazetteer** |
| 109 | **Around the Streets of London** |
| 110 | The Streets and Buildings |
| 121 | The Squares |
| 124 | London's Churches |
| 133 | Statues, Monuments and Plaques |
| 139 | **Thames Bridges** |
| 141 | **The Royal Parks** |
| 148 | **The Public Parks** |
| 153 | **Key Map** |
| 154 | **Central London Map** |
| 166 | **District London Map** |
| 168 | **Street Index** |

# About this Book

**London in your pocket —**
This popular pocket size guidebook is set out in easy-to-use sections, designed to help you to make the most of your visit to London.

**Useful Information**

In planning your trip you may want to obtain as much general information as possible. Here we have researched everything you should want to know, including general tourist information, how to get around the city, sightseeing tours, entertainment, even such detail as the times of Changing the Guard at Buckingham Palace.

**Gazetteer**

All the famous places to visit, listed in alphabetical order throughout. Here we give all the necessary information:- name, address, telephone enquiry number and map location grid reference.

After a brief description of the place of interest we list opening times, admission charge (or free!) and any facilities (such as lectures, guided tours, special exhibitions, etc) available.

**Around the streets of London**

London's history has been preserved in the many fine buildings, churches, squares, monuments, statues, plaques and much else of interest that can be found throughout the capital. Here we give you an insight into London's past and the origins of what makes up the streets of London today.

**London map and Street Index**

The twelve-page central London map and the street index are designed to help you find your way around. Shown on the map are places of interest, car parks, buildings, underground stations etc.

**Opening dates**

The dates quoted in the gazetteer are inclusive, so that Apr-Oct indicates that the establishment is open from the beginning of April to the end of October.

**Donations and Charity Boxes**

Some of the places of interest listed in the book are administered by Charities, Trusts and Associations. They are responsible for carrying out much of the restoration work in order to promote Britain's heritage and rely on public generosity to continue their work. They do not charge for admission, but donations are appreciated.

**Ancient Monuments**

**AM** Ancient Monuments in England are in the care of the Historic Buildings and Monuments Commission for England (popularly known as English Heritage), with the exception of seven properties in and around London which are administered by the Department of the Environment. The address of English Heritage is PO Box 43, Ruislip, Middlesex, HA4 0XW

**The National Trust**

**NT** Indicates properties which are administered by the National Trust for Places of Historic Interest or Natural Beauty, 42 Queen Anne's Gate, London SW1H 9AS.

# USEFUL
# INFORMATION

tourist information, accommodation,
entertainment, transport, shops and markets, sport,
ceremonies, calendar of events, etc.

Pocket Guide to LONDON

# Tourist Information

The London Tourist Board and Convention Bureau (LTB) is the official Tourist Board for London. Full facilities, help and advice from multi-lingual staff on all aspects of tourism, accommodation, theatre and cinema ticket bookings is available.

**Written enquiries to:**
**Correspondence Assistant, Distribution Department,**
**London Tourist Board and Convention Bureau**
26 Grosvenor Gardens, London SW1W 0DU

**Personal callers to:**
**London Tourist Board Tourist Information Centre**
Victoria Station Forecourt SW1.
Open: Easter-Oct, daily 8-8; Nov-Easter, Mon-Sat 8-5, Sun 8-4

**Telephone Information Service (LTB)**
071-730 3488
Open: Mon-Fri 9-6 (automatic queueing system)

**Heathrow (LTB)**
Heathrow Terminals 1, 2, 3, Underground Station Concourse, Heathrow Airport.
Open: daily 8.30-6.30

**Liverpool Street Underground Station (LTB)**
Open: Mon-Sat 9-4.30, Sun 8.30-3.30

**Selfridges (LTB)**
Oxford Street W1 (Basement).
Open during store hours

**Local Tourist Information Centres at:**
**Bloomsbury**
35–36 Woburn Place, WC1
Tel: 071-636 7175

**City of London Information Centre**
St Paul's Churchyard EC4
Tel: 071-606 3030

**Clerkenwell Heritage Centre**
33 St John's Square EC1
Tel: 071-250 1039

**Croydon**
Katharine Street, Croydon, Surrey
Tel: 081-760 5630

**Greenwich**
46 Greenwich Church Street, SE10
Tel: 081-858 6376

**Harrow**
Civic Centre, Station Road, Harrow
Tel: 081-424 1104

**Hillingdon**
Central Library, 14 High Street, Uxbridge
Tel: Uxbridge (0895) 250706

**Hounslow**
Library Centre, The Treaty Centre, Hounslow High Street, Hounslow
Tel: 081-572 8279

**Kingston-upon-Thames**
Heritage Centre, Fairfield West, Kingston-upon-Thames, Surrey
Tel: 081-546 5386

**Lewisham**
Lewisham Library, 366 Lewisham High Street, SE13
Tel: 081-690 8325

**Redbridge**
Town Hall, High Road, Ilford, Essex
Tel: 081-478 3020

**Richmond**
Old Town Hall, Whittaker Avenue, Richmond, Surrey
Tel: 081-940 9125

**Tower Hamlets**
Mayfield House, Cambridge Heath Road, E2
Tel: 081-980 4831

**Twickenham**
The Atrium, Civic Centre, York Street, Twickenham
Tel: 081-891 7272

**The British Travel Centre**
Operated by the British Tourist Authority, British Rail, Roomcentre and American Express, offers a comprehensive tourist service for Great Britain. Services include British Rail ticket bookings, bureau de change, accommodation, theatre, air, coach, sightseeing tours, bookings, etc.

**British Travel Centre (BTA)**
94-12 Lower Regent Street, London SW1
Open: all year Mon-Fri, 9-6.30, Sat, Sun 10-4.
Telephone Information Service 071-730 3400 (Mon-Fri 9-6.30, Sat 10-4)

### Telephones

There are hundreds of public payphones throughout the capital. Most of the traditional red phone boxes have now been replaced by clear glass booths. Additionally, many pubs, restaurants, hotels, post offices, and other places open to the public have payphones which you may use. There are three types of payphone:

**Coin-operated payphones:** dial direct to anywhere in the UK and to all countries to which International Direct Dialling is available. They take 10p, 20p, 50p and £1 coins.

**Phonecard phones** are quickly becoming more widely available. To use these phones you must first buy one of the special cards which are available from post offices and shops displaying the 'Phonecard' sign. You may then make any number of calls up to the value of the card, whenever you wish, without the need for cash but only from special Phonecard phones.

In all cases, instruction on how to use the phones will be clearly displayed by the set.

**Creditcall payphones:** phones that accept Visa, Mastercard, Diners Club, and American Express credit cards have now been installed in the London area and at airports.

Instructions for use are given on notices next to these phones.

Remember, when dialling an Inner London number from Outer London, prefix the number with 071 (for the reverse operation prefix with 081). These numbers should be omitted when dialling a telephone number from within the Inner/Outer London area.

The following telephone numbers can be dialled for telephone assistance:

### Operator

For difficulties in obtaining a dialled number
100 (155 for international calls)

### Directory Enquiries

| | |
|---|---:|
| To find out a London number | 142 |
| To find a number outside London | 192 |
| To find an international number | 153 |

(You will need to give the full name and address)

**Emergency Services**  If you are involved in any serious accident, or if you need the police in an emergency, you should always dial 999 in any telephone box (these calls are free), and ask for Fire, Police or Ambulance. London Transport Police (for reporting thefts and other crimes which take place on London Transport): *tel:* 071-222 5600.

If you are injured and require medical attention in Central London, the following hospitals all have 24-hour casualty departments:

Charing Cross Hospital, Fulham Palace Road, W6
*tel:* 081-846 1234

Guy's Hospital, St Thomas Street, SE1
*tel:* 071-955 5000
Moorfields Eye Hospital, City Road, EC1
*tel:* 071-253 3411
St Bartholomew's Hospital, West Smithfield, EC1
*tel:* 071-601 8888
St George's Hospital, Blackshaw Road, SW17
*tel:* 081-672 1255
St Thomas's Hospital, Lambeth Palace Road, SE1
*tel:* 071-928 9292
University College Hospital, Gower Street, WC1
*tel:* 071-387 9300

Private emergency treatment is available from
Medical Express, 117A Harley Street, W1
*tel:* 071-499 1991 (9am-6pm).

Doctorcall: a private 24-hour visiting doctor service
offering emergency treatment for visitors to London
without a GP is available from: 29 Langton Street,
SW10
*tel:* 081-900 1000

Several chemists have extended opening hours,
and these include:
Boots, Piccadilly Circus, W1 (Mon-Fri 8.30am-8pm,
Sat 9am-8pm)
Boots, 75 Queensway, W2 (daily 9am-10pm)
H D Bliss, 5 Marble Arch, W1 (daily 9am-midnight)

All foreign visitors to Britain can take advantage
of the accident and emergency services of the
National Health Service without charge.

Emergency dental treatment can be obtained, at
a charge, from the Emergency Dental Service,
*tel:* 081-677 8383 (open 24-hours).

**Lost property**  If you lose anything while travelling on buses or
the Underground, you should write or go to the
London Transport Lost Property Office at 200 Baker
Street, NW1, adjoining Baker Street Underground
station. This office is open Monday to Friday,
9.30am-2pm (closed Saturdays and Sundays). (For
Lost Property information *tel:* 071-486 2496.)
For property lost in London taxis or in the street,
report any loss to the nearest police station.
Taxis only: write or go to the Metropolitan Police
Lost Property Office, 15 Penton Street, N1, open
Monday to Friday, 9am-4pm (*tel:* 071-833 0996). It
would be helpful to quote the plate number of the
taxi in which you travelled.
If you lose anything in a store, hotel, airport,
etc., contact the premises in question. Should
property be lost on a train or at a railway station,
contact the arrival/departure station of your
journey.

**Post offices**

In the UK you can buy stamps at post offices and some newsagents. Letters, postcards and small packages can be posted in the hundreds of distinctive red pillar boxes dotted around the capital. Parcels must be posted at post offices. Each district in London has its own chief post office, and there are also many smaller sub offices. The London chief office is in King Edward Street, EC1; it is open for all kinds of postal business on Monday to Friday from 8.30am to 6pm, except on public holidays. The Trafalgar Square post office, 24-28 William IV Street, WC2 (*tel:* 071-930 9580) is open for all kinds of business, Monday-Saturday 8am-8pm. The smaller offices in which to transact your business are often combined with a general shop or newsagent, and are normally open Monday to Friday from 9am to 5.30pm, and on Saturday mornings.

**Banks**

All banks are open between 9.30am and 3.30pm Monday to Friday (3pm in the City), and some now open on Saturday mornings. They are closed on Sundays and public holidays. There are 24-hour banks at Heathrow and Gatwick airports. Most banks now operate a queueing system. When changing foreign currency, banks usually give the best rates at the lowest commission charges. Bureaux de Change are located throughout the capital and are usually open longer hours than banks, in the evenings and at weekends; but check the rates of commission they charge — they can be very high. Wherever you change money or cash cheques, exchange rates and charges should be clearly displayed.

**Public conveniences**

London has a large range of well-signposted public loos, but their opening times are sometimes erratic. New individual coin-in-the-slot, French-style conveniences are being erected in Central London; these cost 10p. There are conveniences in hotels, large stores, pubs, and at stations — but be sure you have plenty of change in advance as charges vary.

**Tipping**

It is customary to tip for the following services: taxi-drivers; porters, doormen, bell-boys, and room-service waiters; tour guides; barbers and hairdressers; cloakroom attendants; and in restaurants, except where the menu specifically says that service is included.

**Foreign Embassies, Consulates and High Commissions**

**Australian High Commission**
Australia House, Strand WC2
Tel: 071-379 4334

**Austrian Embassy and Consular Section**
18 Belgrave Mews West SW1
Tel: 071-235 3731

**Belgian Embassy**
103 Eaton Square SW1
Tel: 071-235 5422

**Canadian High Commission**
Canada House,
Trafalgar Square SW1
Tel: 071-629 9492

**Danish Embassy**
55 Sloane Street SW1
Tel: 071-235 1255

**Finnish Embassy**
32 Grosvenor Gardens SW1
Tel: 071-235 9531

**French Consulate General**
21-23 Cromwell Road SW7
Tel: 071-581 5292

**German Embassy of the Federal Republic of Germany**
23 Belgrave Square SW1
Tel: 071-235 5033

**Greek Consulate General**
1a Holland Park W11
Tel: 071-727 8040

**India High Commissioner**
India House, Aldwych WC2
Tel: 071-836 8484

**Irish Embassy**
17 Grosvenor Place SW1
Tel: 071-235 2171

**Italian Consulate General**
38 Eaton Place SW1
Tel: 071-235 9371

**Japanese Embassy**
101 Piccadilly W1
Tel: 071-465 6500

**Luxembourg Embassy**
27 Wilton Crescent SW1
Tel: 071-235 6961

**Malta High Commission**
16 Kensington Square W8
Tel: 071-938 1712

**Netherlands Embassy**
38 Hyde Park Gate SW7
Tel: 071-584 5040

**New Zealand High Commission**
New Zealand House,
Haymarket SW1
Tel: 071-930 8422

**Norwegian Embassy**
25 Belgrave Square SW1
Tel: 071-235 7151

**Portuguese Embassy**
11 Belgrave Square SW1
Tel: 071-235 5331

**Spanish Consulate General**
20 Draycott Place SW3
Tel: 071-581 5921

**Swedish Embassy**
11 Montagu Place W1
Tel: 071-724 2101

**Swiss Embassy**
16 Montagu Place W1
Tel: 071-723 0701

**United States of America Embassy**
24 Grosvenor Square W1
Tel: 071-499 9000

# Accommodation in London

London offers a wide choice of accommodation, ranging from the luxury hotels of Mayfair to the more modest accommodation around Victoria and Paddington.

## Hotel Booking Service

A provisional bed-booking service for the same or next night is available, to personal callers only, at one of the London Tourist Board and Convention Bureau's four central Information Centres — at Victoria, Liverpool Street and Heathrow Stations, and Selfridges or at the British Travel Centre in Regent Street (see page 6 for addresses and opening hours); you will find all the help you need at these centres. A returnable deposit must be paid when making a reservation there, and this is deducted from your final bill; in addition a small non-returnable booking fee is charged.

The London Tourist Board and Convention Bureau can help with advance hotel booking, by giving at least six weeks written notice to:-

London Tourist Board,
Accommodation Services Department,
26 Grosvenor Gardens SW1 W 0DU

Booking accommodation less than six weeks in advance can be made by telephoning the LTB on 071-824 8844 (credit card holders only).
Listed opposite are brief details of AA Appointed hotels, by Postal District numbers.

KEY   ★   Star classification of AA Appointed hotel
      R   Hotel classified with red stars (considered
          to be outstanding within its star rating)
   Listed Approved hotel
Details of Appointed hotels are in the annual AA
guide *Hotels and Restaurants in Britain*. Details of
Listed hotels are in the AA guide *Bed and Breakfast
in Britain*.

**E1 — Stepney**

| ★★★★ | Tower Thistle | 071-488 4106 |
|---|---|---|

**E18 — South Woodford**

| Listed | Grove Hill | 081-989 3344 |
|---|---|---|

**N8 — Hornsey**

| Listed | Aber | 081-340 2847 |
|---|---|---|

**NW2 — Cricklewood, Willesden**

| Listed | Garth | 081-455 4742 |
|---|---|---|

**NW3 — Hampstead and Swiss Cottage**

| ★★★★ | Holiday Inn, Swiss Cottage | 071-586 5822 |
|---|---|---|
| ★★★ | Charles Bernard | 071-794 0101 |
| ★★★ | Forte Posthouse | 071-794 8121 |
| Listed | Seaford Lodge | 071-722 5032 |

**SE3 — Blackheath**

| ★★ | Bardon Lodge | 081-853 4051 |
|---|---|---|
| Listed | Stonehall House | 081-858 8706 |
| Listed | Vanbrugh | 081-853 5505 |

**SE9 — Eltham**

| Listed | Yardley Court | 081-850 1850 |
|---|---|---|

**SE19 — Norwood**

| Listed | Crystal Palace Tower | 081-653 0176 |
|---|---|---|

**SW1 — West End, Westminster, St James's Park, Victoria Station, Knightsbridge, Lower Regent Street**

| ★★★★★R | Berkeley | 071-235 6000 |
|---|---|---|
| ★★★★★ | Hyatt Carlton Tower | 071-235 5411 |
| ★★★★★ | Hyde Park | 071-235 2000 |
| ★★★★ | Duke's | 071-491 4840 |
| ★★★★ | Forte Crest St James | 071-930 2111 |
| ★★★★R | Goring | 071-834 8211 |
| ★★★★ | Halkin | 071-333 1000 |
| ★★★★ | Stafford | 071-493 0111 |
| ★★★ | Royal Horseguards Thistle | 071-839 3400 |
| ★★★ | Royal Westminster Thistle | 071-834 1821 |
| ★★★ | Rubens | 071-834 6600 |
| ★R | Ebury Court | 071-730 8147 |
| Listed | Belgrave House | 071-828 1563 |
| Listed | Chesham House | 071-730 8513 |
| Listed | Winchester | 071-828 2972 |
| Listed | Windermere | 071-834 5163 |

**SW3 — Chelsea, Brompton**

| ★★★★R | The Capital | 071-589 5171 |
|---|---|---|
| ★★★ | Basil Street | 071-581 3311 |
| Listed | Claverley House | 071-589 8541 |
| Listed | Knightsbridge | 071-589 9271 |

**SW5 — Earl's Court**

| ★★★ | Swallow International | 071-973 1000 |
|---|---|---|

**SW7 — South Kensington**

| ★★★★ | Gloucester | 071-373 6030 |
|---|---|---|
| ★★★ | Rembrandt | 071-589 8100 |
| Listed | Number Eight | 071-370 7516 |

### SW19 — Wimbledon

| | | |
|---|---|---|
| ★★★★ | Cannizaro House | 081-879 1464 |
| Listed | King's Lodge | 081-545 0191 |
| Listed | Trochee | 081-946 1579 |
| Listed | Wimbledon | 081-946 9265 |
| Listed | Worcester House | 081-946 1300 |

### W1 — West End — Piccadilly Circus, Soho, St Marylebone, Mayfair

| | | |
|---|---|---|
| ★★★★★R | Claridge's | 071-629 8860 |
| ★★★★★R | The Connaught | 071-499 7070 |
| ★★★★★R | The Dorchester | 071-629 8888 |
| ★★★★★ | Churchill | 071-486 5800 |
| ★★★★★ | Grosvenor House | 071-499 6363 |
| ★★★★★ | Inn on the Park | 071-499 0888 |
| ★★★★★ | Inter-Continental | 071-409 3131 |
| ★★★★★ | Le Meridien London | 071-734 8000 |
| ★★★★★ | May Fair Inter-Continental | 071-629 7777 |
| ★★★★★ | Ritz | 071-493 8181 |
| ★★★★R | The Athenaeum | 071-499 3464 |
| ★★★★ | Britannia Inter-Continental | 071-629 9400 |
| ★★★★R | Brown's | 071-493 6020 |
| ★★★★ | Cumberland | 071-262 1234 |
| ★★★★ | Holiday Inn — Marble Arch | 071-723 1277 |
| ★★★★ | London Marriot | 071-493 1232 |
| ★★★★ | Montcalm | 071-402 4288 |
| ★★★★ | Park Lane | 071-499 6321 |
| ★★★★ | Portman Inter-Continental | 071-486 5844 |
| ★★★★ | Ramada | 071-636 1629 |
| ★★★★ | St George's | 071-580 0111 |
| ★★★★ | Selfridge | 071-408 2080 |
| ★★★★ | Westbury | 071-629 7755 |
| ★★★ | Chesterfield | 071-491 2622 |
| ★★★ | Clifton-Ford | 071-486 6600 |
| ★★★ | Mandeville | 071-935 5599 |
| ★★★ | Mostyn | 071-935 2361 |
| ★★★ | Mount Royal | 071-629 8040 |
| ★★ | Regent Palace | 071-734 7000 |
| Listed | Bryanston Court | 071-262 3141 |
| Listed | Edward Lear | 071-402 5401 |
| Listed | Hotel Concorde | 071-402 6169 |
| Listed | Georgian House | 071-935 2211 |
| Listed | Hart House | 071-935 2288 |
| Listed | Montagu House | 071-935 4632 |

### W2 — Bayswater, Paddington

| | | |
|---|---|---|
| ★★★★ | Royal Lancaster | 071-262 6737 |
| ★★★★ | White's | 071-262 2711 |
| ★★★ | Central Park | 071-229 2424 |
| ★★★ | Hospitality Inn Bayswater | 071-262 4461 |
| ★★★ | London Embassy | 071-229 1212 |
| ★★★ | Park Court | 071-402 4272 |
| ★★ | Delmere | 071-706 3344 |
| Listed | Byron | 071-243 0987 |
| Listed | Camelot | 071-723 9118 |
| Listed | Mitre House | 071-723 8040 |
| Listed | Mornington | 071-262 7361 |
| Listed | Norfolk Tower | 071-262 3123 |
| Listed | Parkwood | 071-402 2241 |
| Listed | Pembridge Court | 071-229 9977 |
| Listed | Slavia Hotel | 071-727 1316 |

### W4 — Chiswick

| | | |
|---|---|---|
| Listed | Chiswick | 071-994 1712 |

**W5 — Ealing**

| ★★★ | Carnarvon | 081-992 5399 |
|---|---|---|

**W6 — Hammersmith**

| ★★★ | Novotel London | 081-741 1555 |
|---|---|---|
| ★★ | Premier West | 081-748 6181 |

**W8 — Kensington**

| ★★★★★ | Royal Garden | 071-937 8000 |
|---|---|---|
| ★★★★ | Kensington Palace Thistle | 071-937 8121 |
| ★★★★ | The Copthorne Tara London | 071-937 7211 |
| ★★★ | Kensington Close | 071-937 8170 |
| ★★ | Hotel Lexham | 071-373 6471 |
| Listed | Apollo | 071-373 3236 |
| Listed | Atlas | 071-373 2136 |
| Listed | Observatory House | 071-937 1577 |

**W14 — West Kensington**

| Listed | Aston Court | 071-602 9954 |
|---|---|---|
| Listed | Centaur | 071-602 3857 |

**London WC1 — Bloomsbury, Holborn**

| ★★★★ | Hotel Russell | 071-837 6470 |
|---|---|---|
| ★★★★ | The Marlborough | 071-636 0532 |
| ★★★ | Forte Crest Bloomsbury | 071-837 1200 |
| ★★★ | Bonnington | 071-242 2828 |
| ★★★ | London Ryan | 071-278 2480 |
| ★★ | Academy | 071-631 4115 |
| Listed | Mentone | 071-387 3927 |

**WC2 — Covent Garden, Leicester Square, Strand, Kingsway**

| ★★★★★R | Savoy | 071-836 4343 |
|---|---|---|
| ★★★★ | Waldorf | 071-836 2400 |
| ★★★ | Drury Lane Moat House | 071-836 6666 |
| ★★★ | Royal Trafalgar Thistle | 071-930 4477 |
| ★★★ | Strand Palace | 071-836 8080 |

### Camping

Staying overnight at a campsite will provide accommodation that is cheap, and a pleasant alternative for the tourist. During the summer it is advisable to book in advance.

Abbey Wood Caravan Club Site
Abbey Wood, SE2
tel: 081-310 2233 (open all year)

Caravan Harbour
Crystal Palace Parade, SE19
tel: 081-778 7155 (open all year)

Dobbs Weir Caravan Park
Essex Road, Hoddesdon, Herts
tel: (0992) 462090 (open Easter to October)

Sewardstone Caravan Park
Sewardstone Road, Chingford, E4
tel: 081-529 5689 (open April to October)

# Entertainment

**What's on in London
(Newspapers and
Magazines)**

For detailed information on concerts, theatres, films, exhibitions and special events in London, see the entertainment section of the evening newspaper *The Standard*, or the weekly magazines *What's On in London*, *Time Out* or *City Limits* — on sale at bookstalls and newsagents. The London Tourist Board and Convention Bureau also produces regular free leaflets on events and entertainment.

**Booking**

Tickets can be booked, of course, at the box offices of the individual theatres and concert halls. Many now accept credit card booking, which means you can telephone the box office to reserve your seats, quote your credit card number, and then collect the tickets half an hour before the performance begins. Some places have special phone numbers for credit card bookings, and these are pre-fixed cc in the listing which follow. Or you can use the services of ticket agencies such as Ticketmaster (tel: 071-379 4444); or try First Call (tel: 071-240 7200), a telephone booking service for credit card holders wanting theatre and concert tickets. It is open 24 hours a day, seven days a week.

**Late Theatre Booking**

The Half-Price Ticket Booth in Leicester Square is open to personal callers only and sells tickets from 12-2pm for matinée performances and from 2.30pm-6.30pm for evening shows. Tickets are for that day only; a booking fee is charged.
For a credit card booking for the theatre the same night, some seats at reduced prices and no booking fee, try: Theatre Tonight (tel: 071-753 0333) Mon-Sat 12-6.

## Theatres

**Adelphi**
Strand WC2
(tel: 071-836 7611; cc
071-836 7358)

**Albery**
St Martin's Lane WC2
(tel: 071-867 1115; cc
071-867 1111)

**Aldwych**
Aldwych WC2
(tel: 071-836 6404)

**Ambassadors**
West Street WC2
(tel: 071-836 6111; cc
071-379 4444)

**Apollo**
Shaftesbury Avenue W1
(tel: 071-494 5070)

**Apollo**
Victoria, 17 Wilton
Road SW1
(tel: 071-828 8665)

**Arts**
Gt Newport Street WC2
(tel: 071-836 2132)

**Barbican**
Silk Street, Barbican EC2
(tel: 071-638 8891)

**Cambridge**
Earlham Street WC2
(tel: 071-379 5299)

**Coliseum**
St Martin's Lane WC2
(tel: 071-836 3161; cc
071-240 5258)

**Comedy**
Panton Street SW1

(tel: 071-867 1045; cc
071-867 1111)

**Dominion**
Tottenham Court Road
W1
(tel: 071-580 9562; cc
071-413 1411)

**Drury Lane Theatre
Royal**
Catherine Street WC2
(tel: 071-494 5400)

**Duchess**
Catherine Street WC2
(tel: 071-494 5075)

**Duke of York's**
St Martin's Lane WC2
(tel: 071-836 5122; cc
071-836 9837)

**Fortune**
Russell Street WC2
(tel: 071-836 2238)

**Garrick**
Charing Cross Road
WC2
(tel: 071-494 5085)

**Globe**
Shaftesbury Avenue W1
(tel: 071-494 5065)

**Haymarket Theatre Royal**
Haymarket SW1
(tel: 071-930 8800)

**Her Majesty's**
Haymarket SW1
(tel: 071-494 5000)

**ICA Theatre**
Carlton House Terrace
SW1
(tel: 071-930 0493)

**London Palladium**
8 Argyll Street W1
(tel: 071-494 5020)

**Lyric Hammersmith**
King Street W6
(tel: 071-741 2311; cc
071-836 3464)

**Lyric**
Shaftesbury Avenue W1
(tel: 071-494 5045)

**Mermaid**
Puddle Dock EC4
(tel: 071-410 0000)

**The National Theatre**
South Bank SE1
(tel: 071-928 2252)

**New London**
Drury Lane WC2
(tel: 071-405 0072)

**The Old Vic**
Waterloo Road SE1
(tel: 071-928 7616)

**Open Air Theatre**
Regent's Park NW1
(tel: 071-486 2431; cc
071-486 1933)

**Palace**
Shaftesbury Avenue W1
(tel: 071-434 0909)

**Phoenix**
Charing Cross Road
WC2
(tel: 071-867 1044)

**Piccadilly**
Denman Street W1
(tel: 071-867 1118; cc
071-867 1111)

**Playhouse**
Northumberland
Avenue WC2
(tel: 071-839 4401)

**Prince Edward**
Old Compton Street
W1
(tel: 071-734 8951)

**Prince of Wales**
Coventry Street W1
(tel: 071-839 5972)

**Queen's**
Shaftesbury Avenue W1
(tel: 071-494 5040)

**Royal Court**
Sloane Square SW1
(tel: 071-730 1745)

**St Martin's**
West Street WC2
(tel: 071-836 1443)

**Shaftesbury**
Shaftesbury Avenue
WC2
(tel: 071-379 5399)

**Strand**
Aldwych WC2
(tel: 071-240 0300)

**Vaudeville**
Strand WC2
(tel: 071-836 9987)

**Victoria Palace**
Victoria Street SW1
(tel: 071-834 1317)

**Whitehall**
Whitehall SW1
(tel: 071-867 1119)

**Wyndhams**
Charing Cross Road
WC2
(tel: 071-867 1116)

## Cinemas

**Barbican Centre**
Silk Street EC2
(tel: 071-638 8891)

**Cannon (Baker Street)**
Marylebone Road NW1
(tel: 071-935 9772)

**Cannon (Chelsea)**
279 King's Road SW3
(tel: 071-352 5096)

**Cannon**
Fulham Road SW10
(tel: 071-370 2636)

**Cannon**
Haymarket W1
(tel: 071-839 1527)

**Cannon**
Oxford Street W1
(tel: 071-636 0310)

**Cannon**
Panton Street SW1
(tel: 071-930 0631)

**Cannon**
Piccadilly W1
(tel: 071-437 3561)

**Cannon**
Shaftesbury Avenue W1
(tel: 071-836 6279)

**Cannon**
Tottenham Court Road
W1
(tel: 071-636 6148)

**Chelsea Cinema**
King's Road SW3
(tel: 071-351 3742)

**Curzon Mayfair**
Curzon Street W1
(tel: 071-465 8865)

**Curzon Phoenix**
Charing Cross Road
WC1
(tel: 071-240 9661)

**Curzon West End**
Shaftesbury Avenue W1
(tel: 071-439 4805)

**Empire**
Leicester Square WC2
(tel: 071-437 1234)

**Lumiere**
St Martin's Lane WC2
(tel: 071-836 0691)

**Metro**
Rupert Street W1
(tel: 071-437 0757)

**Minema**
45 Knightsbridge SW1
(tel: 071-235 4225)

**National Film Theatre**
South Bank SE1
(tel: 071-928 3232)

**Odeon**
High Street, Kensington
W8
(tel: 071-371 3166)

**Odeon**
Haymarket W1
(tel: 071-839 7697)

**Odeon**
Leicester Square WC2
(tel: 071-839 1929)

**Odeon**
Marble Arch W1
(tel: 071-723 2011)

**Odeon Swiss Cottage**
Finchley Road NW3
(tel: 071-722 5905)

**Odeon West End**
Leicester Square WC2
(tel: 071-930 5252)

**Plaza**
Lower Regent Street
W1
(tel: 071-497 9999)

**Premiere**
Swiss Centre, Leicester
Square W1
(tel: 071-439 4470)

**Prince Charles**
Leicester Place WC2
(tel: 071-437 8181)

**Renoir**
Brunswick Square WC1
(tel: 071-837 8402)

**Screen on Baker Street**
Baker Street NW1
(tel: 071-935 2772)

**Warner West End**
Leicester Square WC2
(tel: 071-439 0791)

---

### Concert Halls

**Barbican Centre**
Barbican EC2
(tel: box office 071-638
8891; information
071-634 4141; recorded
information on events
071-628 9760)

**London Arena**
Lime Harbour E14
(tel: 071-538 1212)

**Royal Albert Hall**
Kensington Gore SW7
(tel: 071-589 8212)

**The South Bank Arts
Complex**
SE1
(tel: 071-928 8800)
This includes three
concert halls,
The Royal Festival Hall,
Queen Elizabeth Hall
and the Purcell Room

**Wigmore Hall**
36 Wigmore Street W1
(tel: 071-935 2141)

---

### Opera and Ballet

**The London Coliseum**
St Martin's Lane WC2
(tel: 071-836 3161; cc
071-240 5258)

**Royal Opera House**
Covent Garden WC2
(tel: 071-240 1066; 071-
240 1911; recorded

information
071-836 6903)

**Sadler's Wells**
Rosebery Avenue EC1
(tel: 071-278 8916;
recorded information
071-278 5450)

Royal Albert Hall

## Church Concerts

There are many churches in London which hold lunchtime recitals or concerts. They are held throughout the week and generally start between 1pm and 1.15pm. For full details and programme tel: 071-260 1456. A few of the popular churches are:

**All Hallows-by-the-Tower**
Byward Street EC3

**Holy Sepulchre**
Holborn Viaduct EC1

**St Anne and St Agnes**
Gresham Street EC2

**St Bartholomew-the-Great**
West Smithfield EC1

**St Botoloph's**
Aldersgate EC1

**St Bride**
Fleet Street EC4

**St John's**
Smith Square SW1

**St Lawrence Jewry**
Gresham Street EC2

**St Martin-in-the-Fields**
Trafalgar Square WC2

**St Martin within Ludgate**
Ludgate Hill EC4

**St Mary-le-Bow**
Cheapside EC2

**St Mary Woolnoth**
Lombard Street EC3

**St Michael-upon-Cornhill**
Cornhill EC3

**St Olave**
Hart Street EC3

**St Paul's Cathedral**
EC4

**St Stephen's**
Walbrook EC4

**Southwark Cathedral**
Borough High Street SE1

## Open-Air Music

During the summer, military bands offer free lunchtime entertainment in the Royal parks, and in certain city parks and squares.

**Royal Parks:**
military and brass bands play free most lunchtimes in Hyde Park, St James's Park, Greenwich Park and Regent's Park.

**City sites:**
(phone the City Information Centre on 071-606 3030 for details)

**Finsbury Circus Gardens**
Moorgate EC2: lunchtime band concerts, usually Wednesdays.

**Lincoln's Inn Fields**
WC2: military bands, usually Tuesday and Thursday lunchtimes.

**Paternoster Square**
EC4: military bands, daily, lunchtimes.

**St Paul's Steps**
EC4: sit in full view of St Paul's and listen to a full military band concert; usually Thursdays.

**Tower Place**
EC3: military bands, usually Fridays.

**Victoria Embankment Gardens**
SW1: riverside setting for military bands, massed bands, and light orchestras, most lunchtimes of the week.

**Other sites:**

**Crystal Palace Bowl**
Crystal Palace Park SE26 (tel: 081-313 0527)
A summer season of concerts is held in the lakeland bowl.

**Holland Park Court Theatre**
W8
(tel: 071-602 7856)
A small open-air theatre which stages opera, ballet and concerts during July.

**Kenwood**
Hampstead Lane NW3
(tel: 071-973 3427)
Leading orchestras give symphony concerts in this beautiful setting by the lake on Saturday evenings during June, July and August. To be seen to be 'in', take a picnic.

**Parliament Hill**
NW3
(tel: 071-485 4491)
Massed bands play beside the lake on Saturday evenings during the summer.

# London's Transport

The visitor arriving in London will need to know first of all how to get about the capital. Fortunately, though Greater London is over 610 square miles in size, twice as large as New York or Paris, it is served by one of the finest transport systems in the world.

You have a choice of three means of public transport: the familiar red London bus, the Underground railway — or 'tube' — network, and the London taxi.

The buses and Underground are controlled by London Transport whose headquarters is at 55 Broadway, Westminster SW1. This authority maintains Travel Information Centres at the following underground stations in Central London:

| | |
|---|---|
| Euston-British Rail | 7.15am (8.15am Sun) — 6pm (7.30pm Fri) |
| King's Cross Station | 8.15am-6pm (7.30pm Fri) |
| Liverpool Street Station | 9.30am (8.30am Sat, Sun) — 6.30pm (3.30pm Sun) |
| Oxford Circus Station | 8.15am-6pm (Closed Sun) |
| Piccadilly Circus Station | 8.15am-6pm |
| St James's Park Station | 9am-5.30pm (Mon-Fri) |
| Victoria-British Rail | 8.15am-9.30pm |
| Heathrow Terminals 1, 2, 3 Underground Station | 7.15am (8.15am Sun) — 6.30pm |

(Also Heathrow Terminal buildings, see page 23)

They answer all queries about travel in London, and also issue tickets, book tours, and sell publications. Or you can telephone 071-222 1234 any time, day or night. Travelcheck gives recorded information on how services are running — telephone 071-222 1200.

**The Underground**

There is a map of the Underground on the back of this book.

As with many capital cities, the quickest and most efficient means of public transport in London is the Underground railway — known as 'the tube'. With 273 stations, the Underground covers a wide area reaching out from central London to the suburbs where it rises above ground as an ordinary surface railway. There is almost always a tube station close at hand throughout London, and trains run frequently between 5.30am and 0.15am (7.30am-11.30pm on Sundays). There are no all-night services, however, and it is important to note that certain stations are closed at weekends.

There are large Underground maps posted at all stations, in the booking halls and on all platforms, and each carriage displays a map of that train's route. Each line has a name and is clearly indicated in a separate colour; it is usually easier to follow the colours than go by the names of the lines.

| | |
|---|---|
| Bakerloo line | — brown |
| Central line | — red |
| District line | — green |

| Circle line | — yellow |
| East London line | — orange |
| Hammersmith and City line | — pink |
| Jubilee line | — grey |
| Metropolitan line | — purple |
| Northern line | — black |
| Piccadilly line | — dark blue |
| Victoria line | — light blue |

Signs throughout the tube stations show the way to the line required, but make sure you wait on the correct platform and board the right train by checking the direction indicators both on the platform itself and on the front of the train.

A list of fares is displayed in ticket halls; you must buy a buy a ticket before you begin your journey, either from the booking office or from automatic machines (these will save you queueing and some of them give change), and keep it safe to either show or surrender at your destination.

Under-14s travel at a reduced fare, as do 14- and 15-year-olds with a Child Rate Photocard — these are available free from post offices in the London area. Under-fives travel free.

**The Docklands Light Railway** runs from Bank Underground Station and Tower Gateway (take the Underground to Tower Hill) via Shadwell through the Isle of Dogs to Island Gardens. Another section runs from Stratford (take Underground to Stratford) to Island Gardens (walk from Greenwich through Greenwich Foot Tunnel).

An extension east to Beckton in the Royal Docks is due to open December 1992. (Trains run on weekdays only, until 9.30pm.)

**Buses**
One of the best ways of seeing London is to take a seat on the top deck of one of its famous double-decker buses. The fact that the traffic may be slow on occasions is no great handicap, but offers a wonderful opportunity for leisurely sightseeing. Buses operate from about 6am to midnight on most routes, including those connecting the main-line railway stations, and offer a comprehensive service in central London and the suburbs. A network of special All Night buses runs through central London serving Piccadilly Circus, Leicester Square, Victoria, Trafalgar Square, Hyde Park Corner, Marble Arch, and many other parts convenient for theatres, cinemas, and restaurants. However, do check times before using these buses; their stops have distinctive blue and yellow route numbers.

You should pick up a free, detailed bus map from any Travel Enquiry Office or Underground station. Each bus route is identified by a number which appears on the front, sides and back of each bus. The final destination also appears on the front, and a short list of major ports of call on the sides. Bus-stop signs, which generally list the numbers of the buses which stop there, are displayed on a red or white background. Red backgrounds denote

'Request Stops', where the bus will only stop if hailed in good time; the white background signs are compulsory stops.

On double-decker buses, there are usually conductors who control the number of passengers allowed on and collect fares; on single-decker buses you give your fare to the driver.

Under-14s pay a reduced flat fare until 10pm, as do 14- and 15-year-olds with a Child Rate Photocard, and up to two under-fives per person travel free. Remember to keep your ticket until you leave the bus.

**Concessionary Fares**

If you intend using public transport in London extensively, there are a number of special 'Travelcards' available which will save you money and time. With most of them you can travel when you like, as often as you like; there's no need to queue for separate tickets in the normal way or search for change on buses. They can be bought from any London Transport or LTB Information Centre, Underground Stations and nearly 2,000 newsagents.

The combined British Rail, Underground, and bus network in Greater London is divided into six concentric fare zones. You just choose which zones you wish to travel in, and buy the appropriate Travelcard. You can then travel on any combination of train, tube and bus within your selected zones, any number of times, for the duration of the ticket's validity (one day, seven days, or a month).

**One Day Travelcard** gives you unlimited off-peak travel for the day throughout the whole of greater London. The only restriction is you have to travel after 9.30am, Monday to Friday (no restrictions at weekends). They are not valid on Night Buses.

**Seven Day Travelcard** — adults and children (5-15 yrs). Before buying one, you will need a Photocard: just take a passport–size photograph of yourself with you when you buy your first ticket and you will be issued with one free. (There are instant–photo booths at the major railway and tube stations; these are coin operated, so be sure you have the right change with you.)

**The LT Card** gives you unlimited travel for the day (Monday to Friday) on buses, tube, and the Docklands Light Railway. There are no restrictions on the time of day when you can set off.

**The Visitor Travel Card** is available to overseas visitors for one, three, four or seven days, but must be bought abroad. It offers unlimited travel on buses and tube and includes a selection of tourist discount vouchers. It can be bought from travel agents and London Transport sales agents abroad.

You can also buy a combined British Rail ticket and a one day, seven day, or monthly travel card from most stations outside greater London, which is a great saving if you are not actually staying in the capital.

# British Rail

Britain's extensive rail network links all major cities in the country with London. British Rail offer travel facilities at **The British Travel Centre**, 12 Lower Regent Street SW1 (tel: 071-730 3400). Here you can buy tickets and make reservations, book tickets for theatres and sightseeing tours, arrange accommodation, and change foreign money. The Centre is open from 9am to 6.30pm, Monday to Saturday and on Sundays from 10am to 4pm. British Rail also have **Travel Centres** at:
14 Kingsgate Parade, Victoria Street SW1
87 King William Street EC4
and at Heathrow Airport.

Here you can purchase rail tickets and obtain full information on British Rail services/holidays etc. They are open Monday to Friday from 9am to 5pm. There are also Travel Centres at these main London terminals:
Cannon Street, Euston, King's Cross, Liverpool Street, Paddington, St Pancras and Waterloo

**Railway Terminals**

The principal mainline stations linking London with various parts of Britain and timetable telephone numbers are:

| King's Cross | 071-278 2477 | East and north east England and Scotland via the east coast |
|---|---|---|
| Liverpool Street | 071-928 5100 | East Anglia, Essex |
| Fenchurch Street | 071-928 5100 | Essex |
| St Pancras | 071-387 7070 | East Midlands |
| Euston | 071-387 7070 | West Midlands, north west England, Scotland via the west coast and north Wales |
| Victoria | 071-928 5100 | South and south east England |
| Waterloo | 071-928 5100 | South and south west England |
| Charing Cross | 071-928 5100 | South east England |
| Paddington | 071-262 6767 | South west England, south Wales and Oxford area |

Full details of scheduled rail services are shown in local timetables. Free copies are available from British Rail stations and Travel Centres.

British Rail fares vary according to distance and time of travel. Cheap Day Returns for short journeys are generally available after 9.30am Monday to Friday and at any time over the weekend. For longer journeys check for availability of Saver, Super Saver and Apex tickets, but avoid busy times such as Friday afternoons for cheaper

fares. Reservations are strongly recommended for long journeys. You must buy a ticket before travelling, and surrender it either to the guard on the train or to the ticket-collector on the platform at your destination. Children under five travel free; under 16, half-price.

**Rush Hour** From Monday to Friday the buses and trains of London Transport carry a daily average of over 6,000,000 passengers. In Central London all forms of public transport become extremely crowded between 8am-9.30am and 4pm-6.30pm when most of London is travelling to and from work. London's rush hour is really most uncomfortable, and if travel can be arranged outside these times, the visit will be considerably more enjoyable. Buses and tubes also get quite busy at lunchtime, but not as bad as during the rush hour.

**Taxis** The London taxi is one of the friendliest sights a visitor will see. The traditional colour is still black, though in recent years red, blue and yellow vehicles have added a splash of colour to London's fleet. But the distinctive shape remains. Taxis are a salvation for those who get lost; after midnight they are a godsend and the only way to get about. Taxi drivers are also a useful source of information as they know London inside-out — they have to, in order to get their licence.

London taxis can be hailed in the street if the yellow 'For Hire' or 'Taxi' sign above the windscreen is lit, hired from taxi ranks, or called by telephone: for numbers, see 'Taxi' in the Business and Services section of the London Telephone Directory. Charges vary according to the distance covered and are recorded on the meter; additional charges are made for extra people, luggage, and night journeys. It is customary to tip about 10-15% of the fare, or perhaps a little more if the driver has been particularly helpful. For journeys over six miles — for example, from Heathrow Airport to Central London — you should negotiate a fare in advance.

# London City Airport

London City Airport Ltd, King George V Dock, Silvertown, London E16 2PX
tel: 071-474 5555

London City Airport is owned and operated by John Mowlem and Company PLC. It is situated six miles from the Bank of England in the Royal Docks area of Beckton, close to the A13 and A117 (North Circular Road). The modern passenger Terminal Building has a restaurant, coffee shop, business centre, banking facilities, Bureau de Change, Duty Free and various shops, all within the main concourse.

**Airlines**  The following airlines operate regular flights from London City Airport to many UK and European destinations:

| | |
|---|---|
| Brymon Airways | 071-476 5000 |
| Air France | 071-499 9511 |
| British Midland | 071-589 5599 |
| Flexair | 071-511 2266 |
| Sabena | 081-780 1444 |

**Where to leave your car**  Long and short term car parks are situated directly outside the airport terminal.

**Public Transport**  **Buses** London Transport bus routes 69 and 262 pass the airport entrance in Connaught Road. Route 276 serves the airport Terminal Building.
**Rail** The nearest station is Silvertown and City Airport on North London Link. This connects to the Underground at West Ham (District Line) and Stratford (Central Line).
**River Bus** The River Bus operates from Charing Cross Pier, Festival Pier, Swan Lane Pier, London Bridge Pier, West India/Canary Wharf Pier and Greenwich Pier to the Airport Pier. A shuttle bus connects to the airport. Services run Monday to Friday 7am-7.40pm (every 20 minutes). No service on Saturday, Sunday or public holidays.
**Taxi** A taxi rank is situated outside the main door of the terminal building.

**Car Hire**  The following self-drive car hire firms have reception desks in the terminal building

| | |
|---|---|
| Europcar | 071-476 0309 |
| Hertz | 071-476 7151 |

**Facilities for disabled travellers**  Full access facilities are available for disabled travellers.

# Heathrow Airport — London

tel: 081-759 4321

Heathrow Airport has four Passenger Terminals in separate parts of the airport. Terminals 1, 2 and 3 are situated in the central area of Heathrow. Terminal 4 is situated at the south east of Heathrow's perimeter road. The central area is linked to the M4 via a motorway spur and the Bath Road (A4) via twin tunnels. Terminal 4 is linked to the Great South West Road (A30) and the M25 via the A3113 and the airport's Southern Perimeter Road.

**Tourist Information Centre**  London Underground Ltd and the London Tourist Board and Convention Bureau (tel: 071-730 3488) run a travel office with a separate Tourist Information counter in the Heathrow Central Underground Station. There are also information and sales desks near the arrival points in each Terminal.

| Terminals 1, 2, 3 Underground Station | Mon-Sat 7.15am-6.30pm Sun 8.15am-6.30pm |
|---|---|
| Terminal 1 arrivals | Mon 7am-7pm Tue-Fri 7.15am-10.15 pm Sat, Sun 8am-6.30pm |
| Terminal 2 arrivals | Mon-Sat 7.15am-9pm Sun 8.15am-10pm |
| Terminal 3 arrivals | Mon-Sat 6.30am-1.15pm Sun 8.15am-3pm |
| Terminal 4 arrivals | Mon-Sat 6.30am-6.30pm Sun 8.15am-6.30pm |

**Where to leave your car**

**Short-term parking (covered)**
Car Parks are sited at all passenger terminals. Car parks 1, 2 and 3 are managed for Heathrow Airport Ltd by APCOA Parking (UK) Ltd (tel: 081-745 7861) and car park 4 by CPS Ltd (tel: 081-759 4931 or 081-745 7906). No reservations necessary.

**Open-air Long-term parking**
Heathrow Airport long-term car parks for Terminals 1, 2 and 3 are managed by APCOA Parking (UK) Ltd on behalf of Heathrow Airport Ltd and are situated on the Northern Perimeter Road. Terminal 4 is managed by CPS Ltd and is off the Southern Perimeter Road. Entering the airport from the M4 spur or the A4 follow signs to the long-term car parks. A free coach will take passengers to the terminals and return to the relevant car park following arrival at Heathrow. During the hours midnight-6am special direct line telephones are in use at the pick-up points, enabling passengers to contact the coach base to arrange for collection.
**For a period exceeding 4 hours it is more economical to use these car parks.**
For further information telephone 081-745 7160.

**Public Transport**

**Underground**
The extension of the Piccadilly line tube, opened in 1977, provides a direct link from all Heathrow terminals to the West End of London. Departures from the airport start at about 5am on Monday to Saturday and at about 7am on Sunday; the last train leaves at just before midnight, Monday-Saturday, and just before 11pm on Sunday. The first train to Heathrow leaves King's Cross station at about 6am on Monday to Saturday and at about 7.30am on Sunday; the last train leaves just after midnight, Monday-Saturday, and at about 11.30pm on Sunday.

**Buses and Coaches**
An extensive bus and coach service operates from Heathrow Central to local and major destinations in Britain which include:

**Airbus (express services):**
**A1 to Victoria Station:** stopping at Cromwell Road (Earls Court Road), Cromwell Road (Forum Hotel), Hyde Park Corner (Knightsbridge).
**A2 to Euston Station:** stopping at Holland Park Avenue (Kensington Hilton), Notting Hill Gate,

Bayswater Road, Marble Arch, Gloucester Place, Marylebone Road.

This bus service runs every 20–30 minutes from 6.30am to 10.30pm.

**Heathrow/Gatwick Road Links**

A luxury express service, **Speedlink**, operates between Heathrow and Gatwick Airport every 20 minutes with a journey time of 60 minutes. First/last bus from Heathrow 6am-10.30pm, first/last bus from Gatwick 6am-10pm. Tel: 081-668 7261.

**Jetlink 747** Regular fast daily service linking Gatwick with Heathrow Airport and Watford, Hemel Hempstead, Luton, Luton Airport and Stevenage.

Although airbuses and tubes do not operate during the night, there is an all-night bus service — No 97 — which runs at regular intervals from midnight to 5am between central London and Heathrow.

Regular coach services are operated on behalf of British Rail connecting Woking BR Station; also to/from Reading BR Station; bookings can be made at the passenger terminals, railway stations and appointed travel agencies.

Airline buses operate at frequent intervals between Heathrow and certain town terminals in Central London.

**Taxi**

London taxis operate between London and Heathrow Airport.

**Hotels — General Information**

In all the arrival terminals there are reservation desks operated by Hotel Bookings International Ltd.

**Car Hire**

**Avis Rent-a-car** (*all passenger terminals, 24 hour service*) Self-drive tel: 081-897 9321. Chauffeur-driven tel: 081-897 2621. Open 7am-7pm. A one-way service to/from over 80 locations throughout the UK is also available.

**Budget Rent-a-car** (*all passenger terminals*) tel: 081-759 2216 (24 hour service).

**Europcar** (*all passenger terminals*) tel: 081-897 0811 (24 hour service).

**Euro Dollar Rent-a-Car** Heathrow Park Hotel, Bath Road, Longford tel: 081-897 3232 (24 hour service).

**Hertz Rent-a-car** (*all passenger terminals*) Central reservation office tel: 081-679 1799.

**Kenning Car Hire** (Local and One-Way Car & Van Hire) Gt South West Road, Feltham (opposite Hatton Cross Underground Station) tel: 081-890 1167.

**Facilities for disabled travellers**

All terminals have lifts, ramps and specially designed toilets. If special assistance is required, contact the airline being used.

**Queen's Building Roof Gardens**

The Queen's Building Roof Gardens have been designed for the benefit of the public visiting the airport. Refreshment facilities are available. Open daily from 9am-7pm or dusk. Admission charge.

# Gatwick Airport — London

tel: (0293) 535353.
Twenty-eight miles south of London, Gatwick is the second most important airport in Britain.

Access is available from the A23 and the M23. Essential traffic direction signs are situated both inside and outside the airport. For information on flight enquiries telephone (0293) 31299.

**Tourist Information** This is provided by the South East England Tourist Board, situated in the South Terminal International Arrivals Hall, and open 6am-6pm every day.

**Where to leave your car** North Terminal car parks are managed by Europarks Ltd (now owned by NCP Ltd), and the South Terminal car parks are managed by APCOA Parking (UK) Ltd; both as concessionaires to Gatwick Airport Ltd. There is no need to reserve space although enquiries can be made:
tel: (0293) 502737 (Europarks Ltd); 24 hour information service available tel: (0293) 567161;
tel: (0293) 502896 (APCOA Parking UK Ltd).
**Method of payment:**
**North Terminal** Short-term payments should be made at the automatic payment machines in the terminal. Long-term payments should be made at the kiosk on the ground floor (flight arrivals). Credit cards, cash or cheque are all acceptable.
**South Terminal** There are automatic payment machines for long and short-term parking accepting credit cards and cash. Cheques are accepted at the enquiry desk. Drivers must retain a timed coded card which is fed into a card reader at the exit and raises the barrier.

**Parking** **Short-term Multi-storey Car Parks:**
**North Terminal** The short-term car park is connected to the airport terminal by a passenger walkway and provides spaces for 1,010 cars.
**South Terminal** The terminal car park, consisting of three multi-storey car parks connected by passenger walkways to the airport terminal, provides spaces for 3,118 cars.
**Long-term Open-air Car Park:**
**North Terminal** — 5,760 spaces, situated to the west of the terminal, free bus service to terminal.
**South Terminal** — 12,090 spaces, situated to the south of the airport, free bus service to the terminal.

**Public Transport** There are direct express coach services between many major towns and Gatwick Airport and, in addition to these, services from most parts of Britain connect at London Victoria coach station (half a mile from Victoria rail station) with onward services to Gatwick. Gatwich coach station is located on the ground floor at South Terminal. All coach services, except Speedlink, stop at the coach station. (Speedlink set down and pick up on the arrival and departure service roads.)

**Gatwick/Heathrow Road Links**

See Heathrow Airport — page 24.
Full details of all Bus and Coach services are available from the enquiry desk in the South Terminal Building, open daily 6.30am-8.30pm.

*British Rail* — The Gatwick Airport station is part of Gatwick's South Terminal, with station exit leading onto the check-in concourse. The terminals are clearly signed from the station platforms. Direct access to North Terminal from the British Rail station is via the transit, which operates every 3 minutes, with a journey time of 2 minutes.

A free portering service is available between the station and terminals, and free airport baggage trolleys are available at the points of entry to the terminals. These trolleys are not allowed onto station platforms or onto the transit for safety reasons.

Passengers arriving on a flight wishing to purchase rail tickets may do so at the British Rail desk next to the transit in North Terminal, at the desk immediately after passport control in South Terminal, or in the station itself.

The dedicated Gatwick Express service between London Victoria and the airport operates every 15 minutes during the day and hourly at night. Journey time is 30 minutes during the day, 35 minutes on Sundays and between 35 and 45 minutes during the night.

Full details of all rail services are available from the British Rail Travel Centre at Gatwick Airport Station, situated in the station concourse, or from your local station.

**Hotels — General Information**

In both Terminal Buildings there are reservation desks operated by Hotel Plus.
North Terminal desk tel: (0293) 502723
South Terminal desk tel: (0293) 537270

**Car Hire**

Self-drive and chauffeur-driven cars may be hired from the following companies who have desks in North/South Terminal arrival halls:

| | |
|---|---|
| Avis Rent-a-car Ltd | (0293) 529721 |
| Budget Rent-a-car | (0293) 540141 |
| Europcar | (0293) 531062 |
| Hertz Rent-a-car | (0293) 530555 |

*Not on Airport premises*
Euro Dollar Rent-a-Car, Old Brighton Road, Lowfield Heath, Surrey tel: (0293) 513031
Kenning Car and Van Rental, Gatwick Road, Crawley, West Sussex tel: (0293) 514822

**Facilities for Disabled Travellers**

The terminals have lifts, ramps and specially designed toilets. You are advised to contact your airline if you need any special assistance. A brochure incorporating information on facilities for the disabled is available from: Gatwick Airport

Information Public Affairs Department, Gatwick Airport Ltd, PO Box 93, Gatwick, West Sussex RH6 0NP.

**Spectators' Viewing Area** Situated on the roof of the South Terminal (fourth floor), access is from the arrivals concourse. It is open daily from 8am-8pm (Apr to Sep). Admission charge. Catering facilities are available.

# Stansted Airport — London

tel: Bishop's Stortford (0279) 680500.

This is London's third international airport, 30 miles north east with fast access via the M11 motorway.

**Where to leave your car** Short and long-term parking is available opposite the Passenger Terminal entrance. The car parks are operated by Motorpark, tel: (0279) 662373.

**Public Transport** A direct British Rail service operates from Liverpool Street Station, stopping at Tottenham Hale with direct access to the Victoria Line. Trains run every 30 minutes with a journey time of 40 minutes.

**Car Hire** Self-drive and chauffeur-driven cars may be hired from the following companies who have desks in the arrivals concourse:

| | |
|---|---|
| Budget Rent-a-car | (0279) 681194 |
| Europcar | (0279) 680240 |
| Hertz | (0279) 680154 |
| Stanstead Airport Cars | (0279) 662444 |

(*operate a 24 hour taxi service*)

# Sightseeing Tours

An excellent way to get to know London — particularly if this is your first visit — is to join one of the many sightseeing bus or coach tours.
**The Original London Transport Sightseeing Tours** on double-decker red buses start from Piccadilly Circus (Haymarket), Marble Arch (Speakers' Corner), Baker Street Station, and Victoria Station. The 18-mile route (lasting about $1\frac{1}{2}$ hours) passes most of London's landmarks including St Paul's, Westminster Abbey, and The Tower. Tours run frequently throughout the day with live English commentary, or recorded commentary in eight languages. Buy your tickets in advance from any London Transport or LTB Information Centre at a special low rate; or just pay as you board the bus. A special tour includes direct entrance (no boring queueing) to Madame Tussaud's Waxworks or London Zoo. The buses are open-top in

summer. Details from London Transport, 55 The Broadway SW1 (tel: 071-227 3456).

**London Plus** (tel: 071-828 6449/071-877 1722) Daily (except 24 and 25 December), every 15 minutes (30 minutes in winter) from 10am to 5pm. The distinctive red and cream Routemaster buses follow a circular route in Central London passing many places of interest, with over 30 carefully chosen stops. Once you've paid, you can hop on and off all day. You can buy your ticket from the guide on the bus, or from any London Transport or LTB Information Centre. The ticket includes a book of vouchers giving discounts to many of the attractions you may wish to visit on this tour.

**London By Night** sightseeing tour, every evening from 7pm and lasting over an hour. This fascinating tour takes in all the floodlit sights of London. Tickets from the driver, or London Transport's Information Centre at Victoria Station.

Other sightseeing bus/coach tours are run by: Evans Evans Tours Ltd (071-930 2377); Frames Rickards (071-837 3111); Golden Tours (081-743 3300); London Cityrama (071-720 6663); Harrods Sightseeing (071-581 3603); London Coaches (071-828 6449); and The Big Bus Company (071-498 9345).

**Boat trips on the River Thames**

A holiday in London cannot be complete without the unique views offered by a boat trip on the Thames. Passenger boat services operate a full programme during the summer months and a restricted one in the winter. From Westminster Pier (071-930 4097), Charing Cross Pier (071-839 3572), and Tower Pier (071-488 0344), services operate downstream to Greenwich, and from Westminster and Charing Cross Piers downstream to the Tower. Upstream services operate from Westminster Pier to Kew, Richmond, and Hampton Court, and from Tower Pier to Westminster. Check departures times with the enquiry numbers given with each Pier, or telephone the **River Boat Information Service** on 071-730 4812 (weekdays, 9am-5.30pm).
**River Bus** — see page 23.

**London canal trips**

London also has two canals — the Grand Union and the Regent's Canal. Boat trips operate mainly on the Regent's Canal: the London Waterbus Company goes from Camden Lock to Little Venice, via Regents Park and London Zoo, with a stop for admission; also all day trips to the River Lee (071-482 2550). Jason's Canal Cruises (071-286 3428) run luncheon and evening trips along the picturesque part of Regent's Canal using a pair of traditional narrow-boats; there are cruises on the *Jenny Wren* through the Zoo and Regent's Park, and on the *My Fair Lady*, a luxury cruising restaurant (071-485 4433). Telephone for full details and itineraries.

**Seeing London by bicycle**

A different way to get about London is to use a bicycle. Traffic, especially in Central London, is often congested and the cyclist has a freedom denied the motorist. There are many firms in London who offer a cycle hire service and who are able to meet the needs of both the casual and experienced cyclist, whether it be for a traditional three-speed or a fast and sophisticated ten-speed bike. Most firms can also supply items of cycling equipment and can provide information on sights to see. Hire rates are generally on a daily or weekly basis.

**Go By Cycle** 9–15 Templeton Place, SW5 (tel: 071-373 3657). Open Monday to Saturday 9.30am-6.30pm. They also offer guided tours for groups.

**On Your Bike** 52–54 Tooley Street, London Bridge, SE1 (tel: 071-407 1309), and Duke Street Hill, SE1 (071-378 6669). Open Monday to Saturday 9am-6pm (4.30pm Saturday).

**Portobello Cycles** 69 Golborne Road, W10 (tel: 081-960 0444). Open Monday to Saturday 10am-5pm.

**London on foot**    If you want to discover London by foot — one of the best ways to get to know any city — several firms organise guided walking tours. Information from:
City Walks 071-937 4281
London Walks 071-435 6413
Guided Walks of London 081-346 9255
Historical Tours 081-668 4019
Explore London 081-470 6638
Explore Greenwich 081-650 7640
Streets of London 081-882 3414
Exciting Walks 071-624 9981
Discovering London 0277 213704

If you want to explore London on your own, the Silver Jubilee Walkway covers ten miles of historic London. This walkway was created in 1977 to commemorate the 25th anniversary of the Queen's accession to the throne. The entire route is signposted by silver plaques in the shape of a crown set into the pavement. Parliament Square is a good place to start.

**Pedestrians**    At a Zebra street-crossing (one with flashing orange beacons and black-and-white stripes on the road) you have absolute right of way when you have stepped off the kerb — but do use this sensibly and make sure drivers have seen you before you cross.

At Pelican crossings (two lines of studs with traffic lights to halt the traffic), you have to push a button to make the signals stop the traffic for you. When the signal shows a green man, cross. If this signal starts to flash while you are crossing, carry on, you will have plenty of time to reach the other side; do not start to cross when this is flashing nor, of course, when the red man is showing.

Be aware of the bus lanes where buses may travel in the opposite direction to the main flow of traffic.

# Shopping in London

The capital's well-known shopping areas are mostly in the West End, with such world-famous names as Oxford Street, Regent Street, Bond Street, Piccadilly and Knightsbridge. In some cases, shops along a particular road specialise in certain types of goods. Other roads have a more general mixture of shops, where, in a short distance, almost anything can be purchased.

**Oxford Street**

Justifiably famous, Oxford Street is the backbone of London's shopping area. There are no particular specialities, but it is the home of many of London's big department stores and has many clothes, shoe, and fashion shops.

The busiest stretch is between Marble Arch and Oxford Circus, and not far from Marble Arch is **Marks & Spencer's** largest branch, a favourite with shoppers from all over the world for reasonably priced clothing and other goods. Nearby is **Selfridges**, London's second-largest department store and especially popular for its food hall, restaurants, kitchenware and cosmetics departments. Other department stores along Oxford Street include **D H Evans**, **Debenhams**, and **John Lewis**.

Other inexpensive clothing stores include **British Home Stores** and **C&A**, while nearly every fashion and shoe store chain has at least one branch in Oxford Street. The **HMV** record shop can lay claim to being one of the largest and most comprehensive of its kind anywhere in the world.

**Regent Street**

More department stores and fashion shops are to be found in Regent Street, which crosses Oxford Street at Oxford Circus. The department stores include **Dickins & Jones**, and **Liberty & Co**, world-famous for its classic fabrics and patterns. Classic British-style clothing will be found at shops such as **Jaeger**, **Austin Reed** and **Aquascutum**. Also on Regent Street is the well-known **Hamleys** toy store and **Garrard**, the Queen's jeweller.

**Bond Street**

New Bond Street runs down from Oxford Street to Burlington Gardens, where it becomes Old Bond Street, and continues to Piccadilly. This is one of London's most expensive streets, where leading names in fashion and jewellery alternate with premises of famous art dealers. Fashion shops such as **Saint Laurent**, **Rive Gauche**, **Valentino**, **Gucci**, **Kurt Geiger**, and **Magli** are the sort of establishment where anyone who has to ask the price can't afford it. **Asprey & Co** specialises in the fine, rare, and beautiful in leather, gold, silver, jewellery and antiques, and there is one department store — **Fenwick** — which sells mainly women's fashions. Here also is **Cartier**, the leading international jewellers, and **Sotheby's**, the world famous fine art auctioneers — worth a visit, if only to look at what you can't afford.

**Piccadilly**

There seem to be more airlines and tourist boards represented in Piccadilly than shops, but those that are here are some of the most important names in London. On Piccadilly Circus is the old-established clothes and sportswear store of **Lillywhites**.

Almost opposite the Royal Academy is **Hatchards**, an excellent general bookshop, and **Fortnum & Mason**, which stocks the finest food and drink as well as a variety of other goods. **Swaine, Adeney, Brigg & Sons** nearby is the place to go for high-quality leather goods, umbrellas and riding equipment. Burlington Arcade, off Piccadilly, has some of the most elegant small shops in London, where ties, woollen goods, and antique and modern jewellery can be bought.

**Simpson** is a first-class tailor and outfitter in Piccadilly, but the well-heeled gentleman will buy his clothing in streets off either side of Piccadilly. He will have his shirts hand-made in Jermyn Street, and his suits supplied from a Savile Row or Sackville Street tailor. Those who can't afford such things will go to **Moss Bros**, in King Street, off the Strand, where good-quality men's dress clothing for any occasion can be hired or bought.

**Tottenham Court Road**

Running up from New Oxford Street to Euston Road, Tottenham Court Road was once thought of as the furniture centre for London. Today it is predominantly known for its hi-fi and electrical equipment shops such as the many branches of **Hi-Fi Care**, selling the latest sound systems, and **Laskys** the computer specialists. There are still, however, a number of good furnishing stores, notably **Heal's** and **Maples**. Newer and smaller, but no less striking, is **Habitat**, whose popular furniture and furnishings are of a modern design. Other interesting shops on Tottenham Court Road are **Paperchase**, which has a unique range of cards, posters, wrapping paper and other stationery, and **The Reject Shop** which stocks a wide range of seconds in pottery and household goods.

**Charing Cross Road**

Charing Cross Road is at the southern end of Tottenham Court Road and is the home of a great variety of new and second-hand bookshops as well as shops selling music and musical instruments. Of the bookshops, **Foyles** must be the most famous, and **Macari's** is one of the many shops stocking musical instruments, though these days most of their trade is in guitars, electric keyboards and synthesizers. Shaftesbury Avenue, which crosses Charing Cross Road at Cambridge Circus, also has many music shops.

**Covent Garden**

Since the old Flower Market closed in 1974 Covent Garden has blossomed in another way — as one of the best and most popular shopping areas in

London. There are shops and stalls of every kind, most selling goods of individual, and excellent quality. The atmosphere of the market is enhanced by musicians and other street entertainers.

**Knightsbridge**

Though the Knightsbridge, Brompton Road and Sloane Street area has some of the most luxurious fashion boutiques, antique shops and department stores in London, they all tend to be overshadowed by the magnificence of **Harrods**, the largest department store in Europe. Equally notable, but not as comprehensive, is the **Harvey Nichols** department store in Sloane Street. It is a luxurious store particularly noted for women's and children's wear as well as all kinds of furniture and furnishings. Also popular is **The Scotch House**, which specialises in Scottish woollens, knitwear, and woven tartans.

**Kensington High Street**

At the western end of Hyde Park, the two roads of Kensington High Street and Kensington Church Street make up this lively and fashionable off-centre shopping area. The department store **John Barker** specializes in household goods. Going down Kensington High Street, chain clothing stores like **C&A**, **Marks & Spencer**, **British Home Stores**, and individual fashion shops mingle with supermarkets and exotic restaurants. Kensington Church Street is a haven for antique collectors at its eastern end, and at its western end for those looking out for the most up-to-date in clothing.

**King's Road**

Fashions may come and fashions may go, but the King's Road seems able to transcend them all, remaining the most fashionable thoroughfare in London. It is best-known for clothes shops, but there are also sophisticated antique, furnishing and fashion shops. The shoppers in the King's Road are usually every bit as fascinating and diverse as the shops themselves.

**Street Markets**

Nothing beats a street market for a particular kind of atmosphere. They are usually good places for such things as fruit, vegetables and inexpensive household goods. Some of London's street markets specialise in such things as antiques, but bargains are few and far between.

**Berwick Street Market**
*Berwick Street, W1*

Fruit and vegetable stalls predominate here, but shellfish, clothing, and household goods are also available, and some of the stalls are attached to neighbouring shops. The market is especially crowded at lunchtimes, as shoppers queue up at stalls which are reputed to sell some of the best quality fruit and vegetables in London.
*Monday-Saturday*

**Brixton Market**
*Electric Avenue, SW9*

As this market is set in an area with a large West Indian population, it is not surprising that many of its stalls are stocked with Caribbean fruit and

vegetables. There are also second-hand clothes and household goods stalls.
*Monday-Saturday (Wednesday am only)*

**Camden Lock Market**
*Camden Lock Place,*
*NW1*

Antiques, bric-à-brac, period and Asian clothes are generally available, and there are also craft and food stalls.
*Saturday and Sunday*

**Camden Passage**
*Camden Passage, N1*

This is a rich and varied mixture of antique shops and stalls, most of the latter appearing on Wednesdays and Saturdays. The arcades of the market become very crowded on Saturdays, and only those arriving early can hope to find a bargain. The goods on display are liberally sprinkled with bric-à-brac and Victorian curios, but Camden Passage is as good a place as any for a wide variety of antiques, with dealers specialising in furniture, jewellery, prints, pottery, books, pub mirrors, period clothing, and silverware.
*Wednesday, Thursday and Saturday*

**Chapel Market**
*White Conduit Street,*
*N1*

This market is very popular with the locals at weekends. Fruit and vegetables are always available, and there are usually stalls selling fish, groceries, household goods and fabric and linens.
*Tuesday-Sunday am*

**Church Street**
*Lisson Grove, NW8*

A mixture of stalls is to be found in these adjacent markets. Antiques are well represented, with some excellent stalls. There are also clothes, household goods and food stalls.
*Monday-Saturday*

**The Courtyard**
*St Martin-in-the-Fields*
*Church, St Martin's*
*Place, WC2*

A popular craft market where over 200 artists and designers sell ceramics, glass, jewellery, fashion, fine art and toys.
*Monday-Saturday pm only and Sunday*

**Columbia Road Market**
*Shoreditch, E2*

An enormous variety of flowers, plants, and shrubs make this market a Mecca for all gardening enthusiasts.
*Sunday am*

**Covent Garden —**
**Jubilee Market Hall**
*Covent Garden, WC2*

Partly under cover, this small general market opened in Covent Garden at about the time that Covent Garden Wholesale Market moved to Nine Elms in the 1970s. There are fruit, vegetables, and bric-à-brac stalls, but the greater part of this market contains souvenirs, clothes, craft, jewellery and record stalls.
*Monday-Sunday*

**East Street Market**
*Walworth, SE17*

This is an old-established general market with some bric-à-brac stalls. Plants, shrubs, and fruit are usually available on Sundays.
*Tuesday-Saturday, Sunday am*

**Leadenhall Market**
*Gracechurch Street, EC3*

Formerly purely a wholesale market, today Leadenhall is open to the general public and, while still specialising in meat and poultry, also offers fish,

vegetables, and plants. The Victorian arcade, containing cafes and pubs in contrast to the rows of carcasses which are suspended on tiers of hooks outside the shops, is noted for its old-time market atmosphere, and is a favourite haunt for City office workers, whether intent on buying, or simply watching the world go by.
*Monday-Friday*

**Leather Lane**
*Holborn, EC1*

Fruit, groceries, vegetables, clothing, household goods of all descriptions — particularly crockery — are always on display here. The sight of an entire dinner service being expertly tossed in the air is a regular occurrence.
*Monday-Friday*

**Lower Marsh**
*Lambeth, SE1*

This busy general market nestles in the shadow of Waterloo Station and becomes very popular during the lunch period.
*Monday-Saturday*

**New Caledonian Market**
*Bermondsey Square, SE1*

This is primarily a dealers' antique market. An enormous selection of articles is on view, set out on closely packed stalls, but those in search of a bargain need to be early risers as a great deal of the trading takes place between 6am and 7am (when the market officially opens). Although something of a closed community, run principally by dealers for dealers, private collectors and casual visitors are made very welcome. Bric-à-brac, silver, jewellery, clocks, pottery, and porcelain are always available, and furniture, coins, and medals are also featured, but stallholders tend to avoid specialisation, displaying oddments and curios of all descriptions.
*Friday am*

**Northcote Road**
*Battersea, SW11*

A fruit and vegetable market situated near Clapham Junction. It is at its busiest on Saturdays, and at that time the atmosphere can be very lively indeed.
*Monday-Saturday*

**North End Road**
*Fulham, SW6*

This general market specialises in fruit and vegetables, and flowers and plants are on sale during the summer months. Other stalls in this cheerful market offer clothes, and household goods.
*Monday-Saturday*

**Petticoat Lane**
*Middlesex Street, E1*

The street acquired the name Petticoat Lane during the 17th century because of the number of old clothes dealers who congregated here. Despite the fact that it offically became known as Middlesex Street as long ago as 1846 the old name has lived on, at least as far as the Sunday market is concerned. It is one of the most famous of all London markets, and opens around 9am, but all the stallholders begin to set up their premises about 7.30am before an interested audience of sightseers. Despite its present-day cosmopolitan

atmosphere, engendered by the Indian, West Indian, and Jewish communities which are prevalent in the area, Petticoat Lane still retains its essential Cockney character. The maze of stalls occupies every available corner, and there is very little in the way of household goods and clothes of every description that cannot be purchased.
*Sunday am*

**Portobello Road**
*Notting Hill, W11*

Portobello Road has been noted for its antique shops and stalls since the 1950s. It reached the height of its fame during the late '60s and early '70s when it became the centre of London's hippy community. A general market with fruit, vegetable and meat stalls operates all the week, but it is on Saturdays that all the stalls and arcades are opened. The stalls and shops, of which there are more than 2,000, contain all kinds of furniture, clothes, jewellery, ancient gramophones and records, books, bottles, coins, medals, toys, a great deal of Victoriana, and an endless selection of junk. Buskers, street singers, and street performers jostle with and cajole the crowds. It is rare to find a genuine bargain in the antique stalls at the lower end of the road these days, since all the traders are experts, but real finds can sometimes be made on the stalls beyond the Westway Flyover.
*Monday-Saturday (Thursday am only)*

**Ridley Road**
*Hackney, E8*

One of the better known of London's East End markets, the stalls here are patronised by the local Jewish and West Indian communities. It is a general market, with many fruit and vegetable stalls, and becomes very crowded on Saturdays.
*Monday-Saturday*

**Roman Road**
*Tower Hamlets, E3*

A busy market with stalls on either side of the road offering a good variety of clothes, shoes, food and fancy goods.
*Tuesday and Thursday am only and Saturday*

**Shepherd's Bush**
*W12*

Stalls specialising in West Indian food, and household goods will be found in the market here. It extends as far as Goldhawk Road beside a railway viaduct.
*Monday-Saturday (Thursday am only)*

**Walthamstow**
*The High Street, E17*

This extensive general market straggles along either side of Walthamstow's main street. It is particularly busy towards the end of the week.
*Monday-Saturday*

**Wembley Market**
*Wembley Stadium, NW10 (See also page 70)*

A large open-air market with accommodation for up to 500 stalls is held here every Sunday between 9am-2pm on part of the stadium car park. A large variety of goods is sold, and usually there is free parking.
*Sunday*

**Wentworth Street**
*Tower Hamlets, E1*

This general market is engulfed by Petticoat Lane on Sundays. For the rest of the week it caters for

locals, and has some excellent stalls selling Jewish and West Indian foods.
*Monday-Friday, Sunday am only*

**Whitechapel Waste Market**
*Whitechapel Road, E1*

Stalls line the pavements of this famous East End thoroughfare, multiplying on Saturdays.
*Monday-Saturday (Thursday am only)*

**Whitecross Street**
*Islington, EC1*

A busy market which caters, to a large extent, for lunch-time shoppers. It is particularly crowded on Wednesdays and Fridays.
*Monday-Saturday*

**Woolwich Market**
*Beresford Square, SE18*

This small market is very popular and has a wide variety of stalls.
*Monday-Saturday (Thursday am only)*

## Trade Markets

**Billingsgate Market**
*North Quay, West India Docks, Isle of Dogs, E14*

The first official mention of this historic wholesale fish market was made as long ago as the end of the 13th century, when a royal charter was granted to the Corporation of London for the sale of fish. A market is known to have been held on Billingsgate's old site in Lower Thames Street in the City of London at least 400 years earlier. In 1982, the traders moved to a new site in London's Docklands.

From about 5am the market becomes a hive of activity and the air is pervaded by a pungent aroma of fish and the uninhibited language of the porters. By 8am most of the business is over and about 300 tons of fish will have changed hands.

**Borough Market**
*Southwark Street, SE3*

This market occupies buildings beneath the railway arches of the viaduct serving London Bridge Station to the south of Southwark Cathedral.

It operates from Monday to Saturday, with traders commencing business as early as 3am. Activity builds up in a crescendo of noise and bustle between 6 and 7am, and most of the business has been completed by the middle of the morning.

Covent Garden

**New Covent Garden**
*Nine Elms, SW8*

The original Covent Garden (the area to the east of Charing Cross Road) owes its name to the fact that the monks of Westminster Abbey had a 40 acre walled garden here. It grew to become the most important fruit, vegetable and flower market in the country, and in 1830 the first specially-built market premises were erected on the site. These buildings were rapidly outgrown, and by the middle of the 20th century wholesalers had taken over all the streets in the area. Traffic congestion had become a serious problem by this time, and it was decided that the only solution was to move the market to specially-built premises at Nine Elms. The move was made in 1974, to the sorrow of many people, as Covent Garden had a unique and irreplaceable character.

The market has now settled into its new home at Nine Elms, and there is no doubt that the vast building makes up in increased efficiency what it lacks in character.

**Smithfield Market**
*West Smithfield, EC1*

Smithfield is London's principal wholesale meat market, and is one of the largest meat, poultry and provision markets in the world. The total area covered by all the market buildings is over eight acres.

Smithfield, which is derived from 'Smoothfield', was originally an open space located just outside the old city walls.

Up until the middle of the 19th century all cattle sold at Smithfield were driven through the narrow and congested streets of Central London. At one time the number of beasts flowing in and out of the market amounted to 70,000 a week. It was not until 1867 that a government statute placed restrictions on the droving of cattle through the capital's thoroughfares. It was at this time that the present Central London Meat Market was constructed. It was designed by Sir Horace Jones and is a Renaissance-style building consisting of iron and glass arcades fronted with red brick and flanked by domed towers. To the west of the cattle market is the Poultry Market building, which was built in 1963 to replace a Victorian structure that was destroyed by fire in 1958.

**Spitalfields Market**
*Ruckholt Road, E10*

The original market in Commercial Street was named after the priory of St Mary Spital which was founded here in 1197. Spitalfields refers both to the area and to the wholesale market, which trades in fruit, vegetables and flowers. In 1928 a new market building was opened by Queen Mary and included extensive underground chambers, used principally for ripening bananas. The market outgrew this site and in 1991 moved to a new modern building in Leyton. Trading begins at 3am every weekday and is generally completed by 10am.

### Fine Art Auctioneers

The three big names in London are Sotheby's, Christie's and Phillips, all of which have international connections and hold sales all over the world. The public is admitted to previews and sales except on very rare occasions when admission is by ticket only, and all three auction houses welcome people bringing objects for free inspection and estimation of value.

**Christie, Manson & Woods Ltd**
*8 King Street, SW1*

Founded in 1766, Christie's holds as many as three or four sales a day in its King Street salerooms. Over 150,000 pictures, pieces of furniture, silver, porcelain, jewellery, books, arms and armour, and *objets d'art* are sold each year, two-thirds of them for less than £300. There are a number of specialist sales, and sales in the lower price range are held at Christie's South Kensington.

**Phillips**
*101 New Bond Street, W1*

Phillips was founded in 1796, and today regular sales are held for antiques of all sorts and works of art. In addition there are a great number of specialist sales ranging from coins and stamps to musical instruments and suits of armour.

**Sotheby's**
*34/35 New Bond Street, W1*

Sotheby's, founded in 1744, is the oldest and largest fine art auctioneer in the world. The London headquarters has been in the same white-fronted Georgian house in New Bond Street since 1917 and is open from 9am to 4.30pm Monday to Friday. With around 300 auctions a year, each being on view to the public for at least two days before the sale, the galleries host a fascinating and constantly changing free exhibition. Sotheby's strength is its internationally renowned expertise in over 70 different collecting fields from paintings, furniture, silver and ceramics to musical instruments, toys and dolls, coins, stamps and vintage cars. Sotheby's experts are available during the above hours to give free verbal opinions on the age, identity and saleroom value of any items which members of the public care to bring along.

# Sport

Spectator sport remains popular in London, despite television, and the tarnished reputation of fans of some sports. To be at the finals of a football tournament, or at a cricket test match, or urging your horse to be first past the post is very exciting.

**Association Football**

The Football Association (FA) was not founded until 1863, and the first FA Challenge Cup Final was played at the Oval, Kennington, in 1872. Today London has 13 teams in the four divisions of the Football League, and it has had at least one team in the top category, Division One, every year since 1904. In addition, London boasts Britain's foremost football stadium — Wembley (see page 70). The football season runs from August to May.

**London's Football Clubs**

**Arsenal**
*Arsenal Stadium, Highbury, N5*

**Barnet**
*Underhill Stadium, Barnet Lane, Barnet*

**Brentford**
*Griffin Park, Braemar Road, Brentford*

**Charlton Athletic**
*The Valley, Floyd Road, Charlton, SE7 (Now playing at West Ham United)*

**Chelsea**
*Stamford Bridge, Fulham Road, SW6*

**Crystal Palace**
*Selhurst Park, Whitehorse Lane, SE25*

**Fulham**
*Craven Cottage, Stevenage Road, Fulham, SW6*

**Leyton Orient**
*Leyton Stadium, Brisbane Road, Leyton, E10*

**Millwall**
*The Den, Cold Blow Lane, New Cross, SE14*

**Queen's Park Rangers**
*South Africa Road, W12*

**Tottenham Hotspur**
*748 High Road, Tottenham, N17*

**West Ham United**
*Boleyn Ground, Green Street, Upton Park, E13*

**Wimbledon**
*Plough Lane Ground, 45 Durnsford, Wimbledon, SW19*

**Athletics**  London has witnessed many great moments in athletics history, including the staging of the 14th Olympic Games at Wembley in 1948. The White City stadium has also been the scene of many memorable events. Built at the beginning of this century, it was the venue for the 4th Modern Olympic Games and was London's principal athletic stadium for more than half a century.

In 1964 the Crystal Palace National Sports Centre opened and the White City finally ended its long and honourable association with athletics. The purpose-built Sports Centre has an all-weather track and covered accommodation for spectators, and stages all manner of athletics competitions.

**Crystal Palace National Sports Centre**
*Crystal Palace Park, Sydenham, SE19*

**New River Sports Centre**
*White Hart Lane, Wood Green, N22*

**Parliament Hill Fields**
*Gospel Oak, NW3*

**Victoria Park**
*Victoria Park, E9*

**West London Stadium**
*White City, W12*

**Cricket**

Cricket is widely played in London, on commons and playing fields, but the two major venues are Lord's Cricket Ground in St John's Wood and the Oval in Kennington.

Lord's is probably the best-known ground in the country and is the home ground for two clubs — Middlesex County Cricket Club and the famous Marylebone Cricket Club, perhaps even better known by its initials, MCC. Until recently the MCC was effectively the governing body for the game, and its collection of cricket memorabilia forms the MCC Museum (See page 93).

The game of cricket accompanied the British to the colonies and it became equally popular in Australia, New Zealand, South Africa, the West Indies, India and Pakistan. It is these countries who play England in the Test Matches, which are played here and in their own countries. A Test Match is usually five days long and there can be as many as six in a series, played on various pitches throughout the country. Both Lord's and the Oval are traditional venues for Test Matches, the latter being the site of the first-ever Test in 1877.

The Oval is the home ground of Surrey County Cricket Club, and today it is usually the venue for the final Test in a series.

Lord's, too, has Test Matches, and many other countries as well as the eight Test countries are being drawn into international cricket by the new World Cup competition. Begun in 1975, it takes place every four years, and is now held at various venues throughout the world. The many other matches played at Lord's include county cricket, the finals of the NatWest Cup and the Benson and Hedges Cup, and the annual match between Eton and Harrow.

**Lord's Ground**
*St John's Wood Road, NW8*

**The Oval**
*The Oval, Kennington, SE11*

**Greyhound Racing**

'Going to the dogs' has always been a popular pastime, especially with East End Londoners. Pure-bred greyhounds chase after an artificial hare on an electrified rail at speeds of up to 40mph. Races, either on the flat or over hurdles, are over varying distances and attract a good deal of betting and prize money. The most famous track is probably Walthamstow. Several of the tracks have restaurants overlooking the races.

**Catford**
*Greyhound Stadium, SE6*

**Wembley**
*Stadium Way*

**Hackney Wick**
*Waterden Road, E15*

**Wimbledon**
*Plough Lane, SW19*

**Walthamstow**
*Chingford Road, E4*

**Horse Racing** Horse racing is as much a part of the social calendar as it is a sport. Many go to the races to see and to be seen. There is plenty of excitement for those who go for the actual racing, and of course there is the possibility of winning a bet. The flat-racing season is from March to November, and steeplechasing takes place between August and June.

**Ascot Racecourse**
*Ascot, Berkshire*

**Epsom Racecourse**
*Epsom, Surrey*

**Kempton Park Racecourse**
*Sunbury-on-Thames, Greater London*

**Sandown Racecourse**
*Esher, Surrey*

**Windsor Racecourse**
*Windsor, Berkshire*

**Rugby Union Football** Throughout the rugby season, which extends from September to early May, there are always attractive games to see in the London area. Major matches which are played at the Rugby Football Union's splendid stadium at Twickenham include internationals (which are well publicised), the Oxford v Cambridge match in early December, the Pilkington Cup Final and the Middlesex Sevens Finals, both at the beginning of May. Tickets for these events are usually in short supply — for ticket information call 081-744 3111. The Inter-Services Championships are played at Twickenham during March and April as are the finals of the county and junior clubs knock-out championships. In addition to the major clubs listed below, there are a host of games played by club, college, hospital and school teams, all of them acting as nurseries for future great players.

**Blackheath RFC**
*Rectory Field, Charlton Road, Blackheath, SE3*

**Harlequin RFC**
*Stoop Memorial Ground, Craneford Way, Twickenham, Greater London*

**London Irish RFC**
*Pavilion, The Avenue, Sunbury-on-Thames*

**London Scottish RFC**
*Richmond Athletic Ground, Richmond, Surrey*

**London Welsh RFC**
*Old Deer Park, Kew Road, Richmond, Surrey*

**Metropolitan Police RFC**
*Police Sports Club, Imber Court, Embercourt Road, East Molesey, Surrey*

**Richmond RFC**
*Richmond Athletic Ground, Richmond Surrey*

**Rosslyn Park RFC**
*Priory Lane, Upper Richmond Road, Roehampton, SW15*

**Saracens RFC**
*The Pavilion, Bromley Sports Ground, Green Road, Southgate, N14*

**Wasps RFC**
*Repton Avenue, Wembley, Greater London*

**Speedway**

This highly specialised motorcycling sport, which developed from dirt-track racing in open fields, is now usually held within large football or greyhound stadiums. The fearless riders need a great deal of skill and daring to execute the long, broadside drifts on the sweeping curves at each end of the track, sending showers of the loose shale surface into the air.

**Arena Essex**
*Arena Sports Complex, Arterial Road, Purfleet*

**Rye House**
*Rye House Stadium, Rye Road, Hoddesdon, Herts*

**Tennis**

In the last week of June and the first week in July, the All England Lawn Tennis and Croquet Club hosts what is, in effect, the world tennis championships on grass, though the event is called simply the Lawn Tennis Championships Meeting.

The Wimbledon complex, to which improvements have been made since its opening in 1922 by King George V, consists of 30 grass courts with their cherished and world-famous Cumberland turf, nine hard courts and five indoor courts. The complex includes a post office, bank, and restaurants.

**All England Lawn
Tennis and Croquet
Club**
*Church Road,
Wimbledon, SW19*

# Pageantry, Ceremonies and Events

The most famous events in London's ceremonial calendar are the grand royal pageants, such as Trooping the Colour, which are brilliantly colourful and which attract huge crowds. But London has hundreds of other events, some very big, like the Lord Mayor's Show, and some tiny, like the Ceremony of the Lilies and Roses. For further information on all these events, telephone the London Tourist Board and Convention Bureau — (071) 730 3488. (See also list of events at Earls Court and Olympia, page 70.)

### Changing of the Guard ceremonies

**Buckingham Palace**

This famous ceremony takes place in front of Buckingham Palace daily from the beginning of April to the end of August, and on alternate days from September to March. If the weather is very wet, or if there is some other ceremony on that day, then there may be no change, or the times may be altered. The Guard is changed at 11.30am, but onlookers are advised to be in place outside the palace well before that to get a good viewing position. The Guard is drawn from troops of the Brigade of Guards, the Queen's personal bodyguard. The new guard, usually accompanied by a band, marches to the palace from Wellington Barracks.

**Mounting the Guard**
Horse Guards, Whitehall

This ceremony, which takes about half an hour, takes place at 11.00am Monday to Saturday, and at 10.00am on Sunday. The mounted guardsmen, drawn from the Household Cavalry, ride from Hyde Park to Whitehall.

**St James's Palace**

The detachment of the Queen's Guard which patrols St James's Palace marches to Buckingham

Palace at 11.15am and returns to St James's Palace at 12.10pm. This ceremony does not take place if there is no guard-change at Buckingham Palace.

**Tower of London** If there is a guard-change at Buckingham Palace, the Guard at the Tower is changed at 11.30am.

**Ceremony of the Keys** For 700 years the main gate at the Tower has been locked by the Chief Yeoman Warder of the Tower and an escort of Guards. The ceremony starts at 9.40pm. Permits are essential for this ceremony; they can be applied for from The Constable's Office, Queens House, H M Tower of London, EC3 4AB. At least four weeks advanced booking is necessary.

**Gun Salutes** Royal Salutes take place annually at midday in Hyde Park on February 6 (the Queen's Accession Day), April 21 (the Queen's Birthday), June 2 (Coronation Day), June 10 (the Duke of Edinburgh's Birthday), August 4 (Queen Mother's Birthday). The salutes (of 41 guns) are fired by the King's Troop, Royal Horse Artillery. On the same days, 62-gun salutes are fired at the Tower of London by the Honourable Artillery Company. These salutes take place at 1.00pm.

# Major events

**January** **Lord Mayor of Westminster's New Year's Day Parade** Marching bands, floats and performers parade from Piccadilly to Hyde Park Corner, culminating in a firework display.

**6th January** **Royal Epiphany Gifts Service**
Chapel Royal, St James's Palace

A 700-year-old ceremony in which officers of the royal household offer up gifts of gold, frankincense and myrrh. The gold is subsequently exchanged for currency and distributed for charitable purposes.

**early January** **Old Bailey in Session**
Central Criminal Court, Old Bailey

The opening session of the Central Criminal Court, Old Bailey, is attended by the Lord Mayor of London, who leads a procession from the Mansion House to the Old Bailey attended by the sheriffs, swordbearer, common crier and city marshal.

**Court of Common Council Service**
Church of St Lawrence Jewry, Gresham St

The Lord Mayor of London and his officers walk in procession from the Guildhall to attend a service at the Church of St Lawrence Jewry, Gresham Street, prior to the first sitting of the newly-elected Court of Common Council which presides over the City of London.

| 30th January | **Charles I Commemoration Ceremony** |
| | Trafalgar Square |

Each year members of the Society of King Charles the Martyr and the Royal Stuart Society commemorate the execution of Charles I on 30th January 1649. They walk in procession from St Martin-in-the-Fields to the equestrian statue of the King which stands in Trafalgar Square near the entrance to Whitehall.

# February

**Sunday nearest first day of new Lunar calendar**

**Chinese New Year**
Gerrard St

London's 'Chinatown' is decorated for this event, and a procession led by a 'lion' weaves through the area receiving gifts from shops. This celebration has evolved in recent years to become one of London's most colourful and exciting ceremonies.

**Ash Wednesday**

**Cakes and Ale Sermon**
St Paul's Cathedral

Members of the Stationers Company walk in procession from Stationers' Hall to St Paul's Cathedral where their chaplain preaches a sermon in accordance with the wishes of John Norton, a member of the Worshipful Company of Stationers who died during the reign of James I. Cakes and ale are distributed before or after the service.

**3rd February (St Blaise's Day)**

**Blessing of the Throats**
St Ethelreda Church, Holborn

Throat sufferers congregate at the Church of St Ethelreda, in Holborn, for a service commemorating St Blaise, Bishop of Dalmatia, who saved the life of a child with a fishbone lodged in its throat while on his way to a martyr's death during the 3rd century.

**on the Saturday nearest to 22nd February**

**Scout and Guide Founders' Day Service**
Westminster Abbey

Scouts and guides gather in Westminster Abbey on the shared birthday of Lord Baden-Powell, founder of the Scout and Guide Movement, and his widow. Wreaths are laid on the Baden-Powell memorial.

**Shrove Tuesday (occasionally March)**

**Pancake Race**
Lincoln's Inn Fields, Paternoster Square

**on or near 20th**

**Sir John Cass Commemoration Service**
Sir Botolph's Church, Aldgate

This service commemorates a City Sheriff who founded the school named after him in 1709.

**first Sunday in February**

**The Clown Service — Grimaldi Commemoration Service**
Holy Trinity Church, Dalston

Joseph Grimaldi was one of the most famous clowns of all time, and there is a memorial to him in this church. The service is attended by clowns in full costume.

# March

**(on or near 21st, Spring Equinox)**    **Druid's Observance Ceremony**
Tower Hill

Members of the Druid Order gather to celebrate the spring equinox here.

**(or April)**    **Oxford & Cambridge Boat Race**
Putney — Mortlake

The Boat Race, a contest between two crews of eight rowers and one coxswain representing the universities of Oxford and Cambridge, is one of the most famous sporting events in the world. The first Boat Race took place at Henley-on-Thames in 1829, but in 1845 the event was moved to its present location in London. The course runs on the Thames from Putney to Mortlake, a distance of over 4 miles, and it takes place annually on a Saturday shortly before Easter.

**on or near 28th March**    **Oranges & Lemons Children's Service**
St Clement Dane's Church, Strand

A service to mark the restoration of the bells of St Clement Danes in the Strand, the 'St Clements' of the well-known nursery rhyme 'Oranges and Lemons'. The service is attended by children of the St Clement Danes Primary School and each child receives an orange and a lemon.

# Easter

**Maundy Thursday**    **Distribution of the Royal Maundy Money**
Alternate locations including Westminster Abbey and Southwark Cathedral

This ancient ceremony of royal humility, which dates back to the time of Edward III, once included the reigning monarch washing the feet of the poor. The last sovereign to perform this rite was James II. William III delegated the washing to an aide, and the last foot-washing took place in 1754, after which the ceremony consisted of giving specially-minted Maundy pennies. Today the Queen distributes two purses, one containing the Maundy Money, the other containing money which represents the now discontinued gifts of food and clothing, to senior citizens selected from London parishes. The ceremony is held at various alternate locations including Westminster Abbey and Southwark Cathedral.

**Good Friday**    **Hot-Cross Buns Service**
St Bartholomew-the-Great Church, Smithfield

Under the terms of an ancient charity, the morning service at St Bartholomew-the-Great, Smithfield, is concluded by the distribution of money and hot cross buns to 21 local widows.

**Easter Monday**

**Harness Horse Parade**
Regent's Park

An extensive display of private and commercial horse-drawn vehicles, featuring all types of horses from shire horses drawing brewers' drays to the pony and trap, which takes place on the Inner Circle, Regent's Park.

**second Wednesday after Easter**

**Spital Sermon Procession**
Guildhall to St Lawrence Jewry Church

The Lord Mayor of London walks in procession with aldermen and other City dignitaries from the Guildhall to the Church of St Lawrence Jewry where a bishop nominated by the Archbishop of Canterbury preaches the Spital Sermon. These sermons have an Easter theme and were preached at St Paul's Cross in the Cathedral churchyard prior to the Great Fire.

# April

**on or near 5th April**

**John Stow's Quill Pen Ceremony**
St Andrew Undershaft Church, Leadenhall St

The memorial service for John Stow, who wrote *The Survey of London* in 1598, takes place each year at the Church of St Andrew Undershaft, Leadenhall Street, attended by the Lord Mayor and other dignitaries. During the service the Lord Mayor places a fresh quill in the hand of Stow's statue, which depicts him at work on his *Survey*.

**Spring Flower Show**
Royal Horticultural Society Halls, Vincent Square, SW1

# May

**21st May**

**Ceremony of the Lilies and Roses**
Tower of London

Representatives of Eton College and King's College, Cambridge, both founded by Henry VI, join in a ceremony at the Wakefield Tower, Tower of London on the anniversary of the King's murder. Lilies from Eton and roses from King's are placed on the spot where Henry was killed in 1471.

**29th May**

**Oak Apple Day**
Royal Hospital, Chelsea

The Chelsea Pensioners honour Charles II, the founder of the Royal Hospital, on the anniversary of his escape after the Battle of Worcester (1651). His statue is decorated with oak leaves and branches — in memory of the fact that the King hid in an oak tree.

**(May to July)**    **Royal Academy Summer Art Exhibition**
Royal Academy, Piccadilly

**Royal Windsor Horse Show**
Windsor

**Association Football Cup Final**
Wembley

**Chelsea Flower Show**
Royal Hospital, Chelsea

The Royal Hospital Gardens have been the setting for the Flower Show since 1913. Entire landscapes are created for the show, and new strains of flowers are often unveiled here.

**(April or May)**    **London Marathon**
Greenwich to Westminster

This event has now established itself as one of the highlights of the London year. Thousands of runners, from the very young to the very old and from the fit to the not-so-fit, compete in a good-humoured race through London.

# June

**second Saturday in June**    **Trooping the Colour**
Buckingham Palace to The Mall to Horse Guards Parade

Held on the Queen's official birthday, at Horse Guards Parade, off Whitehall, Trooping the Colour is probably the most spectacular military display in the country. The 200-year-old ceremony, with its roots stretching back to medieval times, begins with the Queen riding from Buckingham Palace, wearing the uniform of one of the regiments of which she is Colonel-in-Chief, to Horse Guards Parade, where the Brigade of Guards and the Household Cavalry await her, massed on the parade ground. Her Majesty takes the salute which is followed by a display of marching and the 'trooping' or carrying of the colours of a selected regiment. Originally the colours were 'trooped' so that the men of the regiment could learn to recognise their own colours. The Queen then leads a contingent of Guards back to Buckingham Palace. The sovereign's official birthday is always held in summer when the chances of good weather are at their best.

**about 24th June**    **The Knollys Red Rose Rent**
Seething Lane to Mansion House

This ceremony commemorates the fining of Sir Robert Knollys in the 14th century for building a footbridge between two of his properties on either side of Seething Lane. In recognition of his recent military service in France the fine imposed was the

presentation of a red rose from his garden to the
Lord Mayor every Midsummer Day. Today
churchwardens of All Hallows-by-the-Tower carry a
red rose to the Mansion House on an altar cushion
where it is presented to the Lord Mayor together
with a bouquet of roses for the Lady Mayoress.

**Epsom Races — The Derby**
Epsom

**Royal Ascot Races**
Ascot

**(2 weeks end June/ beginning July**   **Lawn Tennis Championships**
Wimbledon

**(occasionally July)**   **Cricket — Test Match**
Lord's Cricket Ground

**Grosvenor House Antiques Fair**
Park Lane

**(early June)**   **Beating Retreat — Household Division**
Horse Guards Parade

**(mid June)**   **Royal Artillery**
Horse Guards Parade

An impressive military display of marching and
drilling bands. Each event is held over three days.

# July

**on or near last Monday in July**   **Swan Upping**
London Bridge to Henley

The Vintners' and Dyers' Livery Companies have
the right, shared with the monarch, of keeping
swans on the River Thames between London Bridge
and Henley. Swan Upping takes place when the
cygnets (or young swans) are about two months
old, and entails the Queen's Swan Keeper and the
Swan Wardens and Swan Markers of the two
companies inspecting all the adult swans and
establishing the ownership of the cygnets. These
are duly marked by the officials, who wear
traditional livery, and operate from skiffs rowed by
assistants in striped jerseys and hats.

**late July/early August**   **Doggett's Coat and Badge Race**
London Bridge to Albert Bridge

This, the oldest rowing event in the world, was
instituted in 1715 by Thomas Doggett, an Irish
actor, in honour of the accession to the throne of
George I. Today, under the patronage of the
Fishmongers' Company, six Thames watermen race
against the tide from London Bridge to Albert
Bridge. The winner of what is sometimes called the
'Watermen's Derby' receives a scarlet livery with
silver buttons and a large silver badge on the left
arm.

**mid July/mid August**

**Henry Wood Promenade Concerts**
Royal Albert Hall SW7

Founded in 1895 by Sir Henry Wood, this series of concerts is famous the world over.

**Royal International Horse Show**
Wembley

**Cricket: Benson and Hedges Cup Final**
Lord's Cricket Ground

**Vintners' Procession**
Vintners' Hall to St James, Garlickhythe

After the installation of a Master Vintner, the wine porters sweep a path for the following procession.

# August

**Greater London Horse Show**
Clapham Common

**Notting Hill Carnival**
Portobello Road area

A noisy, friendly, colourful event, with a large contribution by London's Caribbean population.

# September

**28th September or preceding Friday**

**Admission of Sheriffs**
Mansion House to Guildhall

The two sheriffs elected by the livery companies on Midsummer Day go in full procession together with the Lord Mayor, senior City officials, and their fellow liverymen, from the Mansion House to the Guildhall. Here the sheriffs are presented with their chains of office.

**on or near 29th September**

**Election of the Lord Mayor**
Guildhall to Mansion House

The election of the Lord Mayor of London has taken place on Michaelmas Day since 1546. After a service in St Lawrence Jewry, the current Lord Mayor goes in procession to the Guildhall, where he and his aldermen make the final selection from the candidates nominated by the livery companies. After the ceremony the Lord Mayor and his successor ride in the state coach to the Mansion House to the accompaniment of the city bells.

**on or near 15th September 11am-noon**

**Battle of Britain Week**
Greater London and Westminster Abbey

Fly-past of aircraft over London and Thanksgiving service in Westminster Abbey on Sunday.

**Last Night of the Proms**
Royal Albert Hall

**(Autumn Equinox)**

**Druids' Observance Ceremony**
Primrose Hill, Regent's Park

# October

**21st October**   **Trafalgar Service and Parade**
Trafalgar Square

A naval parade in memory of the Battle of
Trafalgar, 1805, including a march from the Horse
Guards Parade to Trafalgar Square followed by a
service and the laying of wreaths at the foot of
Nelson's Column.

**late October/early**   **State Opening of Parliament**
**November**   Buckingham Palace to House of Lords, Westminster

In one of London's most colourful pageants, the
Queen rides in the Irish State Coach from
Buckingham Palace to the Palace of Westminster
via the Mall and Whitehall. At Westminster, the
Queen and other members of the royal family are
greeted by a gun salute fired by the King's Troop of
the Royal Horse Artillery. The royal party then
enters the Houses of Parliament through the great
arch under the Victoria Tower, and the Queen
enters the Robing Room. Later Her Majesty
emerges wearing the royal robes and the crown,
and is conducted, amidst a procession of great
officers of state, heralds, and the sound of
trumpets, to the House of Lords where she ascends
to the throne. The Lords, in their ceremonial robes,
are already present and the Speaker and members
of the House of Commons are now summoned by
the official called Black Rod. After their arrival the
Queen makes her speech outlining the
government's proposed legislation for the new
parliamentary session. A few hours before the
Queen arrives, Yeomen of the Guard search the
vaults of the Houses of Parliament. This exercise
has been carried out each year since the
unsuccessful Gunpowder Plot of 1605. The actual
ceremony of the State Opening of Parliament is
not open to the public, but many thousands of
people line the processional route.

**Horse of the Year Show**
Wembley Arena

**1st Sunday, 3pm**   **Costermonger's Harvest Festival**
St Martin-in-the-Fields

This service, originating in the 19th century, is
attended by the Pearly Kings and Queens in their
tradifional button-covered costumes.

**late October**   **Quit-Rents Ceremony**
Royal Courts of Justice, Strand

This public ceremony, one of the oldest still carried
out in London, is held at the Royal Courts of
Justice, and involves the City Solicitor making
token payments for two properties. The rent takes
the form of two faggots of wood, a billhook, and a
hatchet of land in Shropshire, and six horseshoes
and sixty-one nails, for a forge which once stood in
the Strand.

# November

**first Sunday in November**

**London to Brighton Veteran Car Run**
From Hyde Park Corner

Cars built between 1895 and 1904 take part in this run which starts from Hyde Park Corner and finishes at Madeira Drive, Brighton. The event dates originally from 1896 when the law compelling motorists to have a man with a red flag walking in front of them was abolished and jubilant drivers destroyed their flags and roared off to Brighton. The first organised Run was held in 1933. All the cars taking part in the event are beautifully cared for, and many of the drivers and passengers dress in period costume.

**2nd Saturday in November**

**Lord Mayor's Show**
Guildhall to Royal Courts of Justice, Strand

This is the day when the new Lord Mayor publicly takes office. He rides to the Royal Courts of Justice in a ceremonial 18th-century coach, drawn by six horses, attended by a bodyguard of Pikemen and Musketeers, and preceded by a colourful procession of floats depicting some theme related to London's history. This ceremony is at least 600 years old and is the City's most spectacular showpiece. On the following Monday the Lord Mayor gives a lavish banquet at the Guildhall.

**8th November**

**Installation of the Lord Mayor**
Mansion House to Guildhall

The current Lord Mayor and the Lord Mayor-Elect attend a luncheon at the Mansion House together with liverymen of each of their companies. They then go in procession to the Guildhall where they officially change places and transfer the insignia of office. The two Lord Mayors then return to the Mansion House to the accompaniment of peals of bells from the City churches.

**on Sunday nearest to 11th November**

**Remembrance Day Service**
Cenotaph, Whitehall

A service at the Cenotaph, in Whitehall, to remember the dead of both World Wars, is attended by the Queen, members of the royal family, representatives of the armed services, ex-servicemen's associations and leading politicians. A gun salute is followed by two minutes' silence after which wreaths are laid at the Cenotaph.

**on or near 22nd November**

**Festival of St Cecilia**
St Sepulchre's, Holborn

A service is held at St Sepulchre's, Holborn, in honour of St Cecilia, the patron saint of music. Well-known organists and choirs from Westminster Abbey, St Paul's and Canterbury Cathedral combine to provide a feast of church music in a 16th-century ceremony which was revived in 1946 after having died out in the 19th century.

# December

**around 16th onwards**

**Christmas Tree and Carol Singing**
Trafalgar Square

Every year a giant Christmas tree is donated to London by the people of Oslo, Norway. It is set up in Trafalgar Square and becomes the focal point for evening carol services.

**Christmas Decorations**
Regent St/Oxford St

**Sunday before Christmas**

**Tower of London Parade**
Tower of London

The Yeomen Warders in full uniform are inspected before and after morning service.

**New Year's Eve Celebrations**
Trafalgar Square

On New Year's Eve the square is the scene of tumultuous celebrations as hundreds see the new year in, many of them demonstrating their joy by dousing each other in the fountains.

**Occasional Ceremonies**

**Nosegays for Judges**
Central Criminal Court

Whenever a High Court judge hears cases at The Central Criminal Court (The Old Bailey) between May and September, nosegays are presented to all presiding judges. This ceremony dates from the days when evil smells from Newgate Jail pervaded the court during the summer months and judges were given bunches of strong smelling herbs to protect their sensitive noses.

**Beating the Bounds**
Tower of London

Once every three years a service is held on Ascension Day (May) at the Tower of London in the Chapel Royal of St Peter Vincula attended by all the dignitaries of the Tower. After the service the Chaplain leads a procession to each boundary stone where he shouts 'Cursed is he who moveth his neighbour's landmark' and the Chief Warder orders the choirboys to beat the stone with their willow wands. This curious custom dates from the Middle Ages and similar ceremonies are still held in a number of parishes throughout the country. Its purpose (it is thought) was to teach young boys their local parish boundaries.

CHRISTMAS CAROLS IN TRAFALGAR SQUARE

# DRIVING AND PARKING IN LONDON

car hire, parking regulations, car parks,
exhibition centres, Wembley, etc

# Driving a car in London

The best advice for the visitor wanting a worry-free time in the capital must be: don't take your car into Central London. Parking and traffic congestion is a problem and driving can be difficult. Many one-way street systems have been introduced, which do create difficulties for the visitor. However, those unfamiliar with the complexities of London traffic can take advantage of the services offered by larger car-hire agencies, which will provide a driver to meet the client at a specific point and drive or guide him in his own car into or across central London or the suburbs. Information on car-hire agencies and chauffeur-driven cars is available from any London Tourist Board Information Centre.

For those who still wish to drive themselves and are unfamiliar with conditions in the capital, the best advice is to avoid the rush-hour traffic, which is at its height around 8-9.30am and 4–6.30pm. Areas to avoid are Buckingham Palace and The Mall between 11am and 12am, when the changing of the Guard at the Palace causes traffic delays. Additionally, no cars are allowed to use Oxford Street between 7am-7pm from Monday to Saturday.

### Street Parking

**Parking zones**   Street parking in central London is controlled by a parking policy of meter zones known as the Inner London Parking Area. There are also parking zones in outer London, most of which include meters. The controlled zones are indicated by signs at their boundary points, giving the hours of operation. Special regulations may also apply in areas near to the wholesale markets and where Sunday street markets are held. Street parking other than at officially designated places is prohibited during the specified hours. In many zones, some parking places may be reserved exclusively for residents or other classes of users specified on nearby plates.

**Parking meters**   Parking meters take 10p, 20p, 50p or £1 coins but there are differences in charges and variations in the length of time for which parking is allowed. The car must be parked within the limits of the parking bay, indicated by the white lines on the road. It must also face in the same direction as the traffic flow, unless angle parking is indicated by road markings. Payment must be made on arrival, although unexpired meter time paid for by a previous occupant of the space may be used. After the initial payment has been made, additional parking time may not be bought by making any further payments.

Infringement of these rules results in penalties in the form of expensive '**parking tickets**', which you will find attached to the windscreen of the car.

**Red Routes**   A red route pilot scheme has been introduced between Archway and Commercial Road via A1,

A501, A1202 and A13. Traffic is not permitted to stop on the above roads for any reason between 7am and 7pm, Monday to Saturday. Red line kerbside markings denote the restriction and offenders are fined or their vehicles removed to a police pound.

**Waiting restrictions**

The usual system of yellow lines should indicate these, but their omission does not necessarily mean there is no effective restriction. In addition, any vehicle waiting on a road may be judged to be causing 'unnecessary obstruction', without proof that other vehicles or persons may have actually been obstructed, and a prosecution could ensue. Enforcement is mostly by the use of parking tickets, but in West End, Kensington, City, Camden, Chelsea, Hammersmith and Fulham, immobilisation by wheel clamp has been introduced. If you need to enquire to which pound your vehicle has been removed, tel: 071-252 2222.

**Parking at night**

Cars, motor cycles and goods vehicles under 30cwt unladen weight can park without lights provided that:

a   The road is subject to a speed limit of 30mph or less.

b   No part of the vehicle is within 15 yards of a road junction.

c   The vehicle is parked close to the kerb and parallel to it, and except in one-way streets, with its nearside to the kerb, or in a parking place. Vehicles 30cwt or more unladen weight, or carrying eight or more passengers, must show two white lights to the front and two red lights with an illuminated number plate to the rear, in any night parking situation.

Similarly, if the road is not subject to a 30mph speed limit, any vehicle left standing on the highway at night must conform to the lighting regulations as above.

**The Royal Parks**

There is some free parking on the roads in Hyde Park and Regent's Park. The times may be unusual, but are shown by the normal yellow lines and plates. Read the plates very carefully.

**Disabled Persons — Orange Badge Scheme**
Certain disabled drivers or disabled passengers, including registered blind people, may apply for parking concessions under the Orange Badge Scheme. Application must be made direct to the appropriate County or District Council except in the Greater London area where the London Boroughs are the issuing authority.

The badges are valid throughout the country except for the following areas of Central London: the Cities of London and Westminster, the Borough of Kensington and Chelsea and any part of the Borough of Camden, south of and including Euston Road. In these areas, the Boroughs concerned operate their own concessionary schemes.

# Car Parking in Central London

The following is a list of car parks within the Inner London area. They are operated mainly by National Car Parks Ltd, except where indicated. National Car Parks are easily spotted by their large yellow NCP signs. The classification of areas is by means of the postal district lettering/numbering system e.g. E1, EC1 etc, with a brief description of the district covered. The majority of the car parks listed are shown on the map and can be located by means of the grid reference given alongside.

Most of these car parks are open during normal business hours, or for a slightly longer period at each end of the working day.

It is not possible to quote charges, but the rates in the West End or City of London usually start at around £4 for the first two hours, rising to approximately £15.00 for a 9-hour period, and £20 for a 24-hour period. Cheaper night rates are available between 6pm and 9am. In outer areas the charges are lower, depending on the distance from the central area.

**When parking your car, always remember to secure it against theft and not leave any valuable property inside.**

## Main Operators' Addresses

APCOA Parking — UK, 111 Windmill Rd, Sunbury-on-Thames, Middx TW16 7EF *tel:* Sunbury 789812

(MLCP) M L Car Parks Ltd, 44A Elmsdale Road, E17 *tel:* 081-509 0127

Motorpark, 15 Phillimore Walk, W8 7SA *tel:* 071-976 1239

National Car Parks Ltd, 21 Bryanston St, Marble Arch, London W1A 4NH *tel:* 071-499 7050

Sterling Guards Ltd, Olympia Exhibition Centre, 'L' Gate, Blythe Road, Kensington, London W14 8UX *tel:* 071-602 9788 (Earls Court and Olympia only).

Details of small operators are given in the text.

## Abbreviations used in text/type of car park

| | |
|---|---|
| C,Ch & L | Car, coaches & lorries |
| M/S | Multi-storey |
| S | Surface |
| U/C | Under cover |
| U/G | Underground |
| P | Petrol facilities |
| * | Open 24 hours |
| Mdnt | Open until midnight |
| LB | London Borough |
| LUL | London Underground Ltd |
| BR-NSE | British Rail (Network SouthEast) |

| Page | Map Ref | | Type | Capacity |
|------|---------|---|------|----------|
| | | **E1 Stepney, Whitechapel** | | |
| 12 | N8 | Shoreditch High Street (one-way, north/south direction), near junction Commercial Street | S*, C & L | 300 |
| 12 | N7 | Rodwell House, Middlesex Street | U/G* | 180 |
| 12 | N7 | Spitalfields, Whites Row | M/S* | 450 |
| | Not on Map | Fieldgate St, (off Whitechapel Rd; south side) (entrance in Fieldgate St via Plumber's Row) (*MLCP*) | S* | 120 |
| | | **EC1 Finsbury** | | |
| 12 | L7 | Aldersgate Street | M/S | 740 |
| 11 | K8 | Bowling Green Lane | S | 150 |
| 12 | L8 | Charterhouse Square | S | 100 |
| 11 | K7 | Cowcross Street, Caxton House | U/G | 63 |
| 11 | K8 | Great Sutton Street | U/C | 40 |
| 11 | K8 | Saffron Hill, St Cross St | M/S | 400 |
| 11 | K8 | Skinner Street | U/G | 250 |
| 11 | K7 | Smithfield Central Market | U/G | 450 |
| 11 | K7 | Smithfield Surface, Hosier Lane | S | 50 |
| 11 | K7 | Smithfield Street | S | 100 |
| 11 | K7 | Snowhill (off Farringdon Street) | U/G | 128 |
| | | **EC2 Moorgate, Liverpool St** | | |
| 12 | L7 | Barbican Centre | U/G | 500 |
| 12 | M7 | Finsbury Square | U/G, P (7am-6pm) | 285 |
| 12 | L7 | London Wall | U/G | 250 |
| 12 | N8 | Rivington Street | S | 60 |
| | | **EC3 Aldgate, Tower Hill** | | |
| 12 | N7 | Houndsditch, Ambassador House | M/S | 196 |
| 12 | M6 | Tower Hill, Lower Thames Street | U/G, C, Ch | 210 |
| | | **EC4 St Paul's, Cannon Street, Ludgate Circus** | | |
| 12 | L6 | Baynard House, Queen Victoria Street | U/G* | 300 |
| 11 | K7 | Shoe Lane, Atlantic House | U/G | 75 |
| 12 | L6 | Distaff Lane (off Cannon Street) | U/C | 100 |
| 12 | L7 | Paternoster Row, Ave Maria Lane | U/G* | 265 |
| 11 | K7 | Seacoal Lane, Hillgate House | U/G* | 180 |
| 11 | K7 | Shoe Lane, International Press Centre | U/G | 70 |
| 12 | M6 | Swan Lane | M/S* | 450 |

| Page | Map Ref | | Type | Capacity |
|------|---------|---|------|----------|
| | | **N1 Islington** | | |
| 12 | L9 | Britannia Walk (off City Road) | S | 100 |
| 11 | K9 | Business Design Centre, Upper Street | M/S 7am-11pm | 270 |
| 12 | M9 | Provost Street | S Mon-Fri 7am-6.30pm | 100 |
| 11 | K9 | Torrens Street | S | 60 |
| | | **NW1 Camden Town, Euston, Marylebone** | | |
| 8 | E7 | Bell Street (MLCP) | M/S* | 205 |
| 10 | H8 | Euston Station (British Rail) | U/G* | 235 |
| 10 | I9 | Kings Cross Station (British Rail) | S | 70 |
| 8 | E7 | Lisson Grove, Bell Street | S 7.30am-8pm | 86 |
| 9 | F7 | Marylebone Road, Gloucester Place | U/G* | 180 |
| 8 | E8 | Park Road, Regent's Park | U/G | 97 |
| 10 | I9 | St Pancras Station (British Rail) | S | 50 |
| | | **NW6 Kilburn** | | |
| | Not on Map | Kilburn Square, off Kilburn High Road | U/G | 120 |
| | | **NW8 St John's Wood** | | |
| 8 | D9 | Acacia Garage, Kingsmill Terrace (MLCP) | M/S* | 250 |
| 8 | E7 | Church Street, Penfold Street (MLCP) | U/G | 150 |
| | | **SE1 Elephant and Castle** | | |
| 6 | L4 | Elephant and Castle | U/G | 150 |
| | | **SE1 Waterloo — Royal Festival Hall — National Theatre Complex** | | |
| 6 | N5 | Butlers Wharf, Gainsford Street | S 7am-8pm | 110 |
| 5 | J5 | Doon Street (entrance in Upper Ground) | S, C 8am-Mdnt | 300 |
| 5 | J5 | Hayward Gallery, Belvedere Road | S 8am-Mdnt | 120 |
| 5 | J5 | Hungerford Bridge | S 8am-Mdnt | 120 |
| 5 | J5 | Jubilee Gardens (overflow) | S 8am-Mdnt | 100 |
| 11 | J6 | National Theatre, South Bank | U/G 8am-2am | 410 |
| 5 | J5 | Waterloo Station Approach (British Rail SR) Note: *due to work on the Channel Tunnel terminal, is likely to have capacity reduced.* | S* | 140 |
| 5 | K4 | Westminster Bridge Road | S | 80 |
| | | **SE1 Southwark, Bermondsey** | | |
| 6 | M5 | Snowsfields, Kipling Street | M/S* | 500 |

| Page | Map Ref | | Type | Capacity |
|------|---------|---|------|----------|
| | | ***SW1 Westminster, Victoria*** | | |
| 4 | I4 | Abingdon Street (entrance: Gt College Street) | U/G* | 250 |
| 4 | H5 | Arlington Street, Arlington House | U/G* | 108 |
| 3 | F4 | Cadogan Place, off Sloane Street | U/G* | 349 |
| 4 | H2 | Dolphin Square Garage, Grosvenor Road | U/G* P. Servicing | 250 |
| 3 | F4 | Knightsbridge, Park Tower Hotel | U/G* | 90 |
| 2 | E4 | Knightsbridge Green, Raphael Street | U/G | 65 |
| 3 | F4 | Pavilion Road | M/S* | 311 |
| 4 | H4 | Rochester Row (*Motorpark*) | M/S* | 299 |
| 3 | G3 | Semley Place, Ebury Street | M/S* | 422 |
| 4 | I5 | Trafalgar Square, Spring Gardens (*Motorpark*) | U/G* | 340 |
| | | ***SW5 Earls Court*** | | |
| 1 | C3 | Cromwell Road, Swallow International Hotel | U/C | 40 |
| 1 | B2 | Earls Court Exhibition (*Sterling Guards*) | S, U/C | 1,300 |
| | | ***SW6 Fulham*** | | |
| 1 | B2 | 47/67 Lillie Road, Ramada West Hotel | U/G* | 140 |
| | | ***SW7 South Kensington*** | | |
| 2 | E4 | 70/71 Ennismore Gardens (Kingston House Garage, tel: 071-589 6726) | U/G Mon-Fri 7.30am-11pm, Sat & Sun 8am-11pm | 60 |
| 1 | D3 | Cromwell Road, The London Forum Hotel | U/G* | 95 |
| | | ***SW8 South Lambeth*** | | |
| | Not on Map | Wandsworth (Arndale Centre), Buckhold Road | M/S | 1,060 |
| | | ***SW10 Brompton*** | | |
| 2 | D1 | Edith Yard, Worlds End Estate (*Motorpark*) | U/C | 50 |
| 2 | D2 | Park Walk Garages | S | 44 |
| | | ***SW17 Tooting*** | | |
| | Not on Map | Upper Tooting Road, Castle Hotel | S | 75 |
| | | ***W1 West End*** | | |
| 9 | G6 | Adams Row, Britannia Hotel | U/G* | 175 |
| 3 | G5 | Audley Square, South Audley Street | M/S* | 310 |
| 10 | H7 | Berners Street | M/S | 110 |
| 10 | H6 | Brewer Street, Piccadilly Circus | M/S* | 450 |

| Page | Map Ref | | Type | Capacity |
|------|---------|--|------|----------|
| 9 | G8 | Carburton Street, Regent Crest Hotel | U/G* | 65 |
| 3 | G5 | Carrington Street, Shepherd Market | M/S | 310 |
| 9 | G7 | Cavendish Square | U/G Mon-Sat 7am-11pm | 545 |
| 9 | G7 | Chandos Street, Queen Anne Mews (MLCP) | U/G* | 390 |
| 3 | G5 | Chesterfield House, Chesterfield Gdns | U/G | 50 |
| 9 | F7 | Chiltern Street, Paddington Street | M/S* | 395 |
| 10 | H7 | Cleveland Street | U/G | 84 |
| 9 | G7 | Clipstone Street (MLCP) | U/G* | 347 |
| 9 | F7 | Cramer Street | S | 200 |
| 8 | E7 | Crawford Street | S, U/C | 90 |
| 10 | H6 | Denman Street | U/G* | 143 |
| 10 | H6 | Dufours Place, Broadwick Garage (MLCP) | UG* | 65 |
| 9 | F7 | Gloucester Place, Portman Square Garage | M/S* | 443 |
| 9 | F6 | Gt Cumberland Place, Bilton Towers | U/G* | 160 |
| 9 | G6 | Grosvenor Hill, Bourdon Street | M/S | 216 |
| 9 | F6 | London Marriot Hotel (off Duke Street) | U/G | 85 |
| 9 | F6 | (Marble Arch) Bryanston Street | M/S* | 310 |
| 10 | H6 | Old Burlington Street Burlington Garage (APCOA) | M/S | 477 |
| 3 | G5 | Old Park Lane, Brick Street | U/G | 65 |
| 9 | F6 | Orchard Street (enter from Duke Street) (Selfridge Garage, 071-493 5181) | M/S P | 700 |
| 9 | F6 | Park Lane | U/G* P (not 24hrs) | 1,000 |
| 3 | G5 | Park Lane, Hilton Hotel | U/G* | 235 |
| 10 | H6 | Poland Street (APCOA) | M/S Mon-Sat 6am-Mdnt, Sun & Bank Hols closed | 150 |
| 9 | G7 | Portland Place, Weymouth Mews | U/G | 35 |
| 9 | F6 | Portman Square, Churchill Hotel | U/G | 51 |
| 9 | G7 | Welbeck Street | M/S | 392 |

### W2 Paddington, Bayswater

| Page | Map Ref | | Type | Capacity |
|------|---------|--|------|----------|
| 1 | C5 | Bayswater Road, Kensington Gardens | S, C, Ch | 240 |
| 7 | C6 | Bishop's Bridge Road Colonnades, Porchester Terrace North | U/G* | 152 |
| 10 | I6 | Cambridge Place, Newport Circus (Motorpark) | U/G* | 365 |
| 8 | E7 | Edgware Road, Burwood Place (Water Gardens; Flats) | U/G* | 300 |

| Page | Map Ref | | Type | Capacity |
|---|---|---|---|---|
| 8 | E7 | Edgware Road (Marks & Spencer) | U/G open store hours only | 55 |
| 8 | E7 | Harrow Road, London Metropole Hotel | M/S* | 80 |
| 8 | E6 | Kendal Street South | U/G* | 45 |
| 8 | E6 | Park West | U/G | 100 |
| 8 | D7 | Paddington Station (*British Rail*) | S U/C | 60 |
| 7 | C6 | Queensway (*MLCP*) | U/G* | 300 |
| 7 | C6 | Queensway, Arthur Court (north end of Queensway) | U/C* | 85 |
| | | **W6 Hammersmith** | | |
| | Not on Map | Hammersmith Broadway (Queen Caroline St) | S Mon-Sat 8am-10pm | 300 |
| | Not on Map | King's Mall, Glenthorne Road (eastern end) | M/S Mon-Sat 8am-6.30pm | 960 |
| | | **W8 Kensington** | | |
| 1 | B4 | Hornton Street, Kensington Town Hall (*APCOA*) | U/G* | 410 |
| 1 | C4 | Royal Garden Hotel, Kensington | U/G* | 160 |
| 1 | C4 | Young Street | M/S* | 250 |
| | | **W14 West Kensington** | | |
| 1 | A3 | Holland Road, Ladbroke Kensington Hotel | U/G | 70 |
| 1 | A3 | Maclise Road (Olympia) (*Sterling Guards*) | M/S* | 750 |
| 1 | A4 | Olympia Way | S | 400 |
| 1 | A4 | Russell Road | S | 250 |
| 1 | B3 | Warwick Road (west side) | S* C Ch & L | 350 |
| 1 | B3 | Warwick Road, Fenelon Place | S 6am-6pm | 170 |
| | | Note: *All Warwick Road car parks are on the west side and north of junction West Cromwell Road, and are listed in sequence of approach.* | | |
| | | **WC1 Bloomsbury, Holborn** | | |
| 10 | I7 | Bloomsbury (*EP*) | S 8am-10pm Mon-Sat | 45 |
| 10 | I7 | Bloomsbury Square | U/G* | 450 |
| 10 | I8 | Brunswick Square | U/G* | 443 |
| 10 | I7 | Museum Street | M/S* | 250 |
| 10 | H7 | Ridgmount Place | S | 35 |
| 10 | I8 | Russell Court, Woburn Place | U/G* | 110 |
| 10 | I8 | Russell Square, Imperial Hotel | U/G | 140 |
| 10 | I7 | Tottenham Court Road, Adeline Place YMCA | M/S* | 140 |
| 10 | I8 | Woburn Place, Royal National Hotel | U/G 7am-9pm | 150 |
| | | **WC2 Leicester Square, Strand** | | |
| 10 | I6 | Bedfordbury | U/G | 62 |

| Page | Map Ref | | Type | Capacity |
|------|---------|---|------|----------|
| 10 | I7 | Drury Lane, Parker Street | U/G 6am-Mdnt | 450 |
| 10 | I6 | Savoy Place, Victoria Embankment (*Adelphi Garage tel*: 071-836 4838) | U/G* | 70 |
| 10 | I6 | Swiss Centre, Leicester Square | U/G | 90 |
| 10 | I6 | Upper St Martin's Lane | M/S | 165 |
| 10 | I6 | Whitcomb Street (*MLCP*) | M/S* | 300 |

KENSINGTON ROAD

# Car Parking
# Main approach routes into London

This section provides information about parking at railway or underground stations on the outskirts of London, to assist visitors who may prefer to park their car and continue their journey by railway or underground train to the centre. In some cases where no reasonable facilities exist at the station, other types of car park have been included, but these are usually adjacent.

It is not a comprehensive list of surburban off-street parking: neither does it include details of parking-meter zones in suburban areas.

Stations are grouped into sectors, commencing from North West and continuing in clockwise order. The order of priority is then the route number of the main approach road into London, followed by the name of the station and relevant information.

**Opening times** The hours of opening of BR station car parks vary according to the opening and closing hours of the station, which are subject to the current timetable. London Underground Ltd (LUL) car parks are open from the time of the first train to the time of the last train. Where parking facilities operated by London Borough Councils (LB) or companies are shown, details are given within the text alongside the entry for the station. Car parks open 24 hrs are indicated by an asterisk*.

**Charges**   Charges are displayed at all British Rail and London Underground car parks.

Some car parks operated by London Boroughs and other operators are free of charge but this policy could be varied at short notice. There is no standard rate of charges. This depends on the locality and availability of the car park. At some car parks charges are raised above the standard rate during the morning peak hours or a car park is closed completely to discourage commuter parking. On Saturdays some car parks double the weekday charges.

**Main Operators**   Chiltern District Council, King George V Road, Amersham, Bucks HP6 5AW
London Underground Ltd. Travel Information, 55 Broadway, London SW1H 0BD, tel: 071-222 1234 (24-hour service)
Network SouthEast, British Railways Board, Euston House, 24 Eversholt Street, London NW1 1D2 (contact individual station as required)

| App-roach Route | Station | Operator/Location | Opening Times | Type/Capa-city |
|---|---|---|---|---|
| **NORTH WEST** | | | | |
| M1/M25/ A41 | Croxley | LUL | | Open 106 |
| M25/ M40/A40 | Hillingdon | LUL | | Open 285 (free) |
| | Ruislip | LUL | | Open 121 |
| | Uxbridge | LB Hillingdon Uxbridge Station | * | M/S Open 1,400 |
| M25/ A404 | Rickmans-worth | LUL | | Open 260 |
| A40 | South Ruislip | (1) LUL | | Open 42 |
| | | (2) LB Hillingdon Long Drive (adjacent to station) | * | Open 86 |
| A404 | Chalfont & Latimer | LUL | | Open 500 |
| | Northwood | LUL | | Open 189 |
| | Pinner | Sainsbury's | | Open 400 |
| A413 | Amersham | Chiltern Dist. Council | | M/S 700 (Pay & Display) |
| **NORTH** | | | | |
| M1/A1/ A40/ A406 | Wembley Park | LUL | | Open 634 |

| App-roach Route | Station | Operator/Location | Opening Times | Type/Capacity |
|---|---|---|---|---|
| M1/A1/A41 | Canons Park | LUL | | Open 196 |
| | Edgware | (1) Sainsbury's | | Open 276 |
| | | (2) NCP | Mon-Sat 8am-6.30pm | Open 65 |
| | Stanmore | LUL | | Open 457 |
| M25/A1/A10 | Cockfosters | LUL | | Open 440 |
| | Southgate N14 | LB Enfield, Winchmore Hill Road | *Mon-Sat (Sun free) | M/S 492 |
| M25/A1 | Finchley Central | LUL | | Open 365 |
| | High Barnet | LUL | | Open 227 |
| A10/A406 | Arnos Grove N11 | LUL | | Open 291 |
| A1000/A406 | East Finchley | LUL | | Open 333 |
| A1000 | Totteridge | LUL | | Open 80 |
| | Woodside Park | LUL | | Open 214 |

**EAST AND NORTH EAST**

| App-roach Route | Station | Operator/Location | Opening Times | Type/Capacity |
|---|---|---|---|---|
| M11/A11/A12 | Blackhorse Road (entrance in Forest Road) | LUL | | Open 380 |
| | Leytonstone E11 | LUL Grove Green Road | Mon-Sat 6am-9.30pm | Open 197 |
| | Stratford E15 | LB Newham, Stratford Bus Station, Great Eastern Rd | | M/S 460 |
| M11/A12 | Redbridge | LUL | | Open 186 |
| M11/B1393 | Epping | LUL | | Open 592 |
| A13/A406 | Barking | LB (1) London Rd. | | M/S 650 |
| | | (2) George Street/North Street | | Open 120 |
| A13 | Dagenham Heathway | LB Barking, Church Elm Lane (near station) | | M/S 260 |
| A12 | Gants Hill | LB Redbridge, Bramley Crescent (off Cranbrook Rd) | * | M/S 321 |
| | Newbury Park | LUL | | Open 540 |
| A12/A118/A1112 | Chadwell Heath | (1) Station Road | * | Open 125 |
| | | (2) Wangey Road | * | Open 53 |
| A118 | Ilford | LB Redbridge, Balfour Road (off Ley Street) | * | M/S 483 |
| A11/A12 | Snaresbrook | LUL | | Open 142 |
| A11/A406 | South Woodford | LUL | | Open 140 |
| A127 | Upminster | BR-NSE and LUL | * (Sat free) | Open 501 |

| App-roach Route | Station | Operator/Location | Opening Times | Type/Capacity |
|---|---|---|---|---|
| **SOUTH EAST** | | | | |
| A2 | Bexley | BR-NSE | | Open 250 |
| A2/A20 | Blackheath | LB Lewisham | Pay & Display 8am-6.30pm | Open 88 |
| A20 | Sidcup | BR-NSE | | Open 250 |
| A20/A21 | Lewisham | (1) LB Lewisham, Clarendon Rise | * Pay & Display 8.30am-6.30pm | Open 150 |
| | | (2) Molesworth Street | * (attendant charging time 8am-6.30pm Mon, Tue, Sat; -8pm Thu & Fri) | M/S 1,000 |
| | | (3) Molesworth Street | Pay & Display 8.30am-6.30pm | Open 180 |
| A21 | Bromley North | LB Bromley junction London Rd/Beckenham Lane | * (attendant charging time all hours Mon-Sat. reducing 6.30pm) | M/S 702 |
| | Bromley Nth or Sth | LB Bromley junction Kentish Way/Stockwell Close | All day (reducing 6.30pm Mon-Sat) | M/S 721 |
| | Bromley South | LB Bromley junction Westmoreland Rd/Masons Hill (opposite station) | * (attendant charging time all hours Mon-Sat. reducing 6.30pm) | M/S 593 |
| | Orpington | LB Bromley, Station Road | * Pay & Display 7.30am-7.30pm Mon-Sat | M/S 562 |
| A21/ A205 | Catford or Catford Bridge SE6 | LB Lewisham: (1) Adenmore Road | Mon-Sat 8am-6.30pm | Open 150 (free) |
| | | (2) Holbeach Road | * Pay & Display (charging time 8.30am-6.30pm) | M/S 500 |
| **SOUTH** | | | | |
| A22/A23 | Brixton | LB Lambeth, Popes Rd SW9 | Mon-Sat 7am-9pm | M/S 488 |
| | East Croydon | LB Croydon: (1) Dingwall Rd | * | M/S 600 |
| | | (2) Fairfield (Barclay Road) | * (after 6pm charge reduced) | M/S 1,300 |
| | South Croydon | BR-NSE | * (charging time Mon-Sat 7.45am-5.45pm) | Open 90 |
| | West Croydon | LB Croydon, West Croydon (next to station in London Road) | * Pay & Display (Mon-Sat) | Open 70 |
| | Purley | (1) BR-NSE | * Pay & Display (Mon-Sat) | Open 130 |
| | | (2) LB Croydon, Dale Road | * Pay & Display (Mon-Sat) | Open 140 |
| A23 | Smitham | LB Croydon, Lion Green Rd, Coulsdon | * Pay & Display (Mon-Sat) | Open 180 |
| **SOUTH WEST** | | | | |
| M3/A30 | Feltham | LB Hounslow, 2 parks in Bedfont Lane by the level crossing | * Pay & Display | Open 92 Open 60 |

| App-roach Route | Station | Operator/Location | Opening Times | Type/Capacity |
|---|---|---|---|---|
| M3/A308/A309 | Hampton Court | BR-NSE | | Open 250 |
| M3/A316 | Richmond | NCP Richmond Station | Mon-Sat 7am-Mdnt | M/S 426 |
| A3 | Surbiton | BR-NSE | * | Open 496 |
| | Worcester Park | BR-NSE | | Open 100 |
| A24 | Morden | LB Merton | | |
| | | (1) Kenley Road | * | Open 120 |
| | | (2) Peel House | * | M/S 359 |
| | | (3) Station CP | * | Open S 126 |
| | | (4) York Close | Mon-Sat 7.30am-9.30pm | Open 247 |
| A238 | Raynes Park | LB Merton, Coombe Lance | Pay & Display (Mon-Sat) Mdnt-6.30pm | Open 120 |
| **WEST** | | | | |
| M3/M4/A30/A4 | Hammersmith | NCP Queen Caroline Street (near flyover) W6 | Mon-Sat 8.00am-10pm | Open 300 |
| M4/A4/A30 | Hatton Cross | LUL | * | Open 101 |
| | Hounslow West | LUL | | Open 398 |
| | Osterley | LUL | | Open 122 |
| A40/A406 | North Ealing | LUL | | Open 100 |

# Exhibition Centres

### Earls Court and Olympia

These are the two traditional major exhibition centres in London, hosting a wide variety of events throughout the year.

Parking facilities at the exhibitions are limited and street parking is difficult. It may be worth considering using public transport.

Parking at Earls Court and Olympia is controlled by: Sterling Parking Services, Olympia Exhibition Centre, 'L' Gate, Blythe Road, London W14 8UA (tel: 071-370 8458).

Contact the company direct for current details and advance parking reservations.

**Parking at Earls Court**  Parking is available during shows only, and prices may vary for different exhibitions. Parking for 1,000 cars is available in Seagrave Road.

**Parking at Olympia**  There is parking for 750 cars in the two car parks at the rear of Olympia.

The NCP operate a number of car parks in the vicinity. For further information see page 63 W14.

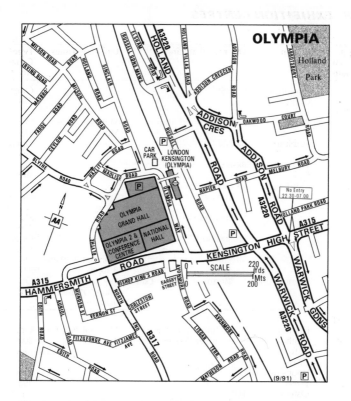

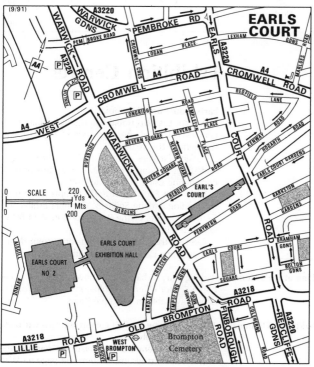

**Forthcoming events**

A selection of exhibitions being held throughout each year at the two venues is shown below. Visitors are advised to check the exact date and venue with the organisers before planning a visit.

For enquiries regarding fixtures at either Earls Court or Olympia please contact: The Press Office, Earls Court and Olympia Ltd, Warwick Road, London SW5 9TA *tel:* 071-385 1200.

| | | |
|---|---|---|
| London International Boat Show | Earls Court | January |
| 'Daily Mail' Ideal Home Exhition | Earls Court | March |
| Fine Art & Antique Fair | Olympia | June |
| Royal Tournament | Earls Court | July |
| International Music Show | Olympia | July |
| European Computer Entertainment Show | Earls Court | September |
| Business Computer | Earls Court | September |
| Motorfair — The London Motor Show | Earls Court | October |
| 'Daily Mail' International Ski Show | Earls Court | November |
| The Caravan Show | Earls Court | November |
| The Royal Smithfield Show | Earls Court | December |
| National Cat Club Show | Olympia | December |
| Olympia International Show Jumping | Olympia | December |

**Other exhibition centres in the London area are at:**

**The Barbican Centre** (central map, page 12, L7) Silk Street, Barbican, EC2Y 8DS *tel:* 071-588 8211

**Alexandra Palace** (district map, page 167, D5) Wood Green, N22 4AY *tel:* 081-365 2121

# Wembley Complex

**District map, page 166, B4.** The Wembley complex is situated 6 miles north west of Central London and is close to the southern terminal of M1 motorway. The A40/M40, M4, M25 motorways and the North Circular Road A406 are also within easy reach.

The main buildings in the 73-acre complex are:-
**Wembley Stadium** 80,000 capacity, famed for its Football and other major sporting and entertainment events.

**Wembley Arena** an indoor venue with 12,500 seats, where ice-shows, rock concerts, horse shows and many varied events are held.

**Conference Centre** for conferences and exhibitions; the Thames Suite alone provides over 3,000 sq metres of display space, while there are many other display and hospitality areas.

WEMBLEY STADIUM

**Wembley Grand Hall** The main conferences area with a seating capacity of over 2,500, also hosts regular sporting and entertainment events.

**Wembley Exhibition Hall** A new multi-purpose venue with 5,000 square metres of exhibition space.

**Catering at Wembley**
The Grandstand Restaurant overlooks the greyhound race course and pitch.
Wembley Stadium *tel:* 081-902 8833
Wembley Conference Centre *tel:* 081-902 8833
Wembley Arena Restaurant, a new 150-seater restaurant for pre-show suppers and interval refreshments.

**General Information**
Box Office arrangements (all enquiries *tel:* 081-900 1234). Postal enquiries: Wembley Stadium Ltd, Main Box Office, Wembley, Middx HA9 0DW.

**Facilities for the Disabled**
Easy access to all buildings. In the conference centre there are special ramps and lifts to all floors. Toilet facilities for the disabled are available in all buildings. Wheelchair users are advised to telephone in advance to make arrangements for their visits *tel:* 081-902 8833.

**Guided Tour,** see page 107.

**Sunday Market,** see page 36.

**Parking at Wembley**
The space available will accommodate up to 6,000 cars or up to 1,000 coaches. Parking charges can vary according to the size and class of events.

**Parking outside the Wembley Area**
Limited parking facilities are available at a few underground railway stations, if you decide to proceed to Wembley by rail for the final stage of the journey. Parking cannot be booked in advance, neither can accommodation be guaranteed. From Monday to Friday the car parks are used extensively by commuters and on Saturday by shoppers. The stations listed on page 74 have been selected because they have reasonably large car parks. *London Underground Ltd car parks are open from the time of the first train to the time of the last train.*

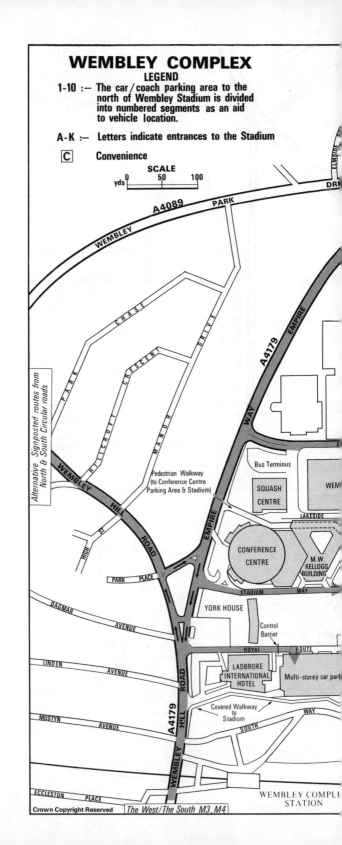

# WEMBLEY COMPLEX

## LEGEND

**1-10 :—** The car/coach parking area to the north of Wembley Stadium is divided into numbered segments as an aid to vehicle location.

**A-K :—** Letters indicate entrances to the Stadium

**C** Convenience

**SCALE**
yds 0   50   100

A4089   PARK

WEMBLEY

ELMSIDE DR

DR

CHASE

DRIVE

A4179

EMPIRE

PARK

CRESCENT

MANOR

HILLCROFT

WEMBLEY

WAY

Alternative Signposted routes from North & South Circular roads

HILL

ROAD

Pedestrian Walkway
(to Conference Centre
Parking Area & Stadium)

Bus Terminus

SQUASH
CENTRE

WEM

LAKESIDE

EMPIRE

HIGH ST

CONFERENCE
CENTRE

M.W.
KELLOGG
BUILDING

PARK PLACE

STADIUM WAY

DAGMAR

YORK HOUSE

Control
Barrier

AVENUE

ROYAL

ROUTE

LINDEN

AVENUE

LADBROKE
INTERNATIONAL
HOTEL

Multi-storey car park

A4179

HILL

ROAD

Covered Walkway
to
Stadium

WAY

MOSTYN

AVENUE

SOUTH

WEMBLEY

ECCLESTON   PLACE

  *The West/The South M3, M4*

WEMBLEY COMPLE
STATION

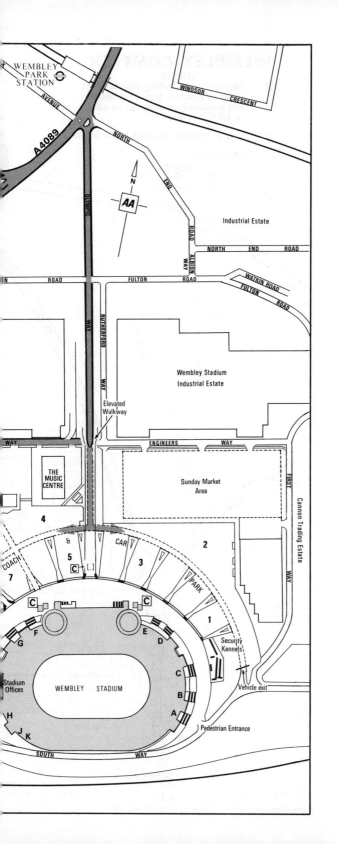

### A40/M40 and the West
Hillingdon Underground Station — Long Lane, B466, 150yds north of Hillingdon Circus (Western Avenue A40), open car park, capacity 300, free. Metropolitan Line to Wembley Park Station.

### M1, A1, A41 and the North
Stanmore Underground Station — London Road, A410, open car park, capacity 457, charges as displayed. Jubilee Line to Wembley Park Station.

### Accommodation
A selection of hotels and guesthouses (GH) at, or within a short radius of the Stadium is given below. The widest choice of accommodation is in Central London, from where there are ample transport facilities operating at frequent intervals to Wembley. For further details see page 10.

### Hotels and guesthouses in the locality
Within 3 miles:

**Harrow**

| | |
|---|---|
| ★★ | Cumberland Hotel, 1 St John's Road tel: 081-863 4111 |
| ★★ | Harrow Hotel, Roxborough Bridge, 12-22 Pinner Road tel: 081-427 3435 |
| GH | Central Hotel, 6 Hindes Road tel: 081-427 0893 |
| GH | Hindes Hotel, 8 Hindes Road, tel: 081-427 7468 |
| GH | Kempsford House, 21/23 St John's Road tel: 081-427 4983 |
| GH | Lindal Hotel, 2 Hindes Road tel: 081-863 3164 |

Within 4 miles
**Ealing W5**

| | |
|---|---|
| ★★★ | Carnarvon Hotel, Ealing Common tel: 081-992 5399 |

### Public Transport:
**By Rail**
**Wembley Park Station** (Underground — Metropolitan and Jubilee Lines)
**Wembley Stadium Station** (British Rail from Marylebone)
**Wembley Central Station** (within $\frac{3}{4}$ mile) (British Rail from Euston; also Bakerloo Line, peak hours only).

**By Bus**
London Transport 83, 92 and 182 routes all pass the complex. Other buses that pass nearby are routes 18, 79, 204, 224, 245 and 297 (Monday to Saturday only), also night service N18.

**By Taxi**
Taxi ranks are situated outside the Conference Centre and Wembley Park Station.

# GAZETTEER

principal places of interest, including
museums, art galleries, etc

### Africa Centre

38 King Street, WC2
Central map: page 10, I6
☎ 071-836 1973

The centre is a charity and of
particular interest to those who wish
to learn more about African culture.
There are displays of paintings,
photographs and craftware by African
artists.

*Open: Mon-Fri 10-6, Sat 10-4.
Admission free.*

### Agnew's Galleries

43 Old Bond Street, W1
Central map: page 4, H5
☎ 071-629 6176

Annual exhibitions held here include
a watercolour exhibition devoted to
English watercolours and drawings of
the 18th and 19th centuries, and a
selling exhibition of Old Master
paintings from the 14th and 19th
centuries. There are also exhibitions
of French and English drawings from
about 1800 to the present day, work
by English painters of this century,
and loan exhibitions in aid of charity.
Many works pass through Agnew's
on their way to famous art galleries
and museums.

*Open: all year Mon-Fri 9.30-5.30
(6.30pm Thu, during major exhibitions;
closed BH).
Admission free (admission charge for
some loan exhibitions).*

### Bank of England Museum

Bartholomew Lane, EC2
Central map: page 12, M7
☎ 071-605 5545
*recorded information 071-601 5792*

The museum is arranged in
chronological order and traces the
history of banking from its Royal
Charter in 1694 to the modern high-
tech world of today. Displays include
a reconstruction of Sir John Soane's
Stock Office of 1793, complete with
original ledgers and other documents.
Elsewhere there are gold bars dating
from Roman times and a display of
part of the world's finest collection of
Bank of England notes, including a

few forgeries. An interactive video
display tests your skill and knowledge
of banking today.

*Open: all year, Mon-Fri 10-5, Sun &
PHs from Good Fri to Sep 11-5
(closed 25-26 Dec & 1 Jan).
♿ Shop*

### Banqueting House

Palace of Whitehall, SW1
Central map; page 4, I5
☎ 071-930 4179

Built in 1619 for James I to a design
by Inigo Jones, the Banqueting House
is in a severe classical style, but the
interior is enriched by Rubens'
paintings. It is one of the most
important buildings of its period.
London court life was centred here
during the 17th century and it was
the scene of many historic events,
including the execution of Charles I
in 1649, the restoration of Charles II,
and the offer of the throne to Prince
William of Orange and Princess Mary.

*Open: Mon-Sat 10-5 (closed Good Fri,
23 Dec-2 Jan & BH). May also be
closed at short notice for government
functions.
Admission charge.*

### Bethnal Green Museum of Childhood

Cambridge Heath Road, E2
District map: page 167, 1 E4
☎ 081-980 2415

The principal exhibits here are toys,
dolls and dolls' houses, model
soldiers, puppets, games, model
theatres, wedding dresses, children's
costume and Spitalfield silks — all
housed in a very attractive building.

*Open: Mon-Thu & Sat 10-6, Sun 2.30-
6 (closed: Fri, May Day, Spring BH
Mon, 24-26 Dec & 1 Jan).
Admission free.
♿ Shop ⌀ (ex guide dogs)*

### Brass Rubbing

Given below are descriptions of three
places where brasses (which can be
described as commemorative
plaques) can be seen and rubbed.
Admission is free, but charges are

made for rubbing, and for rubbing materials. The churches themselves are described separately.

### All Hallows Church by the Tower

Byward St, EC2
Central map: page 12, M6
☎ 071-481 2928

The church contains 19 original brasses dating from 1389-1591. There is also an exhibition of 26 medieval facsimile brasses from which visitors can take rubbings. Staff are available to assist.
(All Hallows Church — see page 124).

*Open: daily Mon-Sat 10.30-5, Sun 12.30-5 (closed Good Fri, 25 & 26 Dec & 1 Jan).*
*Admission free, charge for making rubbings.*

### St Martin-in-the-Fields Church

Trafalgar Square, WC2
Central map: page 10, I6
☎ 071-437 6023

A collection of around 90 facsimile brasses from churches in all parts of Britain, from which rubbings can be made. These include some of Henry VIII's courtiers, such as Anne Boleyn's father Sir Thomas Bullen. Classical music plays while you work. Staff are available to assist making rubbings.
(St Martin-in-the-Fields Church — see page 129).

*Open: Mon-Sat 10-6, Sun 12-6 (closed Good Fri, 25-26 Dec & 1 Jan).*
*Admission free, charge for making rubbings.*

### Westminster Abbey

Broad Sanctuary, SW1
Central map; page 4, I4
☎ 071-222 2085

In the North Cloisters there is a collection of around 100 facsimile brasses. These include facsimiles of original brasses in Westminster Abbey. Some of the facsimiles are taken from the foot supports of larger brasses. These include animals, shields, and coats of arms. Staff are available to assist making rubbings.
(Westminster Abbey — see page 132).

*Open: daily Mon-Sat 9-5 (closed Good Fri, 25 & 26 Dec & 1 Jan).*

WESTMINSTER ABBEY

*Admission free, charge for making rubbings.*

## British Museum

Great Russell Street, WC1
Central map: page 10, I7
☎ 071-580 1788

Founded in 1753, this is one of the world's great museums, showing the works of people from all over the world, from prehistoric to comparatively modern times. The imposing building which houses the museum was designed by Sir Robert Smirke and completed in the mid-19th century. The galleries are the responsibility of the following departments: Egyptian; Greek and Roman; Western Asiatic; Prehistoric and Romano-British; Medieval; Renaissance and Later; Coins and Medals; Oriental; Prints and Drawings, and Ethnography (based at the Museum of Mankind). The museum also displays famous books and manuscripts from the British Library collections. Most visitors wish to see the superb Elgin marbles, from

ELGIN MARBLES

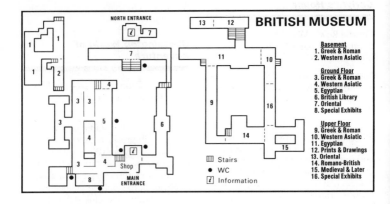

NORTH ENTRANCE

**BRITISH MUSEUM**

**Basement**
1. Greek & Roman
2. Western Asiatic

**Ground Floor**
3. Greek & Roman
4. Western Asiatic
5. Egyptian
6. British Library
7. Oriental
8. Special Exhibits

**Upper Floor**
9. Greek & Roman
10. Western Asiatic
11. Egyptian
12. Prints & Drawings
13. Oriental
14. Romano-British
15. Medieval & Later
16. Special Exhibits

MAIN ENTRANCE

▥ Stairs
● WC
𝑖 Information

temples and other buildings in Athens. British treasures include the beautiful 7th-century Sutton Hoo Treasure and the 12th-century Lewis Chessmen. Each year, special exhibitions focus more detailed attention on certain aspects of the collections. Programmes on request. There is a regular programme of gallery talks, lectures and films. Children's trail at all times.

*Open: Mon-Sat 10-5, Sun 2.30-6 (closed: Good Fri, May Day, 24-26 Dec & 1 Jan).*
*Admission free.*
*🍴 (licensed) ♿ shop ✖ (ex guide dogs)*

### Bromley Museum

The Priory, Church Hill, Orpington
District map: page 167, 40 F1
📞 (0689) 873826

This is a 13th- to 14th-century clergy house with the addition of a 15th-century manor house. It is now a museum of local interest, and special exhibitions are held during the year.

*Open: daily 9-5 ex Thu & Sun (closed: PH).*
*Admission free.*
*♿ (ground floor only) ✖*

### Bruce Castle Museum

Lordship Lane, N17
District map: page 167, 3 E5
📞 081-808 8772

An E-shaped part Elizabethan, part Jacobean and Georgian building, with an adjacent circular 16th-century tower, which stands in a small park. The museum contains sections on local history, postal history and the Middlesex Regiment, also known as the 'Diehards'.

*Open: daily 1-5 (closed: Good Fri, Xmas & New Year's Day).*
*Admission free (donations).*
*shop ✖*

### Cabinet War Rooms

Clive Steps, King Charles St, SW1
Central map: page 4, I5
📞 071-930 6961

The rooms comprise the most important surviving part of the underground emergency accommodation provided to protect Winston Churchill, his War Cabinet and Chiefs of Staff of Britain's armed forces against air attacks in World War II. Among the rooms are the Cabinet Room, the Transatlantic Telephone Room, the Map Room (where information about operations on all fronts was collected) and the Prime Minister's Room. The more important rooms have been preserved intact since the War, while others have been carefully restored to their wartime appearance.

*Open: daily 10-6, last admission 5.15pm (closed 24-26 Dec & 1 Jan).*
*Admission charge.*
*♿ shop ✖ (ex guide dogs)*

## Carlyle's House

Cheyne Row, SW3
Central map; page 2, E2
☎ 071-352 7087

Built in 1708, this is a fine example of an 18th-century town house. Thomas Carlyle lived here from 1834 until his death in 1881, and entertained among others Dickens, Thackeray, Browning and Tennyson. Many of Carlyle's letters, personal possessions and furniture are preserved here, including an early piano on which Chopin played and the desk where Carlyle wrote his books.

*Open: Apr-Oct, Wed-Sun & BHs 11-5 (closed Good Fri).*
*Admission charge.*
*No parties over 20 persons. (NT)*

## Central Criminal Courts

Old Bailey, EC4
Central map: page 12, K7
☎ 071-248 3277

Most of the major trials of this century have been heard here, including those of Crippen, Christie and Haig. On the first two days of each session the judges carry posies of flowers and the courts are strewn with herbs, a custom dating from the time when it was necessary to disguise the stench of Newgate Prison. When the courts are in session visitors may sit in the public galleries. It is often necessary to queue. (Entrance in Newgate Street.)

*Open: Mon-Fri, 10.30-1 & 2-4.*
*Admission free.*

## Chelsea Physic Gardens

Royal Hospital Rd, SW3
Central map: page 3, F2
☎ 071-352 5646

This is the second oldest botanic garden in England, about 50 years younger than the one at Oxford. It was set up in 1673 to grow plants for recognition and study, for medicinal and general scientific use.

*Open: 22 Mar-18 Oct, Wed & Sun 2-5. Additional opening during Chelsea Flower Show week.*

*Admission charge.*
  ♿ *shop*

## Chessington World of Adventure

Chessington (on A243, off M25 Jct9)
District map: page 166, 4 B1
☎ *Epsom (0372) 727227*

Dare you ride the Vampire, the UK's only hanging roller coaster and the Dragon River Water Ride with the most exciting single drop in the UK? Plus Chessington's latest attraction, Professor Burp's Bubble Works, a unique, crazy, colourful, musical indoor water ride for all the family. Over 100 attractions and rides in all, and including an international circus and world famous zoo.

*Open: Theme Park, daily 28 Mar-1 Nov; Zoological Gardens, all year, last admission 3pm.*
*Admission charge.*
*shop* ☕ ⊗

## Chislehurst Caves

Off A222 near Bromley, Kent
District map: page 167, 2 F2
☎ *081-467 3264*

The labyrinth of caves as been called the enigma of Kent. Miles of mysterious caverns hewn out of the chalk over some 8,000 years can be explored, with experienced guides to tell the history and legends of the caves.

*Open: daily 11-4.30, longer tours Sun & BHs (closed: 25 Dec).*
*Admission charge.*
☕ *shop* ⊗

## Chiswick House

Burlington Lane, W4
District map: page 166, 5 C3
☎ *081-995 0508*

Considered to be the finest example of Palladian architecture in Great Britain, this domed mansion was built between 1725 and 1730.

*Open: daily Apr-Sept 10-6; Oct-Mar 10-4 (closed 24 & 25 Dec).*
*Admission charge.*
*shop* ♿ ⊗

### Church Farm House Museum

Greyhound Hill, NW4
District map: page 166, 6 C5
℡ 081-203 0130

A gabled house, dating from 1660s,
which is now a museum of local
interest. Notable features include a
period furnished kitchen and dining
room. There is a programme of
changing exhibitions.

*Open: Mon-Sat 10-1 & 2-5.30 (Tue
10-1 only), Sun 2-5.30 (closed: Good
Fri, 25 & 26 Dec, 1 Jan).
Admission free.*
♿ (garden only) shop ✖

### Claremont Landscape Garden, Esher

Entrance on edge of Esher (west of
A307)
District map: page 166, 8 A1
℡ (0372) 469421

This is the earliest surviving example
of an English landscape garden. Its 50
acres include a lake with an island
pavilion, and a grotto.

*Open: Nov-Mar 10-5 or sunset if
earlier; Apr-Oct, Mon-Fri 10-6, Sat,
Sun & BH 10-7.
Admission charge.
(NT)*

### The Clink Exhibition

1 Clink St, SE1
Central map; page 12, L6
℡ 071-403 6515
Housed within the ancient walls of
the original Clink Prison, the
exhibition gives a true insight into the
sordid world of prostitutes, debtors,
heretics and criminals who languished
and were tortured here during the
Middle Ages. It also houses the only
working armoury in Europe.

*Open: daily 10-8 (closed: 25-26 Dec &
1 Jan).
Admission charge.*

### Commonwealth Institute

Kensington High St, W8
Central map: page 1, B4
℡ 071-603 4535

Life in the countries of the
Commonwealth is depicted here by a
large number of exhibitions. Also
library, art gallery, and arts centre.

*Open: Mon-Sat 10-5, Sun 2-5 (closed:
Good Fri, May Day, 24-26 Dec & 1
Jan).
Admission free. Occasional charge for
special exhibitions.*
♿ shop ✖ (ex guide dogs)

### Contemporary Applied Arts

43 Earlham Street, WC2
Central map: page 10, I6
℡ 071-836 6993

The regular programme of special
exhibitions and retail displays held
here includes wallhangings, furniture,
studio ceramics, pottery, wood,
jewellery, etc. There are also books
and magazines specialising in craft
and design. It is an excellent place to
see the best of contemporary British
crafts.

*Open: Mon-Sat 10-5.30 (closed: Xmas
& BH).
Admission free.*
♿ (ground floor only) ✖

### Courtauld Institute Galleries

Somerset House, Strand, WC2
Central map: page 11, J6
℡ 071-873 2526

These galleries contain the most
important collection of Impressionist
paintings in Britain, including work by
Monet, Renoir, Degas, Cézanne, Van
Gogh, Gauguin and Toulouse-Lautrec.
There are also Old Master paintings
and drawings, including woks by
Peter Bruegel. Michelangelo and
Rubens, as well as works by the
Bloomsbury Group.

*Open: Mon-Sat 10-6, Sun 2-6 (closed:
Good Fri, Xmas & 1 Jan).
Admission charge.*

### Craft Centre of Silk

Bourne Rd, Crayford
District map: page 167, 7 F3
℡ Crayford (0322) 559401

A guided tour takes visitors along a
kind of 'silk road' through the

working mill and craft centre which shows the history of silk, associated craft tools and sericulture. As well as the audio-visual presentation, craftspeople can be seen at work hand-printing silk.

*Open: Mon-Fri 9.30-5, Sat to 4.30 (closed: BHs).*
*Admission charge.*
shop ⌷ ♿ ⌘

## Cuming Museum

155/157 Walworth Rd, SE17
Central map: page 6, L3
📞 071-701 1342

The museum traces the history of Southwark from Roman and medieval times to the present day, with rare reminders of everyday life. Also on display is the worldwide art collection of Richard and Henry Cuming, and the unique Lovett collection of London superstitions.

*Open: Mon-Sat 10-5 (closed BHs).*
*Admission free.*
shop ⌘

## Cutty Sark Clipper Ship

Greenwich Pier, SE10
District map: page 167, 9 E3
📞 081-858 3445

Probably one of the most famous ships in the world, the *Cutty Sark* was launched in 1869, and was built for speed — she once covered 363 miles in a day. Her cargoes were tea, and latterly wool. In 1922 she was converted into a nautical training school, and in 1957 was transferred to dry dock at Greenwich. In her holds are displays explaining her history and even a collection of ships' figureheads.

*Open: daily 10-5, Sun 12-5; 6pm in summer (closed 24–26 Dec & 1 Jan.)*
*Admission charge.*
♿ ('tween-deck only) shop ⌘

## Darwin Museum

Down House, Downe (off A233)
District map: page 167, 34 F1
📞 Farnborough (0689) 859119

Down House was the home of

Charles Darwin from 1842 until his death in 1882. The drawing room and Old Study are restored and furnished as they were when Darwin was working on his famous and still controversial book, *On the Origins of Species by means of Natural Selection*, first published in 1859. The museum also includes collections and memorabilia from Darwin's voyage on *HMS Beagle*. There is one room dedicated to his illustrious grandfather Dr Erasmus Darwin. The garden is maintained as laid out by the Darwins, beyond which lies the famous Sand Walk or thinking path, along which Darwin took his daily walk.

*Open: Wed-Sun 1-6, also BH (closed: 14 Dec-1 Jan & Feb).*
*Admission charge.*
shop ♿ ⌘

## Denis Sever's House

18 Folgate St, E1
Central map: page 12, N8
📞 071-247 4013

This unique town house is a living example of 18th and 19th century life, 'touched' with the atmosphere that is so missing from stately homes of this period. Visitors are told that a fictitious family has walked out of the door, but that everything that your senses behold indicates their imminent presence: children's toys lying on the stairs, meals half eaten, a kettle steaming on the open fire, the air of the house scented with pipe tobacco, candle wax and toasted scones.

*Open: 1st Sun in each month 2-5pm.*
*Admission charge.*
*(There are special evening performances three times a week.)*

## The Design Museum at Butler's Wharf

Butler's Wharf, Shad Thames, SE1
Central map: page 6, N5
📞 071-403 6933

A museum of everyday objects. It is the first of its kind to show design in mass production and in the context of our lives. There is also a library and a lecture theatre.

*Open: Tue-Sun 11.30-6.30 (closed:
Mon ex BH).*
*Admission charge.*
shop 🖵 *(licensed)* & 🚫

### Dickens' Old Curiosity Shop

13–14 Portsmouth St, WC2
Central map: page 11, J7
☎ 071-405 9891

Established in the 16th century, this
half-timbered shop is the oldest in
London. It is said to be the shop
immortalised by Dickens in his novel
of the same name. Inside is a desk
containing items owned by Dickens.

*Open: April-Oct, Mon-Fri 9-5.30; Nov-
Mar, Mon-Fri 9.30-5.30; Sat, Sun & BH
9.30-5.*
*Admission free.*

### Dickens' House

48 Doughty St, WC1
Central map: page 11, J8
☎ 071-405 2127

Dickens lived here during his twenties
and here completed *Pickwick Papers*
and wrote *Oliver Twist* and *Nicholas
Nickleby*. Pages of the original
manuscripts of his early books and
others are on view, together with
valuable first editions in the original
paper parts of his works; his special
marriage licence; his family Bible
which contains a personal record of
his children, and many other personal
relics. Entrance includes Suzannet
Rooms.

*Open: 10-5, last admission 4.30 pm
(closed Sun, BH, Good Fri & Xmas
wk).*
*Admission charge.*
shop & *(ground floor only)* 🚫

### Docklands

London Bridge — Woolwich
District map: page 167, 41 E3

Stretching east from London Bridge
to Woolwich, this eight and a half
square mile area, north and south of
the Thames, is the largest
redevelopment site in Europe,
breathing new life into the
Docklands, once the heartland of
Britain's trade-based Empire. The old
warehouses have been imaginatively
renovated and are now 'up-market'
apartments, offices, shopping and
entertainment complexes. The
regenerated dock system has been
painstakingly restored. Many are
yacht marinas and centres for water
sports. Much of traditional London
still remains and many of the
Docklands pubs are enjoying a new-
found popularity.

These changes have been
incorporated with the many new
modern buildings to create a city of
the 21st century. St Katharine's
(central map: page 12, N6) was the
first dock to be redeveloped, and is
now a popular waterside attraction.
Tobacco Dock in Wapping is
probably the finest example of a
converted bonded warehouse
retaining its original charm and now
a stylish shopping centre, overlooking
two replica pirate ships (see page 98).
The modern commercial
developments at the Isle of Dogs are
dominated by the fifty floor, 800ft
Canary Wharf skyscraper. Further
east in the Royal Docks is London
City Airport (see page 22). It lies
between two deep-water basins once
used for berthing liners the size of
the *Mauritania*, but today a popular
watersports venue. Surrey Docks on
the south side of the Thames is being
transformed, with the water and
leisure facilities complementing the
housing and commercial
developments. An exciting way to
visit Docklands is to take a ride on
the Docklands Light Railway (see
page 19), which in places travels high
above the ground with great views
over the surrounding area.
Alternatively you can travel on the
Thames Riverbus (see page 29), a fast
boat service stopping at many piers
along the Thames. Once there, visit
the Docklands Visitor Centre, an
exhibition area with displays and
information showing the development
of the area. (Free tours of Docklands
available every Thursday —
telephone for details.)

*Docklands Visitor Centre,
3 Limeharbour, Isle of Dogs, E14*
☎ 071-512 1111
*Open: Mon-Fri 10-6, Sat & Sun 10-
4.30 (closed: Xmas & 1 Jan).*

## Dr Johnson's House

17 Gough Sq, EC4
Central map: page 11, K7
☎ 071-353 3745

Gough Square was built in about 1700 and this house has changed very little since that time. Dr Johnson lived here (1749-1759) and it was here that he completed his famous English dictionary (a first edition is on display) and wrote *The Rambler* and *The Idler*. The house was opened as a museum in 1914 and contains a fine collection of prints as well as letters and other relics.

*Open: May-Sep 11-5.30; Oct-Apr 11-5 (closed Sun, BH, Xmas Eve & Good Fri).*
*Admission charge.*
*shop* ✖

## Dulwich Picture Gallery

College Rd, SE21
District map: page 167, 10 E2
☎ 081-693 5254

Few art galleries are as beautiful to look at as this; it was specially designed by Sir John Soane in 1811 and was the first public picture gallery in England. Among the notable paintings here are works by Gainsborough, Poussin, Raphael, Rembrandt, Rubens and Van Dyck.

*Open: Tue-Sat 10-1 & 2-5, Sun 2-5 (closed Mon & BH).*
*Admission charge.*
*shop* ♿ ✖

## East Ham Nature Reserve

Norman Road, E6
District map: page 167, 23 F4
☎ 081-470 4525

This 10-acre nature reserve has two nature trails. There is a visitor centre with displays relating to natural history and history of the churchyard nature reserve.

*Open: Visitor Centre, Sat & Sun 2-5; Nature Reserve, Mon-Fri 9-5, Sat & Sun 2-5 (winter closes 4pm).*

## Eltham Palace

Off Court Rd, Eltham, SE9
District map: page 167, 11 F2
☎ 081-781 2242 (ext 4232)

Henry VIII was the last monarch to live at Eltham Palace, notable for the great hall with its 15th-century hammer beam roof. An old bridge spans the moat.

*Open: Winter, Thur & Sun 10-4; Summer, Thu & Sun 10-6.*
*Opening arrangements subject to possible alteration; you are advised to phone before your visit.*
*Admission free.*
*(AM)*

## Fenton House

Hampstead Grove NW3
District map: page 166, 12 C4
☎ 071-435 3471

This is an elegant William and Mary house, built around 1693, and set in a walled garden. Collections housed here include notable Oriental, Continental and English china, needlework, furniture and the fascinating Benton Fletcher Collection of early keyboard instruments. Concerts are held here in summer.

*Open: Mar, Sat & Sun 11-6; Apr-Oct, Sat, Sun & BH 11-6, Tue & Wed 1-7.*
*Admission charge.*
♿ ✖ *(NT)*

## Florence Nightingale Museum

2 Lambeth Palace Rd, SE1
Central map: page 5, J4
☎ 071-620 0374

Set on the site of the first School of Nursing, this museum shows clearly that Florence Nightingale was more than 'the Lady with the Lamp'. Beautifully designed, the museum creates a personal setting in which are displayed Florence's prized possessions, a lamp from the Crimean War and nursing artefacts. The centrepiece is a recreated ward scene from the Crimea, and audio-visual technology takes the museum beyond its four walls.

*Open: Tue-Sun 10-4 (closed: Xmas, 1 Jan, Good Fri & Etr Sun).*
*Admission charge.*
shop ♿ 🖥 🚫

## Forty Hall Museum

Forty Hill, Enfield
District map: page 167, 13 E5
📞 081-363 8196

Built in 1629 for Sir Nicholas Raynton, Lord Mayor of London, this mansion was modified in the early 18th century. Contemporary plaster ceilings and a screen can be seen here, as can 17th- and 18th-century furnishings and paintings, ceramics and glass.

*Open: Tue-Sun 10-5.*
*Admission free.*
🖥 shop 🚫

## Freud Museum

20 Maresfield Gardens, NW3
District map: page 167, 44 D4
📞 071-435 2002

In 1938 Sigmund Freud left his home in Vienna as a refugee from the Nazi occupation and chose exile in England, transferring his entire domestic and working environment to this house. He resumed work until his death here a year later. Freud's extraordinary collection of Egyptian, Greek, Roman and Oriental antiquities, library and papers, and his famous desk and couch are all here. The house was bequeathed by his daughter Anna Freud (1895-1982), whose pioneering development work is also represented.

*Open: Wed-Sun 12-5 (closed BH).*
*Admission charge.*
shop ♿ 🚫

## Geffrye Museum

Kingsland Rd, E2
Central map: page 12, N9
📞 071-739 8368

The former almshouses of the Ironmongers' Company. Built in the 18th century it now houses an interesting collection of furniture and woodwork from the Elizabethan period to 1939. It includes a

reconstruction of John Evelyn's closet of curiosities.

*Open: Tue-Sat 10-5, Sun 2-5 & BH 10-5 (closed Mon, Good Fri, 24-26 Dec & 1 Jan).*
*Admission free.*
shop 🖥 ♿ (ground floor only) 🚫

## Gipsy Moth IV

Greenwich Pier, King William Walk, SE10
District map: page 167, 14 E3
📞 081-858 3445

The yacht in which Sir Francis Chichester sailed single-handed round the world in 1966–67, starting the fashion for 'Round the World' sailing races.

*Open: daily, Apr-Oct 10-6 (Sun 12-6).*
*Admission charge.*

## Grange Museum of Community History

Neasden Lane, NW10
(centre of roundabout)
District map: page 166, 15 C4
📞 081-452 8311

Dating from around 1700, this building originally formed part of the outbuildings of a large farm and was later converted into a 'gothic' cottage. Permanent collections inside tell the story of the area that is now the London Borough of Brent. There are also temporary exhibitions, a local history library and a display on the British Empire Exhibition for which Wembley Stadium was built. Two period rooms of late 19th century and early 20th century, and a reconstructed draper's shop form part of the display.

*Open: Tue-Thu 12-5, Sat 10-12 & 1-5.*
*Admission free (donations).*
shop ♿ 🚫

## Guildhall

Gresham St, EC2
Central map: page 12, L7
📞 071-606 3030

Parts of this magnificent building date from 1411. Particularly fine is the crypt, which is the largest of its kind

GUILDHALL

in London. It was severely damaged in the Great Fire of 1666 (after which Wren restored it) and during the Blitz. Restoration work, completed in 1954, was carried out to designs by Sir Giles Scott. Here the Court of Common Council, which administers the city, meets and entertains. The Guildhall Library contains an unrivalled collection of books, manuscripts, and illustrations on all aspects of London. The Guildhall Clock Museum, with 700 exhibits, illustrates 500 years of time-keeping.

*Open: May-Sep daily 10-5; Oct-Apr, Mon-Sat 10-5 (closed: Xmas, New Year, Good Fri, Etr Mon & Civic occasions).*
*Admission free.*
*shop* 🚻 ♿ ✂

## Guinness World of Records

The Trocadero, Piccadilly Circus, W1
Central map: page 10, H6
☎ 071-439 7331

Through the use of life-size models, videos and the latest audio-visual techniques, many of the records from within the famous *Guinness Book of Records* come alive. There are six theme areas, corresponding with the sections of the book: the Human World, the Animal World, Our Planet Earth, Structures and Machines, the Sports World, the World of Entertainment, and British Innovation and Achievement.

*Open: daily from 10am, last admission 10pm, Sun 9.30pm (closed: Xmas day).*
*Admission charge.*
*shop* ♿ ✂

## Gunnersbury Park Museum

Popes Lane, W3
District map: page 166, 16 B3
☎ 081-992 1612

This 19th-century former Rothschild mansion, set in a fine park, is now a museum of local interest for the London Borough of Ealing and Hounslow, showing archaeological discoveries, transport items, costume and topographical and social material. Rothschild coaches are on display. The Victorian kitchens are open to the public on certain summer weekends.

*Open: Mar-Sept, Mon-Fri 1-5, Sat, Sun & BH 1-6; Oct-Feb, daily 1-4 (closed: Good Fri & 24-26 Dec).*
*Admission free.*
*shop* ♿ *(ground floor only) Nursery* ✂

## Hall Place

Bexley (near junction of A2 & A233)
District map: page 167, 17 F2
☎ Crayford (0322) 526574

A 15th-16th-century mansion building with contrasting elevations of chequered flint and brick, Hall Place is surrounded by ornamental gardens, with topiary in the form of Queen's Beasts, rose, rock, water, herb and peat gardens. There are also conservatories and recreation facilities.

*Open: House: Mon-Sat 10-5, Sun 2-6 (summer); Mon-Sat 10-dusk (winter). Gardens: Mon-Fri 7.30-dusk, Sat & Sun 9-dusk.*
*Admission free.*
*shop* 🍽 ♿ ✂

## Ham House

Ham St, Ham (annexe of Victoria & Albert Museum)
District map: page 166, 18 B2
☎ 081-940 1950

An outstanding Stuart house, built in 1610, redecorated and furnished in the 1670s by the Duke and Duchess of Lauderdale. Much of this furniture is still in its original rooms today.

*Open: House: closed in 1992 for major restoration work. Garden: Tue-Sun & BH 10.30-6 or dusk.*
*House: admission charge. Grounds: free.*
✗ ☐ (NT)

### Hampton Court Palace

Hampton Court
District map: page 166, 19 B2
℡ 081-977 8441

Hampton Court Palace was started in the 16th century by Cardinal Wolsey, Lord Chancellor to Henry VIII. It was to have been his personal palace, but he gave it to Henry VIII in a vain attempt to stave off his downfall. It has since been added to and altered by many monarchs, and it has been the setting of many historic events. Sir Christopher Wren was commissioned by William and Mary to convert it to a palace on the lines of Versailles, and much of the exterior dates from this time. The last monarch to live here was George II, after which it became a series of 'grace and favour' residences. Today it is full of priceless paintings, tapestries and furniture, some of which were saved from a fire which caused great damage in 1986. The gardens and grounds, which include the famous maze, set the palace off to perfection.

*Open: Gardens and grounds, see page 144; Palace and Maze: daily 9.30-6 (4.30 mid-Oct-Mar) (closed: 23-26 Dec & 1 Jan).*
*Admission charge.*
*shop* ♿ ☐ ✗ *(ex in grounds)*

### Hayward Gallery

South Bank Centre, SE1
Central map: page 5, J5
℡ 071-921 0876

THE CLOCK COURT,
HAMPTON COURT PALACE

Opened in 1968, the gallery is a major international venue for temporary exhibitions and also the home of the South Bank Centre's touring exhibitions. Its programme includes contemporary and historical exhibitions, often devoted to a particular theme or artist.

*Open: daily 10-6 (8pm Tue & Wed).*
☐

### HMS Belfast

Morgan's Lane, Tooley St, SE1
Central map: page 6, M5
℡ 071-407 6434

Launched in 1938 this was the Royal Navy's largest cruiser. After being damaged by a mine in 1939 the ship did not re-enter service until November 1942. It then played an active roll for the rest of the war, including duty on the famous Russian convoys, and was also present in 1943 at the sinking of the *Scharnhorst* at the Battle of North Cape. Today as a floating museum you can explore its seven decks and defend the ship against simulated air attacks.

*Open: daily 20 Mar-Oct 10-6, last admission 5.20; Nov-19 Mar 10-4.30, last admission 4 (closed: 24–26 Dec & 1 Jan).*
*Admission charge.*
*shop* ☐ *(summer only)* ✗

### Highgate Cemetery

Swains Lane, N6
District map: page 167, 20 D4
℡ 081-340 1834

One of the private cemeteries which sprang up in the 1830s. The eastern part is well known for the grave of Karl Marx. The western part, decaying and overgrown through years of neglect, provides a marvellous backdrop for the magnificent tombs, vaults and buildings. Other famous Victorians buried here include George Eliot, Michael Faraday, and Charles Dickens' family.

*Open: Eastern cemetery daily 10-5 (4 in winter). Western cemetery, guided tours only, Sat-Sun 11-4 (3 in winter); midweek tours 12, 2 & 4 (12, 2 & 3 in winter).*
*Admission charge.*

## Hogarth's House

Hogarth Lane, Great West Road, W4
District map: page 166, 21 C3
📞 081-944 6757

William Hogarth lived in this 17th-century house for 15 years. Many of his engravings and drawings are on show here, as are other mementoes of the life and times of this great artist.

*Open: Mon, Wed-Sat 11-6, Sun 2-6 (4pm Oct-Mar) (closed: Tue & Good Fri, 1st two weeks Sept, last 3 weeks Dec & New Year's Day).*
*Admission free.*

## Horniman Museum

London Road, SE23
District map: page 167, 22 E2
📞 081-699 2339

Displays from different cultures and large natural history collections, including living creatures, can be seen here, and there is also an exhibition of musical instruments from all parts of the world. Extensive library, and lectures and concerts in spring and autumn. Special exhibitions. Educational Centre programmes.

*Open: Mon-Sat 10.30-6, Sun 2-6 (closed: 23-26 Dec).*
*Admission free.*
*shop* 🚻 🐕 *(ex guide dogs)* ♿

## Houses of Parliament

Westminster, SW1
Central map: page 4, 14
📞 071-219 4272

From Edward the Confessor to Henry VIII, the Palace of Westminster was the principal residence of the monarch. Almost all of the old palace was destroyed in a fire in 1834, the only substantial survivor being the superb Westminster Hall (see below). The Commons and the Lords had sat in various parts of the palace (including the Hall) since the time of Henry VIII. Immediately after the fire a competition was held for a building to replace it, and this was won by Sir Charles Barry. Although the basic design was Barry's, much of the detailed work was done by Augustus Pugin, and together they created a Gothic masterpiece which is now one of the most famous buildings in the world. Although most people now know it as the Houses of Parliament, it is still, strictly, the Palace of Westminster. The two principal chambers are set either side of a central hall and corridor — the House of Lords to the south and the House of Commons to the north. The clock tower, 320ft high, contains Big Ben, the hour bell weighing $3\frac{1}{2}$ tons, while the Victoria tower stands 340ft high. The House of Commons suffered bomb damage in 1941 and a new chamber was constructed to the design of Sir Giles Gilbert Scott and opened in 1950.

*To gain admission to the Strangers' Galleries join the queue at St Stephen's entrance from approx 5.30pm Mon-Thu, approx 9.30am Fri (House of Commons). From approx 2.30pm Tue & Wed, from 3pm Thu & 11am Fri (House of Lords) or by arrangement with an MP (House of Commons) or Peer (House of Lords).*
*Admission free, although guides require payment if employed.*
♿ *(by arrangement)*
*bookstall* 🐕 *(ex guide dogs)*

## also Westminster Hall

📞 071-219 4272

Built in 1097–99 by William Rufus, it is the oldest remaining part of Westminster Palace. The glory of the hall is the cantilever, or hammerbeam roof, the earliest and largest of its kind in existence, built between 1394 and 1401. The Hall has been the setting for many momentous national events, including the trial of Charles I in 1649, and the lying in state of monarchs and statesmen.

*Open: Mon-Thu am by arrangement with an MP only.*
*Free, although guides require payment if employed.*
&#9855; *(by arrangement)*
&#8555; *(ex guide dogs)*

## Imperial War Museum

Lambeth Road, SE1
Central map: page 5, K4
&#9743; *071-416 5000*

Housed in the buildings of the former lunatic asylum universally known as 'Bedlam', this museum illustrates and records all aspects of the two World Wars and other military operations involving Britain and the Commonwealth since 1914. Recent major renovations have resulted in the spectacular use of technology to bring to life many events. These include a 'Blitz Experience' and 'The Trench War', in which you walk through a World War I trench at night, passing dug-outs and hearing the sounds of battle from beyond the barbed wire. There is also an art gallery and a cinema offering a weekend programme of documentary and feature films.

*Open: daily 10-6 (closed: 24-26 Dec & 1 Jan).*
*Admission charge.*
*Shop* &#9855; &#8555;

## The Inns of Court

There used to be 12 Inns of Court, but only three still exist in their traditional capacity — Gray's Inn, Lincoln's Inn and Temple. To pass through the gateways of any of these is to step back in time — their peace and tranquillity is anachronistic, more in keeping with their monastic origins than the secular hubbub outside their walls.

### Gray's Inn

Gray's Inn Road, WC2
Central map: page 11, J7
&#9743; *071-405 8164*

A late 17th-century gatehouse opens from Holborn into the confines of Gray's Inn Square. Of particular interest are the 16th-century Hall, with its contemporary windows, the Library, with a statue of Francis Bacon, the most famous member of the Inn, and the chapel. The gardens here are lovely. They are said to have been laid out by Sir Francis Bacon — famous Elizabethan statesman and essayist — who kept chambers here from 1577 to 1626. The ancient catalpa trees in the garden are reputed to be the ones that Bacon planted.

*Open: Gardens May-Sep, Mon-Fri 12-2.30, Buildings by prior application to the Undertreasurer.*
*Admission free (children not admitted).*
&#8555;

### Lincoln's Inn

Chancery Lane, WC2
Central map: page 11, J7
&#9743; *071-405 1393*

The buildings here date mainly from the 16th and 17th centuries. The Gatehouse was built in 1518, and still has its original oak doors. Old Hall dates from 1506, but was extensively restored in 1928. Inigo Jones is said to have designed the 17th-century chapel. The complex is dominated by Victoria New Hall and Library dating from 1843.

*Open: Chapel and gardens, Mon-Fri 12.30-2.30 (closed Etr, Xmas & 1 Jan). Other buildings open by application to the Treasury Office.*
*Admission free.*
&#8555;

### Temple

Fleet Street, EC4
Central map: page 11, J6/K6
&#9743; *071-353 7323 (Prince Henry's Room)*
&#9743; *071-353 8462 (Inner Temple Hall and Church)*
&#9743; *071-353 4355 (Middle Temple Hall)*

Originally, the Temple was the English headquarters of the Knights Templar. The entrance from Fleet Street is through Inner Temple Gateway. Above this is Prince Henry's Room, which retains its original panelling and ceiling. It contains an exhibition relating to Samuel Pepys. The oldest building in the complex is Temple Church, one of only four round churches surviving in England. Middle Temple Hall is a superb example of Tudor architecture.

*Open: Prince Henry's Room (Inner Temple Gateway):Mon-Fri 1.45-5, Sat 4.30 (closed BH).*
*Temple Church, daily 10-4 (except for services).*
*Middle Temple Hall: Mon-Fri 10-11.30, 3-4 (closed: Xmas, week after Etr, Aug-mid Sep).*
*Inner Temple Hall: Mon-Fri 10-11, 1.45-4 (opening subject to porter being available).*
*Admission free.*
❀

### Jewish Museum

Woburn House, Tavistock Square, WC1
Central map: page 10, H8
☎ 071-388 4525

A fascinating exhibition displaying a collection of ceremonial art, portraits and antiques illustrating Jewish life, history and religion. Two audio-visual programmes explain Jewish festivals and ceremonies.

*Open: Tue-Thu & Sun 10-4, Fri Apr-Sep 10-4, Oct-Mar 10-12.30 (closed: Sat, Mon, public & Jewish hols).*
*Admission free (donations).*
*shop* ♿

### Keats' House

Keats Grove, NW3
District map; page 167, 24 D4
☎ 071-435 2062

In fact, this was originally two Regency houses. Keats lived in one with his friend Charles Brown, while next door lived his nurse and lover, Fanny Brawne. It was here that he wrote his greatest poetry, including *Ode to a Nightingale*, which was composed in the garden. The little group lived here between 1818 and 1820. Today the combined houses are furnished in period style and contain many manuscripts, letters and relics.

*Open: Mon-Fri 10-1, 2-6 (Nov-Mar 1-*

*5), Sat 10-1, 2-5, Sun & BH 2-5 (closed: Good Fri, Easter eve, May Day, Xmas & 1 January).*
*Admission free.*
*shop* ♿ *(ground floor only)* ❀

### Kensington Palace State Apartments & Court Dress Collection.

Kensington Gardens, W8
Central map: page 1, C5
☎ 071-937 9561

The palace was acquired by William III in 1689 and remodelled and enlarged by Sir Christopher Wren. Queen Victoria was born and brought up here, and today it is the London residence of the Prince and Princess of Wales, Princess Margaret, and Prince and Princess Michael of Kent. The State Apartments display pictures and furniture from the Royal Collection and there is a section on the Great Exhibition. Also on view is the colourful Court Dress Collection. Its exhibits provide a glimpse into a bygone age, with displays of costumes worn at court from 1750 to the present day.

*Open: Mon-Sat 9-5, Sun 1-5, last admission 4.15pm (closed: Good Fri, 24–26 Dec & 1 Jan).*
*Admission charge.*
*shop* ♿ ❀

### Kenwood, Iveagh Bequest

Hampstead Lane, NW8
District map: page 167, 25 D4
☎ 081-348 1286

This fine mansion was remodelled by Robert Adam between 1767 and 1769. Further changes and additions were made later in the 18th century. The house and wooded grounds, which form part of Hampstead Heath, were bequeathed to the nation by Lord Iveagh in 1927. Adam's Library is especially notable. Outstanding, however, are the works of art, including paintings by Rembrandt, Hals, Reynolds and Gainsborough. Also on display are collections of 18th-century shoe buckles and jewellery. Kenwood is a popular venue for summer events and musical evenings (see page 17).

Open: Good Fri-Sept 10-6, Oct-
Maundy Thu 10-4 (closed: Xmas).
Admission free.
shop ▢ &

### Kew Bridge Steam Museum

The Pumping Station, Green Dragon
Lane, Brentford
District map: page 166, 26 B3
☎ 081-568 4757

London's living steam museum,
containing model engines, steam
engines and six beam engines (five
working) plus traction engines and a
museum of London's water supply.
Old workshops and forges help to
recreate a working site which was
operational from 1820 to 1945.
Various events throughout the year.

Open: daily 11-5. Engines in steam Sat,
Sun & BH (closed: Xmas wk).
Admission charge.
shop ▢ & (ground floor only)

### Kew Gardens

Royal Botanic Gardens, Kew
District map: page 166, 27 B3

See page 150.

### Kew Palace

Royal Botanic Gardens, Kew
District map: page 166, 28 B3

This Dutch-gabled house, built in
1631, was the favourite residence of
George III and used for nearly a
century until 1818, when Queen
Charlotte died. It still reflects the
quiet country life his family enjoyed
here, with displays of personal
souvenirs, furniture and tapestries.

Open: daily, Apr-Sep 11-5.30.
Admission charge.

#### Queen Charlotte's Cottage

Built in 1772 as a summer house for
George III's family, it is a perfect rural
retreat — timber-framed and with a
thatched roof — and stands in the
most 'natural' seeming part of Kew
Gardens. The interior remains as it
was in the 18th century when royalty
were in residence.

Open: Apr-Sep: Sat, Sun & BH 11-5.30.
Joint ticket with Kew Palace.

### Leighton House

12 Holland Park Road, W14
Central map: page 1, B4
☎ 071-602 3316

Leighton House is a uniquely opulent
and exotic example of High Victorian
taste. Built for the President of the
Royal Academy, Frederic, Lord
Leighton, by George Aitchison, the
main body of the house was
completed in 1866. The fabulous
Arab Hall, with its rare Middle-Eastern
tiles, fountain and gilded decoration,
is a 19th-century 'Arabian Nights'
creation finished in 1879. Fine
Victorian paintings by Lord Leighton
and his contemporaries hang in the
rooms, and there are galleries for
exhibitions of modern and historic
art.

Open: Mon-Sat 10-5 (6pm during
temporary exhibitions) (closed: BH).
Gardens open Apr-Sep 11-5.
Admission free.

### Linley Sambourne House

18 Stafford Ter., W8
Central map: page 1, B4
☎ 081-994 1019 (The Victorian Society)

The home of Linley Sambourne
(1845-1910), chief political cartoonist
of Punch. The magnificent interior has
survived almost unchanged, and the
fixtures and fittings have been
preserved together with many of
Sambourne's own pictures.

Open: Mar-Oct, Wed 10-4, Sun 2-5.
Admission charge.
shop ✗

### Livesey Museum

682 Old Kent Road, SE15
District map: page 167, 29 E3
☎ 071-639 5604

Southwark's family museum holds
one major exhibition each year,
popular among children, with
colourful 'hands-on' displays. Past
exhibitions include 'Robots' and 'The
Great Rubbish Show'.

Open: when exhibition is in progress,
Mon-Sat 10-5.
Admission free.
shop ⟑ (ground floor only) ⚡

## Lloyd's of London

1 Lime St, EC3
Central map: page 12, M6
☏ 071-623 7100

The world's leading insurance market
moved into a new headquarters
building of advanced design in Lime
Street in May 1986. It incorporates a
purpose-built exhibition
encompassing Lloyd's 300 years in
the City as well as a viewing area.

Open: Mon-Fri 10-2.30 (3.45 for
booked groups) (closed: PH and
occasional other days).
Admission free.
shop ⟑ ⚡

## London Diamond Centre

10 Hanover St, W1
Central map: page 9, G6
☏ 071-629 5511

A unique exhibition of and about
diamonds, where visitors can see
diamond cutters and polishers
practising their craft, a goldsmith
creating jewellery exclusively for the
London Diamond Centre, and many
other interesting aspects about the
craft and industry. There is a walk-in
diamond mine, and a video on
diamond mining. Another part of the
exhibition displays replicas of some of
the world's most historic diamonds,
and shapes in which diamonds can
be cut.

Open: Mon-Fri 9.30-5.30, Sat
9.30-1.30.

Admission charge (includes a free
memento in the form of a brilliant cut
stone (not a diamond) in a
presentation case, which value far
exceeds the admission fee).
shop ⟑ ⚡

## The London Dungeon

28/34 Tooley St, SE1
Central map: page 6, M5
☏ 071-403 0606

The London Dungeon leads the
visitor through a series of vast, slimy
vaults housing strange and horrifying
scenes of man's inhumanity to man
in Britain's dank past. Methods of
torture and death, the tools of
witchcraft and black magic and some
of the more grisly medicinal practices
are well represented.

Open: daily, Apr-Sep 10-5.30, Oct-Mar
10-4.30 (closed: Xmas).
Admission charge.
shop ⟐ ⟑ ⚡

## London Planetarium

Marylebone Rd, NW1
Central map: page 9, F7
☏ 071-486 1121

'Solar Swoop' is the new star show at
the London Planetarium, which
incorporates laser effects for the first
time. Two eagles come to life under
the Planetarium dome and describe
their adventures through the Solar
System to the audience. 'Space Trail'
is the new interactive 'lift-off' zone at
the Planetarium, where visitors can

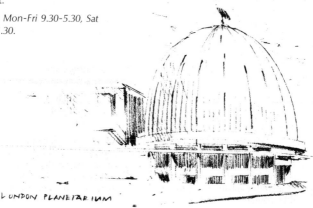

LONDON PLANETARIUM

receive up-to-date information about space through the use of touch-sensitive screens.

*Open: daily, star shows from 12.40, every 40 minutes (earlier at weekends and holidays).*
*Admission charge.*
*shop ⊗*

### London Silver Vaults

Chancery Lane, WC2
Central map: page 11, J7
℡ 071-242 3844

A fine collection of antiques and modern silverware in an underground location. Visitors can browse, and traders are happy to talk about their wares, look up hallmarks and explain histories.

*Open: Mon-Fri 9-5.30, Sat 9-12.30.*
*Admission free.*

### London Toy & Model Museum

21-23 Craven Hill, W2
Central map: page 7, D6
℡ 071-262 9450/7905

This Victorian building houses a fine collection of commercially-made toys and models, with an emphasis on trains, cars and boats. Pleasant garden and extensive garden railway.

*Open: Mon-Sat 10-5.30, Sun 11-5.30 (closed: 25-26 Dec & 1 Jan).*
*Admission charge.*
*shop ⌂ ⅙ ⊗*

### London Transport Museum

The Piazza, Covent Garden, WC2
Central map: page 10, I6
℡ 071-379 6344

Housed in the former Flower Market in Covent Garden, this museum tells the story of the development of London's transport, from its earliest beginnings right up to the present day. Vehicles include steam locomotives, trains, buses, trolleybuses, railway coaches and horse buses. There are also extensive displays using working and static models, posters and audio-visual material. One can 'drive' a modern bus, a tram and a tube train. A

reference library is available by appointment.

*Open: daily 10-6, last admission 5.15pm (closed: Xmas).*
*Admission charge.*
*shop ⅙ ⊗*

### London Zoo (Regent's Park)

NW1
Central map: page 9, F9
℡ 071-722 3333

Set in Regent's Park, the zoo is one of the most comprehensive collections of animals in the world, with over 5000 animals on view. Creatures from every corner of the globe can be seen here, varying from those found in the British countryside, to the rare and endangered species of the world. Among the many world firsts that the zoo can claim are a reptile house opened in 1849, an aquarium in 1853 and an insect house in 1889. In recent years many new pavilions have been built, including a giant walk-through aviary designed by Lord Snowdon. In 'Moonlight World', day and night have been artificially reversed, enabling a fascinating insight into the world of nocturnal animals. The zoo makes every effort to keep its charges in surroundings that are as near like their natural habitat as possible; its success in this can, perhaps, be judged from the high number of breeding successes. Although it is a fine place simply to watch creaturse at close hand, the zoo also has a serious scientific

function, and to this end much research work is carried out. London Zoo and Whipsnade Wild Animal Park are supported by the most professionally complete veterinary and research services to maintain high animal management standards.

*Open: Mon-Sat 9-6 (Mar-Oct), 10-dusk in winter, Sun & BH close at 7 or dusk, whichever is earlier (closed: Xmas day).*
*Admission charge.*
🍽 *(licensed)* ♿ *shop* 🚫

## Madame Tussaud's

Marylebone Rd, NW1
Central map: page 9. F7
📞 071-935 6861

Founded in Paris, Madame Tussaud's Wax Exhibition settled in London in 1844. Exhibits include the Garden Party, 200 Years of Madame Tussaud's, Hollywood Legends, kings, queens, sportspeople and other famous figures.

*Open: all year 10-5.30 (closed: Xmas day)*
*Admission charge.*
🍽 ♿ *shop* 🚫

## Mall Galleries

The Mall, SW1
Central map: page 4, I5
📞 071-930 6845

These are exhibition galleries of the Federation of British Artists, where eight Art Societies administered by the organisation hold theiur annual exhibitions.

*Open: daily 10-5.*
*Admission charge (gallery friends free).*
♿ 🚫

## Marble Hill House

Marble Hill Park, Richmond Rd, Twickenham
District map: page 166, 30 B2
📞 081-892 5115

An example of English Palladian architecture standing in a wooded park near the River Thames, Marble Hill House was built in 1724-9 for Henrietta Howard, mistress of George

II and later Countess of Suffolk. It contains Georgian paintings and furniture, and there are Italian paintings in the Great Room by G P Panini.

*Open: daily, Good Fri-Sept 10-6; Oct-Maundy Thu 10-4 (closed: 24-25 Dec).*
*Admission free.*
🍽 *(Apr-Sep)* ♿ *shop* 🚫

## The MCC Museum

Lord's Ground, St John's Wood NW8
Central map: page 8, D8
📞 071-289 1611

Located in the best known cricket ground in the country, this gallery was founded in 1865. It contains a collection of cricket memorabilia, including the Ashes urn, and 18th-century paintings of the sport. There is also a fine library of cricketing literature, a 'living image' of W.G. Grace and a video area showing moments from famous matches.

*Open: Match days Mon-Sat 10.30-5 to visitors who have paid ground admission. Guided tours throughout the year (details 071-266 3025).*
*Admission charge.*
*shop* 🚫 ♿

## Museum of Artillery in the Rotunda

Repository Rd, SE18
District map: page 167, 31 F3
📞 081-316 5402

At one time this singular circular structure, which was designed by John Nash, stood in St James's Park. Today it contains a collection of artillery dating from the 13th century to the present day.

*Open: Apr-Oct, Mon-Fri 12-5, Sat & Sun 1-5; Nov-Mar, Mon-Fri 12-4, Sat & Sun 1-4 (closed: Good Fri, 24-26 Dec & 1 Jan).*
*Admission free.*
*shop* ♿ 🚫

## Museum of Garden History

St Mary-at-Lambeth, Lambeth Palace Rd, SE1
Central map: page 5, I4
📞 071-261 1891 *(11am-3pm)*

Alongside the south gateway of Lambeth Palace is the former church of St Mary. This historic building is dedicated to the memory of John Tradescant, gardener to Charles I, who was responsible for the introduction of many new plants from abroad. Rescued from demolition in the 1970s, it now houses a Museum of Garden History. In the churchyard is a newly made knot garden, which contains plants popular in the 17th century. Nearby stand the tombs of the John Tradescants (father & son) and Captain Bligh of the *Bounty*. Temporary exhibitions.

*Open: 4 Mar-9 Dec, Mon-Fri 11-3; Sun 10.30-5.*
*Admission free.*
shop 🖵 ♿

## Museum of London

London Wall, EC2
Central map: page 12, L7
📞 071-600 3699 ext 240

This museum is devoted entirely to London and its people, presenting by way of exhibitions and tableaux the story of its development and life. Open-plan and arranged in chronological order, the museum affords a continuous view from prehistoric times to the 20th century. The exhibits include an audio-visual reconstruction of the Great Fire of 1666, an 18th-century prison cell, a music hall, a barber's shop from Islington, sculptures from the Temple of Mithras, a 1930 Ford car, Selfridge's lift, a medieval hen's egg and a Roman bikini.

*Open: Tue-Sat 10-6, Sun 2-6 (closed BH and Xmas).*
*Admission free. Parties by arrangement.*
shop 🖵 (licensed) ♿ 🚫

## Museum of Mankind

6 Burlington Gdns, W1
Central map: page 10, H6
📞 071-636 1555 ext. 8043

Housed here are the exhibitions, library and offices of the ethnography department of the British Museum. Its collections embrace the art and material culture of tribal village and other pre-industrial societies from most areas of the world, excluding western Europe. There are also archaeological collections from the Americas and Africa. A few important pieces are on permanent exhibition, but the museum's policy is to mount a number of temporary exhibitions usually lasting for at least a year. These are always fascinating. A separate store in Shoreditch contains the reserve collection, which can be made available for serious study by arrangement. Film shows and educational services are also available.

*Open: Mon-Sat 10-5, Sun 2.30-6 (closed: Good Fri, May Day, 24-27 Dec & 1 Jan).*
*Admission free.*
shop 🚫 🖵 ♿

## Museum of the Moving Image

South Bank, Waterloo, SE1
Central map: page 5, J5
📞 071-401 2636

A journey through cinematic history from the earliest experiments to all the technical wizardry of modern animation, is what this museum offers the visitor. There are artefacts to handle, buttons to press and films to watch, as well as a detailed explanation of the operations of a television studio. A fascinating insight into the world of film and television, with each section as exciting as the last.

*Open: daily 10-6 (closed: 24-26 Dec).*
*Admission charge.*
shop ♿ 🖵 (licensed) 🚫

## Museum of the Order of St John

St John's Gate, St John's Lane, EC1
Central map: page 11, K8
📞 071-253 6644 ext 135

This museum is housed in a 16th-century gatehouse, the former entrance to the medieval Priory of the Order of St John of Jerusalem. It is now the headquarters of the modern Order, whose charitable foundations include St John's Ambulance and the Opthalmic hospital in Jerusalem. Also to be seen are the Norman crypt and 15th-century Grand Priory Church. The exhibits include paintings, silver, furniture and historical medical instruments, certificates, textbooks and memorabilia of notable early St John personalities and pioneers.

*Open: Mon-Fri 10-5, Sat 10-4, guided tours Tue, Fri and Sat 11 & 2-30 (closed: Etr, Xmas wk & BH).*
*Admission free (donations).*
shop 🚻 ✤

## Musical Museum

368 High St, Brentford (7m west of London off A315)
District map; page 166, 32 B3
☎ 081-560 8108

A unique collection of working musical instruments, from small musical boxes to huge orchestrations. There are demonstrations during opening hours. Regular concert evenings.

*Open: Apr-Oct, Sat & Sun 2-5; also Jul-Aug, Wed-Fri 2-4 (1½ hr tour).*
*Admission charge.*
shop 🚻 ✤

## National Army Museum

Royal Hospital Road, SW3
Central map: page 3, F2
☎ 071-730 0717

A permanent chronological display of the history of the British, Indian and Colonial forces from 1485 is contained here. Among the exhibits are uniforms, weapons, prints, photographs, manuscripts, letters, glass, china, silver and relics of British commanders and mementoes of Britain's soldiers. There is a special display of the orders and decorations of the Duke of Windsor, and also those of five great field marshals — Lords Roberts, Gough, Kitchener and Wolseley and Sir George White VC. The picture gallery includes portraits by Gainsborough and Reynolds, as well as battle scenes and pictures of Indian regiments. A new display looks at the British Army in the Napoleonic Wars and includes a 400-square foot model of the Battle of Waterloo.

*Open: daily 10-5.30 (closed: Good Fri,*
*May Day, 24-26 Dec & 1 Jan).*
*Admission free.*
shop 🚻 ✤ ▱

## National Gallery

Trafalgar Sq, WC2
Central map; page 10, I6
☎ 071-839 3321 & recorded information 071-839 3526

In 1824 the government bought the collection of pictures accumulated by John Julius Angerstein, a London underwriter, and exhibited them at his former residence in Pall Mall. These formed the major part of the collection of the National Gallery. Further bequests and purchases were made and by 1831 space had become cramped, so plans were made for a special building to house the works of art. The present neo-classical building in Trafalgar Square was opened in 1838. All the great periods of European paintings are represented here, although only a limited selection of British works is displayed, as most of the national collection is housed at the Tate. The gallery's particular treasures include Van Eyck's *Arnolfini Marriage*, Valazquez's *Toilet of Venus*, Leonardo da Vinci's cartoon *The Virgin and Child with Saints Anne and John the Baptist*, Rembrandt's *Belshazzar's Feast* and Titian's *Bacchus and Ariadne*. The British paintings include Gainsborough's *Mr and Mrs Andrews* and Constable's *Haywain*. The new Sainsbury Wing includes an exhibition on early Renaissance works. There are many more captivating masterpieces to be seen at the National Gallery, which houses one of the finest and most extensive collections in the world. Lectures, guided tours, children's worksheets and quizzes are available.

*Open: Mon-Sat 10-6, Sun 2-6 (closed: Good Fri, May Day, 24-26 Dec & 1 Jan).*
*Admission free.*
shop ▱ (licensed) 🚻 ✤

## National Maritime Museum

Romney Rd, SE10
District map: page 167, 33 E3
☎ 081-858 4422

The museum illustrates humankind's relationship with the sea, from ancient boats and Roman trade, through centuries of boatbuilding, battles and exploration to 20th-century ships. Features include items from Henry VIII's naval fleet, and great masterpieces of battles at Trafalgar and in the Americas. There are also galleries devoted to Lord Nelson and Captain Cook.

*Open: Mon-Sat 10-5 (6pm summer), Sun 2-5 (6pm summer) (closed: Good Fri, May Day, 24-27 Dec & 1 Jan). Admission charge. shop ⌨ ᕐ ⌘ (ex guide dogs).*

### National Portrait Gallery

2 St Martin's Place, WC2
Central map, page 10, 16
☎ 071-306 0055

This gallery contains the national collection of portraits of the famous and infamous in British history, including paintings, sculptures, miniatures, engravings, photographs and cartoons. The works are arranged more or less in chronological order, and are accompanied by furniture, maps, weapons and other items to set them in their historical context. Beginning in medieval times, they range in quality from masterpieces to works of a more mundane nature. Special exhibitions several times a year.

*Open: Mon-Fri 10-5, Sat 10-6, Sun 2-6 (closed: Good Fri, May Day, 24-26 Dec & 1 Jan). Admission free (charges for special exhibitions). shop ⌘*

### National Postal Museum

King Edward Building, King Edward St, EC1
Central map: page 12, L7
☎ 071-239 5420

What is probably the finest and most comprehensive collection of postage stamps in the world is contained here. Included are the RM Phillips collection of 19th-century Great Britain (with special emphasis on the One Penny Black and its creation);

the Post Office Collection; a world-wide collection including practically every stamp issued since 1878; and the philatelic correspondence archives of Thomas de la Rue and Co, who furnished stamps to over 150 countries between 1855 and 1965. Within these collections are thousands of original drawings and unique proof sheets of every British stamp since 1840. Special exhibitions, reference library and tours by prior arrangement.

*Open: Mon-Thu (ex BH) 9.30-4.30, Fri 9.30-4. Admission free. shop ᕐ ⌘*

### Natural History Museum

Cromwell Road, SW7
Central map: page 2, D4
☎ 071-938 9123

The museum's collections were built up around the specimens collected by Sir Hans Sloane and which formed a part of the nucleus of the British Museum. By 1860 the continued expansion of the collection meant that a separate natural history museum was required; it was not until 1881, though, that the new museum was opened. The vast and elaborate Romanesque-style building covers an area of four acres. The exhibits include most aspects of biology and geology. In the Whale Hall a life-size model of the enormous Blue Whale can be seen, and in the Hall of Human Biology visitors can learn about the way their bodies work (including how it feels to be in the womb). Ecology stresses our relationship with, and responsibility for, the natural world.

   A major new permanent exhibition on dinosaurs includes new skeletons, recreated robotic models, and displays on how dinosaurs lived, why they became extinct and how they were dug up and studied by scientists. The Earth Galleries were formerly the Geological Museum, which contains the largest exhibition on basic earth science in the world, as well as a notable collection of gemstones and a piece of the moon. The entrance to the Earth Gallery is on Exhibition Road, separate from the

Cromwell Road entrance to the main museum. Public lectures and films are given on Tue, Thu and Sat. Leaflet available on request.

*Open: Mon-Sat 10-6, Sun 11-6 (closed: Good Fri, May Day, 24-26 Dec & 1 Jan).*
*Admission charge.*
*shop* 🚻 🅿 ⚿ ⚐

## North Woolwich Old Station Museum

Pier Road, E16
District map: page 167, 35 F3
☎ 071-474 7244

This is an imposing restored station building, with three galleries tracing the history of the Eastern Region Railway in photographs, models and an original turntable pit. Also houses an 1876 Coffee Pot locomotive and a Victorian booking office.

*Open: Mon-Wed, & Sat 10-5, Sun & BH 2-5 (closed: Xmas).*
*Admission free.*

## Old Royal Observatory

Greenwich Park, SE10
District map: page 167, 36 E3
☎ 081-858 4422

Set in Greenwich Park (see page 143), which was laid out to plans by Le Nôtre, a famous French gardener of the time of Louis XIV, the Observatory is part of the National Maritime Museum. It stands at zero meridian longitude and is the original home of Greenwich Mean Time. There are exhibits of astronomical, horological and navigational interest.

*Open: daily 10-5 (6pm summer) (closed: Good Fri, May Day, 24-26 Dec & 1 Jan).*
*Admission charge.*
*shop* ⚿ ⚐

OLD ROYAL OBSERVATORY.

## Old St Thomas's Operating Theatre

9a St Thomas's St, SE1
Central map: page 6, M5
☎ 071-955 4791

This is the only early 19th-century operating theatre to survive in England. The exhibits tell the history of surgery during the 19th century at Guy's and St Thomas's Hospitals.

*Open: Mon, Wed, Fri 12.30-4, and 1st Sun in each month 12.30-4; Tue & Thu by appointment only (closed: Xmas).*
*Admission charge.*

## Orleans House Gallery

Riverside, Twickenham
District map; page 166, 37 B2
☎ 081-892 0221

The original Orleans House in which Louis Philippe, Duc d'Orléans, King of the French (1830-48) lived in exile in the early 19th century was demolished in 1927. All that survives is the octagonal room, designed by James Gibbs in c1720. It has exquisite plasterwork.

*Open: Tue-Sat 1-5.30 (4.30pm Oct-Mar), Sun & BH 2-5.30 (Oct-Mar 2-4.30) (closed: 24-26 Dec & Good Fri).*
*Woodland gardens open all year, daily 9-dusk.*
*Admission free.*
⚿ ⚐

## Osterley Park House

Osterley (off A4, Great West Rd)
District map: page 166, 38 B3
☎ 081-560 3918

An Elizabethan mansion transformed into an 18th-century villa, this elegant building has neoclassical interior decoration designed by Robert Adam, (Osterley Park, see page 152).

*Open: House, Apr-Oct, Wed-Fri 1-5; Sat, Sun & BH 1-5 (closed: Good Fri & 25-26 Dec).*
*Admission charge.*
🚻 ⚿ ⚐ NT

### Passmore Edwards Museum

Romford Road, E15
District map: page 167, 39 F4
☏ 081-519 4296

Greater London and Essex archeology, biology, geology and history are illustrated here by a series of displays and exhibits.

Open: all year, Wed-Fri 11-5, Sat 1-5, Sun & BH 2-5.
Admission free.
♿ shop ✸

### Percival David Foundation of Chinese Art

53 Gordon Square, WC1
Central map: page 10, I8
☏ 071-387 3909

A unique collection of Chinese ceramics, dating from between the 10th and 18th centuries, is housed here. It encompases the Sung, Yuan, Ming and Qing dynasties. It was presented to London University by Percival David in 1950.

Open: Mon-Fri 10.30-5 (closed: BH).
Admission free.

### Pirate Ships at Tobacco Dock

The Highway, E1
District map; page 167, 49 E3
☏ 071-702 9681

These two replica sailing ships, moored alongside Tobacco Dock, paint a gruesome picture of piracy on the high seas, their decks strewn with corpses as a result of a sudden and bloody raid. Below decks, the Three Sisters houses an animated history of piracy and the Sea Lark vividly brings to life the story of Robert Louis Stevenson's Treasure Island.

Open: daily 10-6.
Admission charge.

### Pollock's Toy Museum

1 Scala St, W1
Central map: page 10, H7
☏ 071-636 3452

The museum occupies two little houses joined together: the rooms

are small and connected by narrow winding staircases. The collection is wide-ranging and covers items from all over the world. It includes a 19th-century toy theatre workshop, toy theatre with performances and slide shows, dolls, optical and mechanical toys, young girl's nursery, folk toys, English tin toys and teddy bears.

Open: all year, Mon-Sat 10-5 (closed: Xmas).
Admission charge.
shop ♿

### Public Record Office Museum

Chancery Lane, WC2
Central map: page 11, K7
☏ 081-876 3444

This is the chief repository for the national archives. The Search Rooms contain records from the Norman Conquest to the present day. There is an exhibition of records illustrating major events in British history. Famous documents which can be seen include the Domesday Book, William the Conqueror's survey of 1086. Also on display are letters from Cardinal Wolsey and Guy Fawkes, and Shakespeare's will. A series of special temporary exhibitions is held.

Open: all year, Mon-Sat 10-5.
Admission free.
shop ✸

### The Queen's Gallery

(Buckingham Palace) Buckingham Palace Rd, SW1
Central map: page 3, G4
☏ 071-799 2331

Works of art from the Royal Collection are housed here in a

building originally designed as a conservatory by John Nash in 1831, and later converted by Blore into a chapel. After suffering severe bomb damage in 1940, the building was eventually reconstructed in 1962, partly as the Private Chapel of Buckingham Palace and partly as an art gallery.

*Open: all year, Tue-Sat & BH 10-5, Sun 2-5 (ex for short periods between exhibitions).*
*Admission charge.*
*shop* 🚻 ✍

## The Queens House

Romney Road, Greenwich, SE10
District map: page 167, 56 F3
📞 081-858 4422

The first Palladian style villa in England, designed by Inigo Jones for Anne of Denmark and completed for Queen Henrietta Maria, wife of Charles I. The recent restoration has been carried out to show the house as it appeared when new, with bright silks and furnishings. The Great Hall and State Rooms and a Loggia overlooking Greenwich Park are notable features. There is a fine collection of Dutch marine paintings, including some of the finest seascapes ever painted.

*Open: Mon-Sat 10-5, Sun 2-5 (6pm in summer) (closed: Good Fri, May Day, 24-27 & 29-31 Dec & 1 Jan).*
*Admission charge.*
*shop* 🚻 ✍

## Ranger's House

Chesterfield Walk, SE3
District map: page 167, 42 E3
📞 081-853 0035

The Suffolk collection of Jacobean and Stuart portraits is housed in this 18th-century villa, former home of Philip Stanhope, 4th Earl of Chesterfield. The collection contains a set of portraits by William Larkin, among the finest to survive from the Jacobean period, and a small collection of Old Masters. Three first floor rooms house the Dolmetsch collection of musical instruments, on loan from the Horniman Museum. Chamber concerts and poetry

readings, educational programme, holiday projects and workshop.

*Open: daily Apr-Sep 10-6; Oct-Mar 10-4 (closed: 24-25 Dec).*
*Admission free.*
*shop* 🚻 ✍

## Rock Circus

London Pavilion, Piccadilly Circus, W1
Central map: page 10, H6
📞 071-734 7203

This is the story of rock and pop music from the 1950s to the present day, told through animated wax figures and stereo sound through headsets. Rock Circus re-enacts the great performances of stars such as the Beatles, Cliff Richard and Madonna by use of special effects, memorabilia, and often original clothing and instruments.

*Open: daily, 11-9, Tue 12-9, Fri & Sat 11-10, summer holiday 10-10.*
*Admission charge.*
*shop* 🍴 *(licensed)* 🚻 ✍

## Royal Academy of Arts

Burlington House, Piccadilly, W1
Central map: page 10, H6
📞 071-439 7438

The Royal Academy of Arts was founded in 1768 by George III. It is most famous for its summer exhibitions, displaying the works of living artists. At other times there are loan exhibitions of international importance. Treasures of the Academy include the Michelangelo *Tondo*.

*Open: daily 10-6 (closed: Xmas).*
*Admission charge.*
*shop* 🍴 *(licensed)* 🚻 ✍

## Royal Air Force Museum

Grahame Park Way, Hendon, NW9
District map: page 167, 43 C5
📞 081-205 2266

The museum, on the former Hendon airfield, covers all aspects of the history of the RAF and its predecessors. Over 60 aircraft are on display, from the Sopwith Camel to the Lightning. The Battle of Britain Experience recreates this great air battle with British, Italian and German aircraft, while the 'Blitz' demonstrates its effect on the nation. You can even experience flying in a Tornado flight simulator. In the Bomber Command Museum are the famous Lancaster, Wellington and Vulcan bombers. The museum has a cinema and there are also audio tours.

*Open: daily 10-6 (closed: 24-26 Dec & 1 Jan).*
*Admission charge.*
*shop* ☕ *(licensed)* ♿ ✗

### Royal Artillery Regimental Museum

Old Royal Military Academy, SE18
District map: page 167, 57 F3
☎ 081-781 5628

The story of the Royal Regiment of Artillery from its formation in 1716 is told in this exhibition, housed in the elegant buildings of the Old Military Academy at Woolwich.

*Open: Mon-Fri 12.30-4.30, Sat & Sun 2-4 (closed Good Fri, 24-26 Dec & 1 Jan). Subject to closure at short notice, please telephone for further details.*
*Admission free.*

### Royal Britain

Aldersgate St, EC2
Central map: page 12, L8
☎ 071-588 0588

All the technical wizardry of the 20th century is employed in this unique exhibition on the history of Britain's monarchy. The visitor walks through time, beginning in the mists of prehistory and ending with a revealing look at royalty today.

*Open: daily 9-5.30 (closed 25 Dec).*
*Admission charge.*
*shop* ☕ *(licensed)* ♿ ✗

### Royal Hospital, Chelsea

Royal Hospital Rd, SW3
Central map: page 3, F2
☎ 071-730 0161

Founded in 1682 by Charles II, for veteran soldiers. Sir Christopher Wren

designed most of the buildings, and his work can be seen at its finest in the Figure Court and the Chapel. Alterations and additions were subsequently made by Robert Adam and Sir John Soane. The Hospital now houses 400 army pensioners, who parade in their scarlet frock-coats on Oak Apple Day (29 May).

The **Ranelagh Gardens** were the site of the famous 18th-century Ranelagh Pleasure Gardens. The author and wit Horace Walpole, who was here on the opening night in 1742, said that it was crowded 'with much nobility and much mob'. There was music, opera, gambling, dancing and masquerades — and the entry fee of half-a-crown included coffee and punch. But it declined in favour towards the end of the century and finally closed its gates in 1804. The gardens were later bought by the Royal Hospital and nowadays are famous for the Chelsea Flower Show. (see page 49).

*Open: Hospital, Mon-Sat 10-12 & 2-4, Sun 2-4; Ranelagh Gardens, 10-sunset.*
*Admission free.*

### Royal Mews

Buckingham Palace, SW1
Central map: page 3, G4
☎ 071-799 2331

Designed by John Nash and completed in 1825, the Royal Mews house the state coaches, including the Gold State Coach made in 1762,

ROYAL MEWS

with panels painted by the Florentine artist Cipriani. It has been used for every coronation since. The collection also includes the Irish State Coach, together with private driving carriages and royal sleighs. In the stables are kept the Windsor Greys and the Cleveland Bay carriage horses.

*Open: Apr-mid Jul, Wed & Thu, & mid Jul-Sept, Wed-Fri 12-4; Oct-Mar, Wed 12-4 (closed: if carriage procession or state visit).*
*Admission charge.*
♿ 

### Royal Naval College

Greenwich, SE10
District map: page 167, 45 E3
*081-858 2154*

Its Thames-side setting gives this group of buildings a special elegance. The original architect was Webb, in the late 17th century, with additions by Wren, Hawksmoor, Vanbrugh and Ripley in the 18th century. Originally a Naval Hospital, it became a Naval College in 1873. The Chapel was rebuilt in the 18th century, and the Painted Hall has a famous ceiling painted by Sir James Thornhill.

*Open: Painted Hall and Chapel daily (ex Thu), 2.30-5 (last admission 4.45pm) (closed: Xmas day).*
*Admission free.*
*shop*

### Rugby Football Union

Rugby Rd, Twickenham
District map: page 166, 58 B3
*081-892 8161*

A visit to Twickenham Rugby Football ground captures the marvellous atmosphere of this famous sports ground on match days. Visitors are given a tour of the changing rooms, including the famous double bath and the medical room, followed by a short video. There is also a display of kits and trophies presented to the RFU, and a museum of the game's history.

*Open: Mon-Fri, tours 10.30 & 2.15 (closed: week before internationals).*
*Admission charge.*
*shop (licensed)* ♿

### St Bride's Crypt Museum

Fleet Street, EC4
Central map; page 11, K6
*071-353 1301*

Internationally known as the 'parish church of the press', St Bride's has been the site of seven previous churches, the existing structure having been meticulously restored in Wren's original design. The traditional three-tiered wedding cake of today is a replica of the steeple, and was first copied by a local baker in the 18th century. The crypt museum houses archaeological remains, gravestones, and a display of the history of the church and its connections with the printers and the press. This includes various first editions of the Bible.

*Open: Mon-Sat 9-5, Sun 12-6.*
*Admission free.*

### Schooner Kathleen & May

St Mary Overy Dock,
Cathedral Street (off Clink Street)
Central map: page 12, L6
*071-403 3965*

The last British, wooden, three-masted topsail schooner, now on show to the public in a berth at St Mary Overy Dock, on the south bank of the River Thames. Exhibitions on board, with audio visuals and films.

*Open: daily 10-5 (Nov-Mar 11-4) (closed: Xmas, 1 Jan, & weekends Nov-Feb).*
*Admission charge.*
*shop*

### Science Museum

Exhibition Road, SW7
Central map: page 2, D4
*071-938 8000*

The Science Museum is particularly attractive to children. Among the displays are many working models with knobs to press, handles to turn and buttons to push: exhibits are set in motion, light up, rotate and make noises. The collections cover the application of science to technology, and illustrate the development of engineering and industry through the ages; there are galleries dealing with printing, chemistry, nuclear physics, navigation, photography, electricity, communication and medicine. A popular feature of the museum is the Launch Pad, an interactive children's gallery where children of all ages can carry out their own fun experiments. 'Food for Thought' is a permanent gallery which explains the impact of science and technology on today's food. The centrepiece of the Exploration of Space exhibition is the Apollo 10 space capsule, whilst the Wellcome Museum of Medicine features numerous reconstructions of important events in medical history.

Open: all year, Mon-Sat 10-6, Sun 11-6 (closed: 24-26 Dec & 1 Jan).
Admission charge.
shop &. 🖵 🐾

### Shakespeare Globe Museum

Bear Gardens, Bankside, SE1
Central map: page 12, L6
☎ 071-928 6342

The museum stands on the site of the Hope Theatre and the last bear-baiting ring on Bankside. It occupies a 19th-century warehouse, and houses a permanent exhibition relating to Elizabethan theatre. Following the discovery nearby of the foundations of the Rose Theatre (1988), and The Globe (1989), the Shakespeare Trust is excavating these sites. It is recreating The Globe with an exhibition centre, which is due to open 23rd April (1993), Shakespeare's birthday.

Open: Mon-Sat 10-5, Sun 1.30-5.30.
Admission charge.
&. (ground floor only) 🖵 🐾 (ex guide dogs)

### Sherlock Holmes Museum

221b Baker St, NW1
Central map: page 9, F8
☎ 071-935 8866

221b Baker Street, that famous address of the fictional super-sleuth Sherlock Holmes, was opened as a museum in March 1990, to the delight of admirers of the great detective. The first-floor rooms contain all the features familiar to the Holmes enthusiast, and an authentic Victorian atmosphere has been

maintained throughout the house.

Open: daily 10-6 (closed: 25 Dec).
Admission charge.
shop 🐾

### Sir John Soane's Museum

13 Lincoln's Inn Fields, WC2
Central map: page 11, J7
☎ 071-405 2107

The house of Sir John Soane (1753-1837), the architect, built in 1812 and containing his collections of antiquities, sculpture, paintings, drawings and books, including the Sarcophagus of Seti (1292 BC), The Rake's Progress and the Election series of paintings by Wiliam Hogarth. Architectural Drawings Collection open by appointment. The house itself is designed to show off these objects in surprising and unexpected ways.

Open: all year (ex BH) Tue-Sat 10-5.
Admission free.
&. (ground floor only) 🐾

### South London Art Gallery

65 Peckham Rd, SE5
District map: page 167, 46 E3
☎ 071-703 6120

The gallery presents temporary exhibitions throughout the year. These feature work by local artists and craftspeople, and also that of major artists living and working in Britain. Always on show is the Southwark Art Collection of drawings. paintings and prints by English artists, from Victorian times to the present day.

Open: only when exhibitions are in progress, Tue-Sat 10-6, Sun 3-6 (closed: Mon).
Admission free.
🐾

### Star Trax

The Trocadero, Piccadilly Circus, W1
Central map: page 10, H6
☎ 071-287 8310

Star Trax gives you the opportunity to be a 'pop star'. Using audio and video you can record your own song, or for fun select from their own extensive library. They provide the expertise, sound and special effects, and you can sing the words.

*Open: Sun-Thur 10.30-11, Fri & Sat 10.30-midnight.*
*Admission charge.*

### The Story of Telecommunications

145 Queen Victoria St, EC4
Central map: page 12, L6
☎ 071-248 7444.

Two display floors here feature the past, present and future of Britain's telecommunications. There are many working exhibits, charting 200 years of progress from the earliest telegraphs, to satellites and optical fibres. Cinema shows and children's worksheets.

*Open: Mon-Fri 10-5 (closed: BH).*
*Admission free.*
&#9855; shop &#x2698; (ex guide dogs)

### Syon House

Isleworth (approach via Park Rd off Twickenham Rd)
District map: page 166, 47 B3
☎ 081-560 0881/3

Syon House was founded in 1415 as a monastery and remodelled in the 18th century with splendid interiors by Robert Adam, in particular the superbly coloured ante-room and the gallery library. Fine portraits and furniture are housed here. Capability Brown designed the grounds (see page 152). The house overlooks the Thames. Garden and craft shows are held during the summer.

*Open: Apr-Sep, Sun-Thu 12-5 (last tickets 4.15); Oct, Sun 12-5.*
*Admission charge.*
&#x2709; &#9855; shop & garden centre &#x2698;

#### Heritage Motor Museum

☎ 081-560 1378

Also on display in Syon Park (see page 152) is a collection of more than 100 vehicles covering the history of much of the British motor industry. Special displays during August and September.

*Open: daily 10-5.30 (4pm Nov-Mar) (closed: Xmas).*
*Admission charge.*
&#x2709; &#9855; shop & garden centre &#x2698;

### Tate Gallery

Millbank, SW1
Central map: page 4, I3
☎ 071-821 7128

Sir Henry Tate, the sugar magnate and prominent collector of contemporary British painting and sculpture, offered to finance the building of a new and permanent home for his growing collection of British Art. Sidney J R Smith was commissioned to design the new gallery on the site of the former Millbank Prison, and the building was officially opened to the public in 1897. A number of extensions to the building have followed, the most recent being the Clore Gallery in 1987, which houses the Turner Bequest. In the early part of this century the gallery was able to extend its collection to include foreign 20th-century art. New displays include rooms devoted to Hogarth and his circle, Constable and Early 19th-century Landscape, Romanticism and Pre-Raphaelitism, Whistler and his circle, Art in Germany 1900–1945, British Surrealism, and Post-War painting in Britain and France. The Duveen Sculpture Galleries, restored in 1989, show British Sculpture from Epstein, Moore and Hepworth to contemporaries such as Flanagan, Cox and Kapoor.

*Open: Mon-Sat 10-5.50, Sun 2-5.50 (closed: Good Fri, May Day BH, 24-26 Dec & 1 Jan). Opening times subject to alterations.*
*Admission free. Charge for major loan exhibitions.*
shop &#x2709; &#9855; &#x2698;

### Thames Barrier Visitors' Centre

Unity Way, SE18
District map: page 167, 48 F3
☎ 081-854 1373

Justifiably described as the 'Eighth Wonder of the World', the $\frac{1}{3}$-mile span barrier built to save London from disastrous flooding is the world's largest movable flood barrier, representing an extraordinary feat of British engineering. The nearby exhibition building has displays and an audio-visual programme explaining the flood threat and the construction of the £480 million project. Barrier gates are raised for testing monthly.

*Open: daily 10.30-5 (5.30 Sat & Sun) (closed: Xmas).*
*Admission charge.*
*shop* 🖵 *(licensed)* 🛆 ⟨ *(ex riverside)* ⌗ *(ex guide dogs)*

### Theatre Museum

Russell St, Covent Garden, WC2
Central map: page 10, I6
☎ 071-836 7891

Major developments, events and personalities from the performing arts are featured in this appealing exhibition. Stage models, costumes, prints, drawings, posters, props and a variety of other theatre memorabilia are displayed. There are evening 'live' theatre productions, and monthly talks by professional actors.

*Open: Tue-Sun 11-7.*
*Admission charge.*
*shop* 🖵 ⟨ ⌗

### The Monument

Monument St, EC3
Central map: page 12, M6
☎ 071-626 2717

The Monument was erected by Sir Christopher Wren and Robert Hooke 1671-77 to commemorate the Great Fire of 1666. Its height of 202ft is said to equal the distance from its base to the place in Pudding Lane where the fire started destroying nearly 90 churches and 13,000 houses.

*Open: Apr-Sep, Mon-Fri 9-6, Sat & Sun 2-6; Oct-May, Mon-Sat 9-4.*
*Admission charge.*
⌗

### The Thomas Coram Foundation for Children

40 Brunswick Square, WC1
Central map: page 10, I8
☎ 071-278 2424

The Foundation was formed in 1739, when a royal charter was granted to Captain Thomas Coram to open a Foundling Hospital for destitute children. At the instigation of William Hogarth, various works of art were presented to the Foundation for display in the Court Room, to attract the public and raise funds. The present building, which was built in 1937 on the site of the old one, houses the vast number of exhibits which have been presented to the Foundation over the years. Of particular interest is the portrait of Coram, by Hogarth, which was the first gift.

*Open: Mon-Fri 10-4 (advisable to check) (closed: BH).*
*Admission charge.*

### Tithe Barn Agricultural & Folk Museum

Hall Lane, Upminster
District map: page 167, 50 F4
☎ *Hornchurch (04024) 47535.*

This 15th-century thatched timber building contains a large selection of old agricultural implements, craft and farm tools, domestic bygones and items of local interest. In all, there are over 4000 exhibits.

*Open: 2-6 on the first full weekend of each month.*
*Admission free.*
*shop* ⟨ ⌗

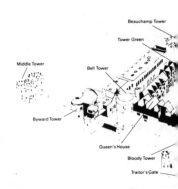

### Tower Bridge Walkway

Tower Bridge, SE1
Central map: page 6, N5
☎ 071-407 0922

The glass-covered walkway, 142ft above the Thames, gives visitors panoramic views over London. Exhibitions illustrating the history and workings of the bridge are in both Towers. The original engine rooms may be seen on the south side of the bridge.

*Open: Apr-Oct 10-6.30; Nov-Mar 10-4.45 (last tickets sold 45 minutes before closing time) (closed: Good Fri, Xmas, New Year's Day).*
*Admission charge.*
*shop* ♿ ✗

### Tower Hill Pageant

Tower Hill Terrace, Tower Hill, EC3
Central map: page 12, N6
☎ 071-709 0081

London's finest dark ride museum. Automated cars take visitors on a journey past life-size scenes tracing the 2000 year history of the City of London and its port. You will visit a Saxon settlement, escape the Great Fire and crew a 'Blitz' bomber. There are also many fascinating archaeological discoveries found along the Thames on display.

*Open: daily, Apr-Oct 9.30-5.30; Nov-Mar 9.30-4.30 (closed: 25 Dec).*
*Admission charge.*
♿

### Tower of London

EC3
Central map: page 12, N6
☎ 071-709 0765

Begun by William the Conqueror in the 11th century in the south-east angle of the Wall of Roman *Londinium*, this is one of the world's most famous fortresses. It soon became the symbol of ultimate power, the place where even the highest and mightiest in the land could be cast down. According to tradition, 1078 marks the start of the building of the original tower (now known as the White Tower). The stronghold was enlarged in later years. Other places of particular interest are the Bloody Tower (15th century), in which the little princes are said to have been smothered in 1483; St Peter Vincula's Chapel Royal in which Anne Boleyn, Lady Jane Grey and the Duke of Monmouth are buried; the Norman St John's Chapel, the oldest in London; and Traitors' Gate, the old water-gate. Adjoining the Beauchamp Tower, near which was the site of the scaffold, is the Yeoman Gaoler's House in which

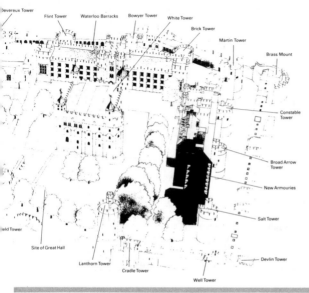

Devereux Tower · Flint Tower · Waterloo Barracks · Bowyer Tower · White Tower · Brick Tower · Martin Tower · Brass Mount · Constable Tower · Broad Arrow Tower · New Armouries · Salt Tower · Devlin Tower · Well Tower · Cradle Tower · Lanthorn Tower · Site of Great Hall · eld Tower

Lady Jane Grey and latterly Rudolf Hess were imprisoned. The White Tower now contains the **Royal Armouries**. These consist of the national collection of arms and armour based on the great arsenal of Henry VIII. Four of Henry VIII's personal armours may be seen. There are also displays of tournament and sporting arms, arms and armour from the Middle Ages to the 17th century and oriental armour. The unique Yeoman Warders, or 'Beefeater' guards are not present merely as a tourist attraction: they guard the Crown Jewels which are exhibited here. Another feature of the Tower are the ravens, whose continued residence is said to ensure the Kingdom does not fail. The first new raven for 300 years was hatched in May 1989, bringing their numbers up to nine.

*Open: Mar-Oct, Mon-Sat 9.30-5.45, Sun 2-5.30; Nov-Feb, Mon-Sat 9.30-4.30 (closed: Good Fri, 24-26 Dec & 1 Jan; Jewel House closed Jan).*
*Admission charge.*
*shop* & ⚡

### Vestry House Museum

Vestry Rd, near Hoe St, E17
District map: page 167, 51 E5
☎ 081-527 5544 ext 439

A small museum located in a former 18th-century workhouse standing in the conservation area 'Walthamstow Village'. Historical items of local interest from the Stone Age onwards include a reconstructed Victorian parlour. Of special interest is the Bremer Car, probably the first British

internal combustion engine car.

*Open: Mon-Fri 10-5.30, Sat 10-5 (closed: BH).*
*Admission free.*
*shop* & *(ground floor only)* ⚡

### Victoria and Albert Museum

Cromwell Road, SW7
Central map: page 2, E4
☎ 071-938 8500

Covering art and design, from all countries and from all periods and styles, this museum has over seven miles of galleries. It is impossible to take it all in on one visit, and so it is advisable to buy a guide book and plan a route before setting off to see the displays. The collection was founded at Marlborough House after the Great Exhibition, and was known as the Museum of Manufactures. In 1857 it moved to its present site and was called the South Kensington Museum. Enlarged and redesigned by Sir Aston Webb at the end of the 19th century, it was reopened in 1909 by Edward VII as the Victoria and Albert Museum. There are two types of galleries: the primary ones which give a comprehensive picture of a period or civilisation; and subject galleries which contain the specialised collections. Features include a series of rooms decorated and equipped with the paintings, furniture and household accessories of particular periods in British history, including the enormous 16th century Great Bed of Ware. The Toshiba Gallery of Japanese Art and Design, the Constable paintings, Raphael cartoons and the costume exhibition displayed

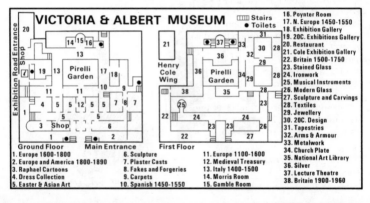

VICTORIA & ALBERT MUSEUM

Stairs · Toilets

**Ground Floor**
1. Europe 1600-1800
2. Europe and America 1800-1890
3. Raphael Cartoons
4. Dress Collection
5. Easter & Asian Art
6. Sculpture
7. Plaster Casts
8. Fakes and Forgeries
9. Carpets
10. Spanish 1450-1550

**Main Entrance**

**First Floor**
11. Europe 1100-1600
12. Medieval Treasury
13. Italy 1400-1500
14. Morris Room
15. Gamble Room
16. Poynter Room
17. N. Europe 1450-1550
18. Exhibition Gallery
19. 20C. Exhibitions Gallery
20. Restaurant
21. Cole Exhibition Gallery
22. Britain 1500-1750
23. Stained Glass
24. Ironwork
25. Musical Instruments
26. Modern Glass
27. Sculpture and Carvings
28. Textiles
29. Jewellery
30. 20C. Design
31. Tapestries
32. Arms & Armour
33. Metalwork
34. Church Plate
35. National Art Library
36. Silver
37. Lecture Theatre
38. Britain 1900-1960

in the Octagon Court all contribute towards one of the world's outstanding collections of fine and applied arts.

*Open: Mon-Sat 10-5.50, Sun 2.30-5.50 (closed: Good Fri, May Day, 27 Aug, 24-26 Dec & 1 Jan).*
*Admission — donation suggested.*
shop 🖵 (licensed) ♿ ⌗

## Wallace Collection

Hertford House, Manchester Sq, W1
Central map: page 9, F7
☎ 071-935 0687

An outstanding collection of works of art bequeathed to the nation by Lady Wallace in 1897, displayed in the house of its founders. Includes pictures by Titian, Rubens, Gainsborough and Delacroix, together with an unrivalled representation of 18th-century French art including paintings, especially by Watteau, Boucher and Fragonard, sculpture, furniture, goldsmiths' work and Sèvres porcelain. Also valuable collections of majolica. European and Oriental arms and armour.

*Open: Mon-Sat 10-5, Sun 2-5 (closed: Good Fri, May Day, 24-26 Dec & 1 Jan).*
*Admission free.*
shop ♿ ⌗

## Wellington Museum

Apsley House, 149 Piccadilly, W1
Central map: page 3, F5
☎ 071-499 5676

Apsley House was designed by Robert Adam, built 1771-8 and extended by Benjamin Wyatt in 1828-1830, under the direction of the Duke of Wellington who purchased it in 1817. It was presented to the nation by the 7th Duke of Wellington in 1947, and opened to the public in 1952. Exhibits include famous paintings, silver, porcelain, orders and decorations and personal relics of the first duke (1769-1852); also Canova's great marble figure of Napoleon.

*Open: Tue-Sun 11-5 (closed: May Day, 24-26 Dec & 1 Jan).*
*Admission charge.*
♿ ⌗ shop

## Wembley Stadium Tour

Wembley
District map: page 166, 52 B4
☎ 081-902 8833

Britain's number one stadium, built in 1923 it holds 80,000 spectators. It is the home of the England football team, and venue for the annual Cup Final and World events. The tour includes a visit to the dressing rooms, Royal Box and retiring room, a walk up the Players' tunnel to the pitch, complete with sound effects. You can then watch a laser disc cinema show and have a ride on the Wembley Land Train. (Wembley Complex, see page 70).

*Open: daily 9.45 — last tour departs 4pm (closed on days of events and 25 Dec).*
*Admission charge.*
shop ♿ (by prior booking) ⌗ 🖵

## Wesley's House & Chapel

47 City Rd, EC1
Central map: page 12, M8
☎ 071-253 2262

This house in which John Wesley lived and died is now a museum, containing a large collection of his personal possessions, etc. The adjoining **Wesley's Chapel**, built in 1778, now houses a museum tracing the history of Methodism from the 18th century to the present day.

*Open: Mon-Sat 10-4; main service 11am Sun followed by tour of chapel and house. (Closed: 25 & 26 Dec.)*
*Admission charge.*
shop ♿ ⌗ 🖾

DUKE OF WELLINGTON

### Whitechapel Art Gallery

Whitechapel High Street, E1
Central map: page 12, N7
℡ 071-377 0107

Opened to contribute to the cultural
life of the East End, this gallery has
achieved widespread fame for the
excellence of its temporary
exhibitions. The building has an
ornate *art nouveau* façade.

*Open: Tue-Sun 11-5, Wed 11-8
(closed: 25, 26 Dec).*
*Admission free (ex special exhibitions).*
shop ⌨

### William Morris Gallery

Water House, Lloyd Park, Forest Rd,
E17
District map: page 167, 53 E5
℡ 081-527 5544 ext 439

William Morris lived in this house,
known as 'Water House', from 1848-
56. There are exhibits of his fabrics,
wallpapers and furniture. Also
ceramics by William de Morgan,
furniture by Gimson and Barnsley and

work by Mackmurdo and the
Century Guild. Pre-Raphaelite
pictures, sculpture by Rodin.

*Open: Tue-Sat 10-1 & 2-5, and 1st
Sun in each month 10-12 & 2-5
(closed Mon & PHs).*
*Admission free.*
♿ shop ✖

### Wimbledon Lawn Tennis Museum

Church Rd, SW19
District map: page 166, 54 C2
℡ 081-946 6131

This museum, within the grounds of
the All England Lawn Tennis and
Croquet Club, is the only one of its
kind in the world. It shows something
of the games which preceded and
helped in the conception of lawn
tennis and traces the development of
the game over the last century. On
display are trophies, postcards,
autographs, pictures and other
memorabilia. Also visit the famous
Centre Court.

*Open: Tue-Sat 11-5, Sun 2-5 (closed:
Mon & BH).*
*Admission charge.*
shop ✖ ♿

### Wimbledon Windmill Museum

Windmill Rd, SW19
District map: page 166, 55 C2
℡ 081-788 7655

Built in 1817, this windmill houses a
museum which displays the history of
windmilling in pictures, models, and
the machinery and tools of the trade.

*Open: Etr-Oct, Sat, Sun & BH 2-5.*
*Admission charge.*
shop ✖ ⌨

# AROUND
# THE STREETS OF
# LONDON

streets, buildings, squares, churches,
monuments, bridges, plaques, etc

*Pocket Guide to LONDON*

# The Streets and Buildings

Apart from places to visit, there is a wealth of history to be found around the streets of London.

Described on the following pages are streets, buildings, churches, monuments, statues, and plaques which mark the homes of famous people.

## Albany

(north side of Piccadilly)
Central map: page 10, H6

This secluded court dates from the early 19th century and was designed to provide exclusive apartments for gentlemen. Many famous men have lived here, including the 19th-century Prime Minister Gladstone and the poet Lord Byron (1788-1824).

## Albert Embankment

Central map: page 5, J3

The earliest section of walkway (1868) was designed by Sir Joseph Bazalgette and built as a river defence for St Thomas's Hospital. Named after the Prince Consort, it stretches between Vauxhall Bridge and Westminster Bridge.

## The Aldgate Pump

(junction of Aldgate and Fenchurch St)
Central map: page 12, N6

This disused drinking fountain stands over what was once St Michael's Well, whose water was renowned for its efficacious qualities as far back as the 15th century. For many years a 'draught [draft] on the Aldgate pump' was a facetious expression for a worthless bill.

## The Anchor Public House (Bankside)

Central map: page 12, L6

This historic pub with its Clink Bar is a reminder that it stands close to the site of the Old Clink Prison. Instruments of torture are on display in the bar — a gruesome reminder of the days when prisons were places of extreme cruelty. The pub has known pirates, smugglers and the Press Gang, who hauled men off to serve in the Navy.

## The Bank of England

Central map: page 12, M7

This most famous of national banks was founded in 1694 when City merchants decided that an independent national bank would be advantageous to all concerned. It operated from the Grocers' Hall until 1734 when the new building was opened in Threadneedle Street. The building was greatly expanded by Sir John Soane at the turn of the 18th century, and was extensively modernised between 1925 and 1939. The Bank was nationalised in 1946 and has special responsibilities for printing and issuing notes, administering the National Debt, and exchange control.

The vaults traditionally house the nation's gold reserves, and the internal security system is therefore of the highest order. After the Bank was attacked by looters during the Gordon Riots of 1780 the Bank Piquet was instituted, whereby a detachment of Guards marched to the building each afternoon and remained on watch throughout the night. This ceremony continued until 1973 when an electronic security system was installed. Bank of England Museum — see page 76.

## Bankside

Central map: page 12, L6

Here in Tudor times were situated the Bear Garden and the Globe Theatre, places of riotous entertainment. The whole area had an evil reputation; being outside the jurisdiction of the City, it became the centre for the darker side of life. Sir Christopher Wren is reputed to have lived at 49 Bankside during the building of St Paul's Cathedral. Shakespeare Globe Museum — see page 102.

## The Barbican

Central map: page 12, L7

This impressive development, built around the remaining portion of the old Roman wall, is an ambitious scheme to promote the City as a residential area rather than a place to be visited only for the purpose of daily work. It contains high-rise blocks of flats, shops, offices, pubs, the new City of London School for Girls, the 16th-century church of St Giles Cripplegate and the Guildhall School of Music. The centrepiece of the development is the Barbican Arts Centre, which is the permanent London home of the Royal Shakespeare Company (Barbican Theatre) and the London Symphony Orchestra (the Barbican Hall). Also here is the Museum of London — see page 94.

**Barton Street**
(off Gt Peter St)
Central map: page 4, I4

Barton Street contains some exceptionally well-preserved Georgian houses. Nos 1-14 (except for Nos 2 and 8) are original and carry a tablet dating them to 1722. T E Lawrence ('Lawrence of Arabia') lived at No 14. An inscription on the wall of No 2 reads: 'Peace on Thy House O Passer-by'.

**Birdcage Walk**
Central map: page 4, H4

Birdcage Walk owes its name to an aviary owned by Charles II which was situated here. It contained, among other rarities, a crane with a wooden leg!

**The Bluecoat School**
Caxton St
Central map: page 4, H4

William Greene, founder of what is now Watney's Brewery, established this charity school in 1688. The building itself, with its charming figure of a charity boy above the doorway, dates from 1709 and now belongs to the National Trust. It is used today as a National Trust shop.

**Bond Street**
Central map: page 9, G6

Famous as one of the world's most exclusive shopping streets, Bond Street is noted particularly for its jewellers and art dealers. It takes its name from Sir Thomas Bond, who, with John Hinde, a goldsmith, built it in 1686.

**Bread Street**
(between Canon St and Watling St)
Central map: page 12, L6

The poet John Milton was born in this street in 1608. Its name is derived from the fact that in medieval times bakers sold their bread here.

**The British Telecom Tower**
Central map: page 9, G7

Completed in 1964, this 619ft-high needle of concrete and glass is one of the tallest buildings in London. The Tower reaches such dizzy heights in order that the telecommunication signals it receives will not be affected by the surrounding buildings. It became famous in the 1960s for the view over London from its rooftop revolving restaurant and viewing gallery, now closed to the public.

**Bruton Place**
Central map: page 9, G6

Emerging from the pavements here are several oddly shaped bollards, which were created by the simple expedient of placing redundant 19th-century cannons upright in the ground:

**Buckingham Palace**
The Mall, SW1
Central map: page 3, G4

Formerly known as Buckingham House, this most famous of royal homes was built in 1703 by the Duke of Buckingham, and subsequently bought by George III in 1762. Nash altered and remodelled it for George IV in 1825, when its name was changed to Buckingham Palace. It was not much used until Queen Victoria came to the throne in 1837, when the court moved here. It has been the London home of the monarch ever since. The east wing, the side the public sees, was added in 1847 and the whole east façade was redesigned in 1913. The west wing remains largely as Nash designed it, but his great gateway, which was to have stood at the end of the Mall, proved too narrow for the State Coach, and the gate was transported bodily to its present site, Marble Arch.

The interior of the palace, with its many splendid rooms, is not open to the public. When in residence, the Royal Family lives in the north wing. When the sovereign is in residence, the Royal Standard is flown. Changing of the Guard — see page 44.

**Burlington Arcade**
(between Old Bond St and Royal Academy of Arts)
Central map: page 10, H6

This delightful Regency arcade is still patrolled by a beadle in traditional dress who also closes the gates at either end each night. The covered walk leads from Piccadilly to Burlington Gardens, and is lined with charming box windowed shops. Built in 1819, the arcade was owned by the Chesham family. Their coat of arms is still above the Piccadilly entrance.

**Carlton House Terrace**
(between The Mall and Pall Mall)
Central map: page 4, I5

John Nash designed this dignified group of buildings as part of his architectural scheme for Regent Street. The terrace gets its name from Carlton House, which stood on the spot now occupied by the southern half of Waterloo Place. At No 6 is the Royal Society (formed 1660, royal charter 1662). Past members include such distinguished scientists as

Sir Isaac Newton, Sir Humphry Davy, and Charles Darwin. No 12 is now the Institute of Contemporary Arts, and houses an art gallery and a theatre.

## Carnaby Street
Central map: page 10, H6

Built in the 18th century for 'poor and miserable objects of the neighbourhood', Carnaby Street was never fashionable. Then in the early 1960s a transformation took place, and the decrepit shops and houses were turned into 'boutiques', at first for men's clothes, later also for girls'. By the mid-1960s it was a teenagers' paradise, but the craze lost momentum as it spread to the King's Road and High Street, Kensington.

## Caxton Hall
Caxton St
Central map: page 4, H4

The name and look of this register office were once familiar to all followers of high society doings, as until 1977 it was the most fashionable place for out-of-church weddings.

## Cecil Court
(off Charing Cross Rd, just past Leicester Sq Station)
Central map: page 10, I6

This narrow pedestrian precinct is filled with antiquarian and secondhand bookshops.

## The Chapel of the Savoy
(junction of Strand and Savoy St)

The buildings and streets with 'Savoy' in their name stand on the site of the ancient Savoy Palace, originally built in 1241, and rebuilt as a hospital by Henry VII in 1510-16. The only part of the hospital to survive is the Queen's Chapel of the Savoy, the private chapel of the reigning monarch as Duke of Lancaster, now used by the Royal Victorian Order. Most of the present building is a 19th-century reconstruction.

## Charles Street
Central map: page 3, G5

Enormous 18th-century houses line both sides of Charles Street. Some of them have ornate ironwork on their exteriors, and all have sumptuous interiors. Also in the street is the curiously named 'I am the only Running Footman' pub. The author Sydney Smith lived at No 32.

## Cheapside
Central map: page 12, L7

This was the high street of the medieval City, a great open-air market called West Chepe (as opposed to East Cheap) from the Anglo-Saxon word for 'barter'.

## Cheyne Walk
Central map: page 2, D1/E2

This fine row of 18th-century houses has been lived in by several famous persons. A plaque at No 23 commemorates the site of Henry VIII's manor house. Henry took a fancy to the village of Chelsea while visiting his

friend and Chancellor, Sir Thomas More (who lived nearby) and decided that the fresh country air would be good for his children. Edward VI, Mary, and Elizabeth all lived here. Sir Hans Sloane bought the manor after his retirement in 1742 and intended to leave it to the nation as a home for his vast collection of treasures. But the government removed the collection (to form the nucleus of the British Museum) and demolished the manor. Many houses in Cheyne Walk have bits of it built into their garden walls.

## City Livery Companies

In 1215 King John signed a charter which gave the citizens of the City of London (that is the area encompassed by the old Roman walls) the right to elect their own mayor annually, rather than accept the choice of the reigning monarch. It was at about this time that the livery companies, who over the centuries have played such a prominent part in the administration of the City, first came into existence. These companies, or guilds, evolved as friendly societies for members of a particular trade or craft, combining this function with the furtherance of their guild's business. As more guilds were founded and those already established become more influential, their leading members took to wearing distinctive costumes or liveries, many of which are still worn during special ceremonies. The original 12 Great Companies — Mercers, Grocers, Clothworkers, Fishmongers, Goldsmiths, Skinners, Merchant

SIR THOMAS MORE

Taylors, Haberdashers, Salters, Ironmongers, Vintners and Drapers — have now been increased to more than 90.

During World War II only two of the guild halls — the Apothecaries' and the Vintners' — escaped bomb damage, and a number were totally destroyed. Several of the halls which exist today, most of which have been restored or rebuilt, contain historical items including ancient plate, works of art, and fine interior decorations. They are not generally open to the public, but special visits can often be arranged by the City Information Centre in St Paul's Church Yard.

Apart from their administrative responsibilities, the livery companies have considerable influence over their trades, being concerned with the binding of apprentices, and trade standards. Many of the companies have considerable charitable responsibilities — including the endowment of schools and alms houses.

Some of the more interesting halls of the companies include —

**Apothecaries**, Blackfriars Lane. A delightful 17th-century range set round a courtyard.

**Drapers**, Throgmorton Street. Some of this building dates from the 17th century but much is Victorian, and some was rebuilt after war damage.

**Goldsmiths**, Gresham

CLARENCE HOUSE

Street. Georgian hall, handsome inside and out.

**Mercers**, Cheapside. Thomas à Becket was born in 1118 in a house which once stood here. The present hall was rebuilt after bomb damage in World War II.

**Skinners**, Dowgate Hill. This hall retains much of the fabric of the building erected after the Great Fire, although the façade is 18th century.

**Vintners**, Upper Thames Street. The medieval courtroom here escaped the Great Fire; the rest was rebuilt in 1671.

## Clarence House
Stable Yard, St James's Palace, SW1
Central map: page 4, H5

Designed by Nash for William IV when he was Duke of Clarence, this house was restored for Princess Elizabeth before her accession in 1952. Princess Anne was born here and it is now the home of Queen Elizabeth, the Queen Mother.

## Clink Street
Central map: page 12, L6

Gaunt 19th-century warehouses overshadow the cobbled alleyways and block the view of the Thames in this atmospheric part of South London. A plaque under the railway bridge tells the story of the 16th-century Clink Prison, from which the term 'in clink' is derived.
The Clink Exhibition — see page 80.

## The College of Arms
Queen Victoria St
Central map: page 12, L6

Sometimes called the Heralds' Office, this is the official authority in Great Britain (except Scotland) and the Commonwealth

on armorial bearings and pedigrees. Its officers, who have resounding titles such as Rouge Dragon Pursuivant, also assist the Earl Marshal, an office hereditary to the Duke of Norfolk since 1672, in arranging state ceremonies such as coronations. The building itself is an imposing 17th-century structure, and stands on a site that has been occupied by the College of Arms since 1555.

## Covent Garden
Central map: page 10, 16

Until 1974, when the famous fruit and vegetable market was moved to Nine Elms, near Vauxhall, there had been a market on this site for over 300 years. The original Covent Garden owed its name to the fact that the monks of Westminster Abbey had a 40-acre walled garden here. In 1631, Inigo Jones was commissioned to lay out the square. This grandly conceived estate, modelled on those he had seen in Italy, included a great Piazza, a church, and, on three sides, arcaded blocks of houses. The square and covered walks in front of buildings attracted market traders, and by 1670 the market had received official recognition. By the middle of the 20th century it had rapidly outgrown its site. After the market had moved, strenuous efforts were made to preserve the attractive old market buildings. These have been renovated and contain many small craft shops, wine bars and restaurants. The atmosphere created here attracts a variety of outdoor entertainment.

### Crosby Hall
Danvers St
Central map: page 2, E2

This 15th-century hall once formed part of a mansion and originally stood at Bishopsgate. Fire destroyed most of the building in the 17th century, but the great hall survived, and was moved to its present site in 1911. At one time the hall was leased by Sir Thomas More, and it now stands on what was part of the gardens of the great house he built here in 1520. His house was demolished in the 1740s, but Crosby Hall still serves to remind passers-by of one of Chelsea's most famous residents.

### County Hall (former)
Central map: page 5, J5

Originally erected in 1912-32, County Hall has since been vastly expanded in size. The colonnaded front facing the River Thames is 750ft long. Formerly the administrative headquarters of the Greater London Council, it was the first component part of the projected South Bank scheme.

### Downing Street
Central map: 4, I5

This world-famous street was built by Sir George Downing, a secretary to the Treasury, in about 1680. At first it was an unimportant residential street with a pub — the Cat and Bagpipes — on the corner. In 1732 George II offered No 10 to Sir Robert Walpole as a town house and since then it has been the official residence of the Prime Minister. No 11 is the official residence of the Chancellor of the Exchequer. The buildings

themselves have unpretentious Georgian façades, but have been extensively modified inside.

### Fleet Street
Central map: page 11, K7

Nearly every national and provincial newspaper or periodical had an office in or near Fleet Street. It is one of the most ancient thoroughfares in London, and has had links with the printing trade since about 1500. The present buildings are mostly modern.

### The George Inn
77 Borough High Street, SE1
Central map: page 6, M5

This is the only galleried coaching inn to be seen in London today.

It dates from the 1670s, and is a replica of an earlier inn on this site which was destroyed by fire. Shakespeare probably enjoyed a drink here. Dickens often frequented the inn and used it as a location in some of his books, notably Little Dorrit.

Today it is run by the National Trust. During the summer you can enjoy a drink in the gallery and watch actors playing scenes from Shakespeare and Dickens in the cobbled courtyard.

### Gerrard Street
Central map: 10, I6

At each end of Gerrard Street stand two beautiful Chinese gateways, erected in 1985 to mark the centre of London's Chinatown. Here and in nearby streets restaurants offer authentic Chinese cuisine. Also here is the Chinese Community Healthcare Centre which offers both orthodox medicine and alternative

Chinese medical treatments.

### Goodwin's Court
(off north end of Charlton St)
Central map: page 10, H9

This narrow alley is entirely lined with the bow-fronted windows of former shops.

### Great Russell Street
Central map: page 10, I7

Celebrated as the home of the British Museum, Great Russell Street has also had some famous residents. At No 46 lived Ralph Caldecott (1846-86), an outstanding illustrator of children's books, while No 91 was the home of George du Maurier (1834-96), who from 1860 drew for Punch but is probably better known for his novel Trilby, in which he created the character of Svengali.

Bloomsbury's association with the world of books is evident in and around Great Russell Street, where there are numerous publishers' offices and small bookshops.

### Greek Street
Central map: page 10, I6

Many famous people are associated with this street. Dr Samuel Johnson, the poet and critic, and Sir Joshua Reynolds, the English portrait painter, founded a Literary Club here; Sir

10 DOWNING ST.

Thomas Lawrence, the 18th-century portrait painter, lived and worked here for 25 years; Thomas de Quincey, who wrote *Confessions of an English Opium Eater*, indulged his addiction here; and Wedgwood had his London showroom here.

### The Greycoat Hospital
Greycoat Place (north side of Greycoat St)
Central map: page 4, H4

This charity school was founded in 1698 as a boarding school for seventy children. The original building, which dated from 1701, was partly destroyed during World War II and has now been restored in the Queen Anne style. The figures of the Greycoat boy and girl over the door are of painted wood, and may date from the early 18th century. Since 1873 it has been a day-school for girls only, who number over 900.

### The House of St Barnabas
Greek St (east side of Soho Square)
Central map: page 10, H7

One of the finest Georgian houses in London, with richly decorated ceilings, woodcarvings, and ironwork, the House of St Barnabas was founded as a charitable institution in 1846 to help the destitute in London. Guided tours available on Wednesday and Thursday.

### Jermyn Street
Central map: page 3, H5

Jermyn Street is famous for its many old-established shops. One of the most interesting is the ancient premises of Paxton and Whitfield, the

cheese shop. Further along is the Cavendish Hotel, with its wrought-iron lamps, which although it has been rebuilt still carries memories of the eccentric hotelier Rosa Lewis, the original 'Duchess of Duke Street'.

### Jubilee Gardens
Central map: page 5, J5

These gardens were laid out as London's tribute to celebrate Queen Elizabeth II's Silver Jubilee in 1977.

### The King's Road
Central map: page 3, F3

It is hard to believe that this bustling thoroughfare was once a quiet country footpath. During the 17th century it was enlarged to become Charles II's private carriage route between St James's and Hampton Court, but did not become a public highway until the beginning of the 19th century. Mary Quant, the designer who revolutionised women's clothing, opened a boutique here in the 1950s, and the whole road promptly achieved a fashionable reputation which it has never lost.

### Lambeth Palace
Central map: page 5, J4

Much of this historic structure, which has been the London residence of the Archbishop of Canterbury for 700 years, was rebuilt during the 19th century. Extensive damage was caused by bombs during World War II. Of the old palace, the most interesting parts are the Lollards Tower and the Gatehouse, both of the 15th century, and the 13th-century Chapel Crypt. The palace is not open to the public.

Adjoining the south gateway of the palace is the former church of St Mary, now restored as a Museum of Garden History in memory of John Tradescant, Charles I's gardener (see page 93). Captain William Bligh, of the *Bounty*, is buried here.

### Laurence Pountney Hill
(off south side of Canon St)
Central map: page 12, M6

Nos 1 and 2 were built in 1703 and are the finest early 18th-century houses in the City. Amid the rich carving of the doorways are two delightful cherubs playing marbles.

### Lawrence Street
(off Cheyne Row)
Central map: page 2, E2

Chelsea China was manufactured at the north end of this street from 1745 to 1784. The Chelsea factory competes with Bow for the honour of being the first to make English porcelain.

### Liberty
Corner of Great Marlborough St and Regent St
Central map: page 10, H6

Liberty, built in 1924, was first planned as a reproduction Tudor building throughout, but was then given a neo-classical façade to match its surroundings. The half-timbering on the north side is not purely decorative — the timbers are structural and come from genuine men-of-war. Every quarter hour, the St George on the clock which adorns the façade fights the dragon, slaying him on the hour. It is now a department store.

LAMBETH PALACE

### Lincoln's Inn Fields
Central map: page 11, J7

Lincoln's Inn Fields were laid out in the 17th century and were a famous haunt of duellists. A tablet here marks the spot were Lord William Russell was executed in 1683. Handsome buildings, including the Sir John Soane's Museum (see page 102), the Royal College of Surgeons and Lincoln's Inn (see page 88) surround the fields.

### Little Dean's Yard and Westminster School
(South side of Westminster Abbey)
Central map: page 4, I4

Westminster Abbey probably had its own school before 1200. When the abbey became a cathedral in 1540, the school became the King's Grammar School, with 40 scholars. It was re-founded by Queen Elizabeth I in 1560. The custom known as the Pancake Greeze is observed here every Shrove Tuesday. The cook, dressed in cap and apron, comes in with a frying-pan and has to toss a pancake over the 16ft-high iron bar that separates the old Upper and Lower Schools. As it falls, representatives from each form scramble for it, and the boy who gets the biggest piece also gets a guinea from the Dean. On the north side of Little Dean's Yard is Ashburnham House, the best example in London of a stately mid-17th-century house.

### London Bridge City
Tooley St, SW1
Central map: page 6, M5

Spreading east from London Bridge is the new commercial development of London Bridge City. This was once Hay's Wharf, one of the busiest wharfs, where tea clippers from the Orient once tied up. Now, new buildings and refurbished warehouses offer a variety of offices, shops and leisure facilities.
Amongst these is **Hay's Galleria**, formerly Hay's Dock, which has been filled in and roofed over with a huge glass and steel dome to form a piazza, with arcades, emporiums, restaurants, wine bars and a centre for live entertainment.
The development has also provided a landscaped riverside walkway and pier.

### The London Stone
Canon St, opposite station
Central map: page 12, M6

This is said to be the milestone from which distances were measured on the great military roads radiating outwards from Roman London.

### The Mall
Central map: page 4, H5

The Mall was originally laid out in 1660-2 as part of Charles II's scheme for St James's Park. It was transformed into a processional way in 1910.

### Marlborough House
Pall Mall, SW1
Central map: page 4, H5

Built by Wren for the Duke of Marlborough, Marlborough House was later occupied by Leopold I of Belgium. In 1850 it became the official residence of the Prince of Wales. George

V was born here and after he became King it became the home of Queen Alexandra, Edward VII's widow. The house is now the Commonwealth Conference Centre.

### Meard Street
(south end of Wardour St)
Central map: page 10, H6

For those who like old houses this short 18th-century street, named after a carpenter, John Meard, is the most rewarding in all Soho. Nos 1-21 are exceptionally well preserved.

### Middlesex Guildhall
(corner of Victoria St and Parliament Sq)
Central map: page 4, I4

This Renaissance-style building was opened in 1913, and stands on the site of an earlier guildhall. It once functioned as the administrative centre for the old county of Middlesex. The friezes on the façade depict Magna Carta, Henry II granting a charter to Westminster, and Lady Jane Grey accepting the crown from the Duke of Northumberland.

### Old Compton Street
Central map: page 10, H6

This street is famous for its exotic provision shops, the legacy of the 19th-century flood of immigrants — particularly French, Italians and Greeks — into the area.

### Pall Mall
Central map: page 4, H5

Pall Mall takes its name from *paille maille*, a French ball game similar to croquet, introduced into England in the reign of Charles I. Numerous famous, and usually exclusive, clubs are situated in Pall Mall. Outside the entrance to the Athenaeum Club, in Waterloo Place, are two slabs of stone, placed here as a mounting-block at the request of the Duke of Wellington.

## Paternoster Row and Panyer Alley Steps

(off south side of St Paul's station)
Central map: page 12, L7

Paternoster (Our Father) is a reminder of the participants in medieval processions who 'told' their rosaries round the precincts of Old St Paul's. Here they recited the Lord's Prayer. For several hundred years Paternoster Row was associated with the book trade, but it was entirely destroyed during the Blitz, and only the ancient name survives. The Steps commemorate the Panyer Boy, an inn whose 17th-century sign is to be seen on the side wall. It shows a baker's boy with his pannier.

## Piccadilly

Central map: page 3, G5

This famous London thoroughfare takes its name from a form of 17th-century ruff (or collar) called a 'piccadil'. At the eastern end of the street is Piccadilly Circus, always packed with shoppers and sightseers. In its centre is the statue known as Eros, erected in 1892 as a memorial to Lord Shaftesbury. This is the centre of London's West End; all around are theatres, cinemas, and restaurants. Further along Piccadilly is Fortnum and Mason's shop. Figures of Mr Fortnum and Mr Mason (who founded the shop in 1707) emerge from the clock high on the wall on the hour and

bow to each other as the carillon plays a tune.

## Piccadilly Arcade

Central map: page 4, H5

This pleasant covered thoroughfare connects Jermyn Street and Piccadilly. It is adorned with hanging baskets of flowers and lined with expensive shops.

## Queen Anne's Gate

(off Birdcage Walk)
Central map: page 4, H4

This quiet close, built in 1704, is undoubtedly one of the most charming streets in London. It has been the home of several distinguished figures in British history, including Lord Palmerston (who lived at No 20), and the statesman, lawyer and philosopher Lord Haldane (No 28). A statue of Queen Anne stands outside No 13, and No 26 still has the snuffer for extinguishing the linkman's torch after he had lighted its owners' home.

## Regent Street

Central map: page 10, H6

Regent Street owes its existence to George IV, who as Prince Regent lived at Carlton House. He wanted to build a country villa on Primrose Hill and connect it to Carlton House by a new road. The villa was never built, but Regent Street was laid out in 1813-20 by the great architect John Nash (1752-1835). The total rebuilding of Regent Street that began in 1900 has made it one of the finest shopping streets in the world, at the expense of some of the greatest architecture.

## Royal Avenue

Central map: page 3, F3

The Avenue is part of a road designed by Sir

Christopher Wren to link the Royal Hospital with Kensington Palace. The road was never finished but the section that remains was completed in 1694. The terraces are 19th century.

## Royal Courts of Justice

Central map: page 11, J7

Generally called the Law Courts, the Royal Courts of Justice were designed in the Gothic style by the distinguished Victorian architect G E Street. The foundation stone was laid in 1874, but the building was not completed until 1882, after Street's death. The Central Hall contains a monument to him. The main entrance, in the Strand, has archways flanked by twin towers in which are stairs to the public galleries.

## The Royal Exchange

Central map: page 12, M7

Opened in 1568 as a meeting place for City merchants. Queen Victoria opened the present building in 1844. Important announcements such as the proclamation of new sovereigns and declarations of war are traditionally made from the broad flight of steps at its entrance.

## Royal Opera House

Covent Garden (corner of Floral St and Bow St)
Central map: page 10, I6

The present building had two predecessors, the second one being the scene of the famous Old Price Riots — the public's protestation against the sharp increase in the costs of seats. The theatre officially opened as an opera house in 1847 and opera has flourished here ever since, achieving its greatest peaks between

1859 and 1939 when it was the entertainment of 'society'.

### St Anne's Soho
(corner of Wardour St and Old Compton St)
Central map: page 10, H6

The remains of a 17th-century church which was almost totally destroyed during World War II; the tower (added in 1801-3) survived. The churchyard has been laid out as a garden where memorials to the essayist William Hazlitt (1778-1830) and Theodore, 'King of Corsica' (1685-1756), can still be seen.

### St Bartholomew's Hospital
Central map: page 12, L7

'Barts' was founded in 1123 as a religious establishment and at the dissolution of the monasteries was given to the City of London by Henry VIII. It is the oldest hospital in London on its original site. Nearby, a half-timbered Elizabethan gatehouse marks the entrance to the Norman church of St Bartholomew the Great (see page 125).

### St James's Palace
St James's Street, SW1
Central map: page 4, H5

The original palace was started by Henry VIII in 1531, and, after the destruction of Whitehall Palace, was the sovereign's official London residence. Foreign ambassadors are still appointed to the Court of St James's. The Gatehouse facing St James's Street is the main remnant of the Tudor building, and has the initials of Henry VIII and Anne Boleyn carved over the doors. The Chapel Royal was originally built by Henry VIII but was much altered in 1837.

However, the ceiling by Holbein is original. Several royal marriages have been solemnised here, including those of William III and Mary II, Queen Anne, George IV, Queen Victoria and George V. Every year on 6th January (the Festival of Epiphany) at Holy Communion in this Chapel, an offering of gold, frankincense and myrrh is made on behalf of the Queen by two of Her Majesty's Gentlemen Ushers.

In Friary Court the new sovereign is proclaimed from the balcony by the Heralds. Charles II, who was born here, made some additions to the palace, commissioning Wren to add some state apartments facing the park. James II, Mary II, Queen Anne and George IV were all born here. George IV employed Nash to restore and redecorate the palace, but Queen Victoria moved the court to Buckingham Palace when she came to the throne. St James's Palace is now occupied by servants of the Crown, and is not open to the public. However, services may be attended in the Chapel Royal between October and July.

### St James's Street
Central map: page 4, H5

Many of the best known gentlemen's clubs in London are situated in this genteel street. They include White's (No 37), Brook's (No 60) and the Carlton Club (No 69), all of which have been established here since the 19th century. Among the old-established shops here are James Lock, hatters for more than 200 years, still with an almost unchanged shop

front, and Berry Bros and Rudd, wine merchants since the 17th century.

### St Martin's Lane
Central map: page 10, 16

St Martin's Lane is easily recognised by the globe on top of the London Coliseum, now the home of the English National Opera. Thomas Chippendale, the greatest furniture maker in England's history, opened his workshop in No 62 in 1753.

### St Paul's Gardens
(south end of New Change)
Central map: page 12, L6

In these gardens is a plaque marking the site of Old Change, a 13th-century building where bullion was stored before being taken to the Royal Mint, and which gave its name to a street, alas destroyed by bombs in 1941. New Change, a much wider street, was built after the war a little to the east of its predecessor and the reconstructed spire of the Wren church of St Augustine, Watling Street.

### Savile Row
Central map: 10, H6

Savile Row is world-famous for its high-class tailoring establishments. No 14, the last home of the playwright Richard Brinsley Sheridan (1751-1816), is now occupied by Hardy Amies, couturier to the Queen.

ST. JAMES'S PALACE

**The Savoy Hotel**
Strand
Central map: page 11, J6

In 1889, Richard D'Oyly Carte, who had already built the Savoy Theatre as a home for Gilbert and Sullivan's comic operas, decided to build a hotel to compete with the best in America. His new Savoy was famous for its 70 bathrooms — such an unheard-of number in those days that the builder asked him if his guests were to be amphibians.

**Shaftesbury Avenue**
Central map: page 10, H6

Laid out in 1877-86, the Avenue is named after the great Victorian social reformer and champion of the anti-slavery cause Lord Shaftesbury. Known for its theatres, it stretches from New Oxford Street to Piccadilly Circus.

**Shell-Mex House**
(between Strand and Savoy Place)
Central map: page 10, I6

Shell-Mex House was originally the Cecil Hotel, which, when it opened in 1886, was the largest hotel in Europe. An old-fashioned street lamp in Carting Lane is always alight, burning gases from the sewers below.

**Shepherd Market**
(off Shepherd St)
Central map: page 3, G5

Set in the heart of Mayfair, this is one of the most delightful areas in all London. Some of the original 18th-century buildings survive, but it is the unique 'village' atmosphere which gives this tiny oasis its special charm. The present web of narrow streets was laid out by the builder and designer Edward Shepherd in 1735.

**The Sir John Cass School**
(north side of Aldgate)
Central map: page 12, N6

Founded in 1710 as a charity school, this philanthrophic establishment was rebuilt in 1909. Over the doorway are two figures of schoolchildren that probably came from the original building.

**South Audley Street**
Central map: page 3, G5

Sir Richard Westmacott (1775-1856), an outstanding sculptor of his day, lived at No 14. At No 57 are the famous gunsmiths, Purdey and Son. No 71 is an exceptionally fine Georgian house. Just after the crossroads with South Street is the blue and white Grosvenor Chapel, where American servicemen worshipped during World War II. It was built in 1730.

**South Bank Trees**
Central map: page 5, J5

The walkway between County Hall and Hungerford Bridge is lined with London plane trees. They probably originated as a hybrid between Oriental and American planes in the 17th century, when cultivated together by the gardeners to the Stuart kings at Lambeth.

**South Bank Arts Complex**
Central map: page 5, J5

This huge assembly of cultural centres was begun in 1951 when the Royal Festival Hall was built for the Festival of Britain. It is one of the most successful examples of modern architecture in London, providing comfortable seating for 3,000 people. The complex was enlarged when, in 1967, two

further concert halls, Queen Elizabeth Hall and the Purcell Room were opened. Also here are the Hayward Gallery (see page 86), the Royal National Theatre, the National Film Theatre, and, opened in 1988, the Museum of Moving Image (see page 94).

**The Strand**
Central map: page 11, J6

In Elizabethan times and long afterwards, the Strand was bordered by noblemen's mansions with gardens running down to the riverside or 'strand'. It is still, as it always was, the principal route between the West End and the City, running for nearly a mile from Charing Cross to the Temple Bar Memorial — where statues of Queen Victoria and Edward VII, and a griffin in the road, mark the boundary of the City. The Temple Bar itself, a triple gateway designed by Wren, was dismantled at the end of the last century and removed to Theobald's Park in Hertfordshire. In much earlier times, the severed heads of traitors and other criminals were impaled on spikes on top of the gateway to the City.

**The Temple of Mithras**
(Queen Victoria St, east of Queen St)
Central map: page 12, L6

Discovered in 1954 during excavations to locate the bed of the River Walbrook, this temple dates from the 2nd century AD. The cult of Mithras, a Persian sun-god, was restricted to men and especially popular with soldiers, and the ceremonies associated with his worship were conducted in great secrecy. This temple is one of the most important Roman remains in London, and has been reconstructed near to the site where it was found.

**Tooley Street**
Central map: page 6, M5

In the 19th century this area was famous for its vast trade in foodstuffs and was known as the 'breakfast table of England'. In 1861 a fire raged in the warehouses along here which, it was said, produced more flames and heat than the Great Fire of London.

**Trocadero Centre**
Shaftesbury Avenue/ Coventry St
Central map: page 10, H6

This modern three-storey complex, built behind its original Edwardian façade, houses shops, restaurants, exhibitions and entertainment facilities including the Guinness World of Records (see page 85).

**US Embassy**
Grosvenor Square
Central map: page 9, F6

This huge building takes up the entire west side of Grosvenor Square. It was designed by Eero Saarinen, the Finnish-American architect, and completed in 1960. An eagle with a wingspan of 35ft dominates the structure. The embassy has been seen on television many times since it has been a focus of demonstrations of all sorts.

**Vauxhall Bridge Garden**
(west side of Vauxhall Bridge)
Central map: page 4, I3

A large bollard here marks the approximate site of Millbank

Penitentiary from which, between 1816 and 1867, convicts sentenced to transportation embarked on their journey. The garden also contains a sculpture by Henry Moore.

**The Victoria Embankment**
Central map: page 11, J6

Stretching from Westminster Bridge to Blackfriars Bridge, the Victoria Embankment forms one of the most interesting and attractive riverside promenades in London. The principal reason for its construction was not, however, to provide a walkway, but to help solve London's pollution problem. By 1855 the river was little more than an open sewer, and the famous scientist Michael Faraday, in a letter to *The Times*, described its appearance as 'an opaque brown fluid . . . near the bridges the feculence rolled up in clouds so dense that they were visible at the surface'. The following year, 1856, became known as the Year of the Big Stink because the stench had become so overpoweringly awful. Sir Joseph Bazalgette had drawn up plans for a comprehensive sewage system by 1856, and it was decided to put these into practice. The system was designed to capture the sewage before it reached the Thames and direct it to outfalls at Barking and Crossness. The Victoria Embankment was constructed to accommodate one of the huge pipes that ran along the north bank. The York Water Gate in Victoria Embankment Gardens marks the position of the original riverbank.

**Victoria Embankment Gardens**
Central map: page 6, I6

To be found here is the old York House Water Gate, the entrance to the Duke of Buckingham's garden from the Thames. In the Duke's day (the 1620s) boats bringing guests would tie up at the Water Gate, which marks the former boundary of the River Thames. There are numerous statues and memorials in the gardens. Of special interest is the little memorial to the Imperial Camel Corps (1921), statues of the poet Robert Burns and Robert Raikes, founder (1780) of Sunday Schools, a bust of the composer Sir Arthur Sullivan and the tree commemorating Queen Elizabeth II's coronation in 1953.

**Victoria Tower Gardens**
(off Millbank)
Central map: page 4, I4

In the thin triangle of Victoria Tower Gardens are the Buxton Drinking Fountain, commemorating the emancipation of slaves in the British Empire in 1834; a statue of the suffragette Mrs Emmeline Pankhurst (1858-1928); and a copy of the famous statue by Auguste Rodin (1840-1917) and called *The Burghers of Calais*.

**Villiers Street**
(off east side of Charing Cross station)
Central map: page 10, I6

In this area in the 17th century stood the mansion and gardens of George Villiers, Duke of Buckingham. He sold them for redevelopment, but insisted that every word of his name and title be preserved in the new street names:

George Street, Villiers Street, Duke Street, Buckingham Street, and Of Alley (now renamed York Place). East of Villiers Street, the area between the Strand and the Thames was named the Adelphi (from the Greek word for brothers, *adelphoi*) after the Adam brothers, who were responsible for laying out the streets in 1768-74. Much of the area has been rebuilt but the name survives in the Adelphi Theatre.

**Wardour Street**
Central map: page 10, H6

During the 1920s and 1930s, Wardour Street became the home of the British film industry. But while film moguls were making (and losing) fortunes here, television was being developed in nearby Frith Street.

**Woburn Walk**
(off east side of Upper Woburn Place)
Central map: page 10, I8

This genteel little thoroughfare has a double row of early 19th-century houses, all of which have picturesque shop fronts. The Irish poet W B Yeats (1865-1939) lived at No 5 for a while.

**Ye Olde Watling**
(east end of Watling St)
Central map: page 12, L6

This interesting old pub which dates from 1668 was used as an office by Sir Christopher Wren during the building of St Paul's Cathedral.

BERKELEY SQUARE

# The Squares

**Belgrave Square**
SW1
Central map: page 3, F4

Sheer size robs Belgrave of its square-like characteristics, because it is not possible to see from one side to the other. To all intents it is a small park, but the carefully tended lawns and gardens have an un-park-like air of exclusiveness undoubtedly lent by the elegant cream-coloured terraces that surround it. The square is one of the largest in London, and centres on attractive private gardens enclosed by ironwork entirely in keeping with the local architecture.

**Berkeley Square**
W1
Central map: page 9, G6

Modern development has detracted somewhat from the original charm of this very famous square. It is doubtful whether the nightingales assigned to it in the song actually existed, though the huge plane trees in which they would have perched are there for all to see. The trees were planted in 1790, a decade before the building of the quaint Pump House that is still so much a part of the square's character. Also in keeping with the atmosphere of slightly time-worn elegance is the fountain — a nymph with a pitcher.

**Bloomsbury Square**
WC1
(off north side of Bloomsbury Way)
Central map: page 10, I7

The name 'Bloomsbury' probably derives from the medieval manor of Blemund'sbury, bought by the Earl of Southampton in 1545. Bloomsbury Square was laid out on its site by one of his descendants in 1661, and was the first open space in London to be called a 'square'. The original mansions have all disappeared, but the houses on the north side date from 1800-14. The gardens were planted in about 1800 by the celebrated landscape gardener Humphrey Repton. No 6 was the home of Isaac D'Israeli, father of Benjamin Disraeli.

**Dorset Square**
NW1 (west side of Gloucester Place)
Central map: page 9, F7

Long before Dorset Square was laid out its site was occupied by the original Lord's Cricket Ground. Here the MCC — the country's most famous cricket club — was begun in the 18th century. However, the grass in the square is no descendant of that upon which early matches were played, for when the square was being developed groundkeeper Thomas Lord left, taking his turf with him.

**Fitzroy Square**
W1
(north side of Fitzroy St)
Central map: page 10, H8

Designed by the famous Adam brothers in the 18th century, Fitzroy Square preserves well-built terraces typical of their designers' work, particularly on the eastern side.

**Golden Square**
W1 (east side of John St)
Central map: page 10, H6

According to popular legend, this Soho square had its name changed from 'Gelding' to 'Golden' by some of its more society-conscious residents. For many years it was the centre for the woollen trade.

**Gordon Square**
WC1
Central map: page 10, H6

Gordon Square is associated with the circle of 20th-century writers, critics and intellectuals known as the Bloomsbury Group. The novelist Virginia Woolf (1882-1941) lived at No 46 for a time before she married. The same house was later the home of the leading economist John Maynard Keynes (1883-1946). The critic and biographer Lytton Strachey (1880-1932) lived at No 51. At the south-west corner of the square stands the Gothic Church of Christ the King.

**Grosvenor Square**
W1
Central map: page 9, F6

Built and rebuilt on the site of a 17th-century citizen's blockade against Charles I, Grosvenor Square is now largely in the hands of a foreign power. This is immediately apparent in the vast brooding eagle

that stretches its 35ft wingspan protectively over the American Embassy, at the same time managing to encompass most of the square in that expansive gesture. The area is popularly known as 'Little America'.

The open garden around which the square is formed was designed by William Kent, a distinguished 18th-century architect and designer, and occupies some six acres. It is a pleasant patch of green amongst the buildings that loom from all sides, and echoes the transatlantic feel of the place in a memorial to one-time US President, Franklin D Roosevelt.

**Hanover Square**
W1
Central map: page 9, G6

Like Berkely Square, Hanover Square once contained elegant Georgian houses, but many of these have now been replaced by modern offices. A statue of William Pitt the Younger stands at the south end of the square facing St George's Church.

**Leicester Square**
WC2
Central map: page 10, I6

This large square gets its name from Leicester House, a mansion built here by the Earl of Leicester in the 17th century. The open space, then known as Leicester Fields, was ideal for fighting duels. The mansion has long since disappeared, and in Victorian times the fields were laid out as a garden, with the statue of Shakespeare in the centre and busts of famous local residents at the four corners.

**Manchester Square**
W1 (between George St and Wigmore St)
Central map: page 9, F7

The leafy centre of Manchester Square contrasts prettily with the dark brick of the Georgian architecture that surrounds it. It is a quiet place, situated just far enough away from Oxford Street to be unaffected by the noise, yet close enough to be a haven for those weary of shopping in the famous thoroughfare.

**Parliament Square**
SW1
Central map: page 4, I4

The square was originally laid out by Sir Charles Barry in 1850, and redesigned in 1951 for the Festival of Britain. There are many statues of British politicians in and around the square.

**Portman Square**
W1
Central map: page 9, F7

Once second only to Grosvenor Square in the eyes of high society, Portman took 20 years to build during the 18th century. The centre of the square is occupied by a garden in which grass, shrubs, and trees combine effectively.

**Russell Square**
WC1
Central map: page 10, I8

James Burton laid out Russell Square in the early 19th century, but few of his original buildings have survived. An exception is No 21, on the north side, which is considered a good example of his work.

The pleasant central garden was originally designed by the architect Humphry Repton, but his layout was later altered.

**St James's Square**
SW1
Central map: page 4, H5

At the centre of this orderly and elegant square, originally created by architect Henry Jermyn, is a garden which is particularly noted for its lovely trees. An equestrian statue of William III forms the central focal point for ranks of tall plane trees, the pastel softness of flowering almond and cherry blossom, the fragrant pyramids of lilac bloom, and golden crowns of laburnum.

**Smith Square**
SW1
Central map: page 4, I4

This square is named after Sir John Smith, who owned and developed the land. Some of the houses were rebuilt after World War II, but No 5 dates from 1726. The streets leading to and from the square are lined with elegant town houses, and this is an excellent area to get a 'feel' of 18th- and early 19th-century London. In the centre of the square is Thomas Archer's fine church of St John. Concerts are often broadcast from the church, which has been specially adapted for the purpose. St John's also has its own orchestra, now of international repute.

**Soho Square**
W1
Central map: page 10, H7

The name 'Soho' is said to come from the cry of huntsmen unleashing dogs to chase hares, *so* meaning 'see', and *ho* 'after him'. The Duke of Monmouth, Charles II's illegitimate son, had a mansion in Soho Square, and when he and his

followers made a bid for the Crown at the Battle of Sedgemoor, 'Soho!' was their battle cry. On the east side of the square is the Roman Catholic Church of St Patrick, built in 1891-3. It has a fine Italianate interior. In the north-west corner is the French Protestant Church of London, founded in 1550 under a royal charter from Edward VI. The present building dates from 1893. Soho has been a foreign quarter since the reign of Charles II, when a great number of French Protestants fled here as the result of religious persecution. Known as 'Huguenots', they were mostly silk-weavers, and in the back gardens around Soho Square there may still be some of the mulberry trees they planted for their silkworms.

**Tavistock Square**
WC1
Central map: page 10, I8

To the right of the central walk through the square's garden is a copper beech tree planted by Pandit Nehru on 13 June 1953 to mark the unveiling of the statue of Mahatma Gandhi in the centre of the garden. The statue in the south-east corner of the gardens is of Dame Louisa Aldrich-Blake (1865-1925), pioneering surgeon to the Elizabeth Garrett Anderson Hospital for women. This memorial is by Sir Edwin Lutyens, who also designed the large building of the British Medical Association on the east side of the square. This building occupies the site of a house where Dickens lived for nine years, and in which several of his novels were written. On

the north side of the square is Woburn House, in which is the fascinating Jewish Museum (see page 89).

**Trafalgar Square**
WC2
Central map: page 10, I6

Pigeons outnumber people in the square. They perch on heads, and shoulders, and are fed, photographed, and fussed over. The square itself, dominated by Nelson's Column, was laid out in memory of Nelson and completed in 1841, but the fountains were added in 1948. On the parapet nearest the National Gallery the Standard British Linear Measures are let into the stonework.

**Trinity Square**
EC3
Central map: page 12, N6

In 1465, during the reign of Edward IV, the first permanent scaffold was set up on Tower Hill. It was situated in what is now Trinity Square, and the site, with its blood-drenched memories, is marked by a rectangle of bricked paving. Public executions were held here until the 18th century; more than 125 people were put to death.

**Vincent Square**
SW1
Central map: page 4, H3

Named after William Vincent, Dean of Westminster 1802-15, the square contains playing fields for the boys of Westminster School. This continues a long tradition, for in medieval times the area was part of the old Tothill Fields, where young men practised military skills such as archery and wrestling.

# Churches

The churches of central London contain some of the capital's greatest treasures, and many of the buildings themselves are architectural gems. But they are surprisingly little visited, and most are havens of tranquillity. A selection of some of the best is on the following pages.

### All Hallows-by-the-Tower
Byward Street, EC3
Central map: page 12, M6

The shell of the church dates from the 12th to 15th centuries, but the interior, which was gutted during the Blitz, was rebuilt in the 1950s. Preserved in the crypt here is a Saxon arch of a church which stood on this site in the 7th century. Also in the crypt are fragments of Roman paving, and the remains of two Saxon crosses. A superb font cover designed by Grinling Gibbons escaped destruction, as did the exquisite brasses in front of the altar (Brass rubbing — see page 76). Samuel Pepys surveyed the results of the Great Fire of London from the tower.

### All Hallows
London Wall, EC2
Central map: page 12, M7

Forming part of the boundary of the churchyard here is a

ALL SOULS'

stretch of the Roman wall which once surrounded the City of London. The church itself was designed by George Dance the Younger in the 18th century and has an elegant and sumptuously decorated interior. It was severely damaged during the Blitz, but was restored during the 1960s.

### All Saints
Margaret Street, W1
Central map: page 10, H7

This striking brick-built church was erected in 1849 to the designs of William Butterfield. He was the most original architect of his time and produced plans that were initially inspired by Gothic architecture. The interior of the church is decorated with coloured bricks, and the decoration becomes much richer nearer the roof, reflecting the Victorian idea that Gothic architecture becomes more elaborate the nearer it gets to heaven.

### All Souls'
Langham Place, W1
Central map: page 9, G7

John Nash designed this large church and had it built in this position to close the northward vista of Regent Street. It was built in 1822 and has a Classical portico surmounted by a needle spire. The interior is designed in such a way that the whole

congregation can view all aspects of the services.

### Brompton Oratory
Brompton Road, SW7
Central map: page 2, E4

This imposing Roman Catholic church was built in an Italian Renaissance style at the end of the 19th century. Its interior is rich in marble and mosaic decoration and the nave is a remarkable 51ft wide.

### Chelsea Old Church (All Saints')
Cheyne Walk, SW3
Central map: page 2, E2

Almost totally destroyed during the Blitz, this church has been restored to its original appearance. The More Chapel, however, survived almost intact. It was built in 1528 for Sir Thomas More and his family, but it is doubtful if he was buried here. The church is extremely rich in monuments, and in the churchyard is an urn commemorating Sir Hans Sloane, the great 18th-century collector and benefactor.

### Holy Trinity
Sloane Street, SW1
Central map: page 3, F3

This church was designed by J D Sedding, one of the principal architects of the 19th-century Arts and Crafts Movement. The interior of the church is based on 15th-century Gothic architecture and is lit by magnificent stained-glass windows designed by Edward Burne-Jones and made by William Morris. During December colourful medieval bible plays are performed at the church. (For details contact the church.)

## St Alfege
Church Street,
Greenwich, SE10
Not on map

Built in 1714, this
splendid Nicholas
Hawksmoor church was
built on the site of the
murder of Archbishop
Alfege by the Danes in
1012. Badly damaged
during the Blitz many of
the treasures which it
had contained were
destroyed. The church
was restored in the 1950s
and houses a memorial
to General Wolfe and the
tomb of the 'father of
English church music',
Thomas Tallis (c.1505-85).

## St Andrew
Holborn Circus, EC1
Central map: page 11, K7

Although this church
escaped the Great Fire, it
was nonetheless rebuilt
by Sir Christopher Wren,
and is his largest parish
church. It did not escape
the Blitz, however, and
had to be largely rebuilt.
It contains a delightful
memorial to Thomas
Coram, who founded the
Foundlings Hospital in
the 18th century. The
church's pulpit, font, and
organ came from the
chapel of the hospital. St
Andrew's is a non-
parochial guild church
and no Sunday services
are held here, but it is
open for prayers on
weekdays.

## St Andrew-by-the-
## Wardrobe
Queen Victoria Street,
EC4
Central map: page 12, K6

Only the shell of this
church survived the Blitz.
It takes its name from
the Great Wardrobe, or
royal storehouse, which
used to stand nearby.
The church was restored
in the late 1950s and
contains furnishings from
other London churches.

## St Andrew Undershaft
St Mary Axe, Leadenhall
Street, EC3
Central map: page 12,
M7

The strange name of this
church is derived from
the fact that a famous
maypole once stood
beside it. It is essentially
a 16th-century building,
although the tower was
restored during the 19th
century. Its most notable
monument is to John
Stow, a 16th-century
historian who wrote the
first topographical
description of London.
Despite bomb damage in
the Blitz, the church still
retains some original
glass in the aisle
windows, and the
magnificent west window
dates from the 17th
century.

## St Anne and St Agnes
Gresham Street, EC2
Central map: page 12, L7

Wren rebuilt this
attractive little church
after the Great Fire. It has
a square tower and a
spacious interior with a
central vault supported
by elegant columns. The
church contains a fine
collection of
ecclesiastical antiquities,
but is only open to the
public on Sundays, when
it is used for Lutheran
services.

## St Anne Limehouse
Commercial Road, E14
Not on map

This was the first of
Nicholas Hawksmoor's
spectacular Classical-style
churches, of which there
are two others in the
East End. It was built in
1712 and is especially
notable for its imposing
tower. Hawksmoor was a
pupil of Sir Christopher
Wren, and followed
closely in the footsteps of
his master.

ALL SAINTS

## St Bartholomew the
## Great
West Smithfield, EC1
Central map: page 12, L7

St Bartholomew's is one
of the few surviving
examples of Norman
architecture in London. It
dates from the 12th
century and is the
chancel of a great
Norman monastery
church which once stood
here. After the
dissolution of the
monasteries it became
private property, and for
300 years was put to a
variety of uses, including
a factory and stables. It
reverted to its original
use during the 19th
century and was restored
by Sir Aston Webb. Its
interior is dominated by
huge Romanesque pillars,
and contains the tomb of
Rahere, the founder of
the church and of St
Bartholomew's Hospital.
The church has a
particularly interesting
gateway, consisting of a
half-timbered gatehouse
above a battered 13th-
century arch which was
the original entrance to
the nave.

## St Bartholomew-the-Less
West Smithfield, EC1
Central map: page 12, L7

This is the chapel of St
Bartholomew's Hospital,
in whose grounds it

stands. All that remains of the original 15th-century building is the tower and vestry, which were incorporated into an octagonal church designed by George Dance the Younger in the 18th century.

### St Benet's (Welsh Metropolitan Church)
Paul's Wharf, off Queen Victoria Street, EC4
Central map: page 12, L6

Wren put the finishing touches to this handsome little church in 1683. Its exterior has elaborately decorated window surrounds and the interior has an abundance of carved woodwork, including the galleries and altar. The church has been used by Welsh Episcopalians since 1879 and is only open for Sunday services.

### St Botolph Aldgate
Aldgate High Street, EC3
Central map: page 12, N7

A church has occupied this site for more than 1,000 years, but the present building dates from the 18th century, when it was built by the architect George Dance the Elder. J F Bentley, the architect responsible for Westminster Cathedral, added the figured ceiling in 1889, and further extensive alterations were made after a fire in 1965.

ST CLEMENT DANES.

### St Botolph
Aldersgate St, EC1
Central map: page 12, L7

Founded in the 11th century and rebuilt in the 18th century, this church stands near the site of one of the old City gates. The simple but very attractive exterior has a brick-built square tower with a cupola capped by a wooden bell turret. The beautifully decorated interior is lit by an odd mixture of stained glass windows, the best of which is undoubtedly an 18th-century representation of the Agony in the Garden.

### St Botolph's
Bishopsgate, EC2
Central map: page 12, M7

St Botolph's was rebuilt in the 18th century by James Gold with the help of George Dance the Elder. It is an impressive brick building surmounted by a clock tower and steeple. The interior was altered in the 19th century and has a coved ceiling supported by huge Corinthian columns.

### St Bride
Fleet Street, EC4
See page 101

### St Clement Danes
Strand, WC2
Central map: page 11, J6

A church has stood on this site since the 9th century. Sir Christopher Wren rebuilt it in the 1680s, and it was rebuilt once more after it had been virtually destroyed during World War II. It is the memorial church of the Royal Air Force, and the crests of some 900 squadrons and Commonwealth air forces are let into the flooring. Many of the church's fixtures and furnishings

ST ETHELBURGA THE VIRGIN

have been donated by overseas air forces. The 115ft tower houses the bells that are immortalised in the famous lines of the nursery rhyme: 'Oranges and Lemons say the bells of St Clement's'.

### St Clement Eastcheap
Clements Lane, EC4
Central map: page 12, M6

Of particular interest in this little church is the beautiful 17th-century woodwork, seen at its best in the canopied pulpit. The church itself was built by Wren in 1683.

### St Dunstan-in-the-West
Fleet Street, EC4
Central map: page 11, K7

Although founded in the 13th century, the present church on this site dates only from the early part of the 19th century. It is an octagonal building with a prominent lantern tower. Many monuments from the church that once stood here have been preserved, and include one to the mythical King Lud and his sons. Also of interest is the clock, which was made in 1671, and was one of the first clocks in London to have minute divisions. The famous angler Izaak Walton is depicted in the north-west window, and it was in Fleet Street that *The Compleat Angler* was published (1653).

### St Edmund The King and Martyr
Lombard Street, EC3
Central map: page 12, M6

This church is dedicated to a king of East Anglia who was killed by the Danes in AD870. It was rebuilt by Sir Christopher Wren in 1670, and has a distinctive spire.

### St Ethelburga-the-Virgin
Bishopsgate, EC2
Central map: page 12, M7

Entered by a 14th-century doorway, this tiny medieval building is one of the best preserved of the City's pre-Fire churches. It was once famous for the picturesque shops which obscured the front, but were demolished in 1932.

### St Etheldreda, or Ely Chapel
Ely Place, EC1
(off Charterhouse St)
Central map: page 11, K7

Originally built in the 13th century, this little chapel was allowed to deteriorate over the centuries, and was finally almost totally destroyed during the Blitz. Only the façade and some Roman foundations survived, and these have been incorporated into the present structure. The chapel is two-storeyed and has a massive vaulted undercroft dating from 1252. It is the oldest pre-Reformation Roman Catholic church in London.

### St George
Bloomsbury Way, WC1
Central map: page 10, I7

Noted for its striking façade, this 18th-century church was built by Nicholas Hawksmoor. It has a Corinthian portico supported by six columns, and a tower and spire crowned by a statue of George I wearing a Roman toga.

### St George
Borough High Street, Southwark, SE1
Central map: page 6, L5

Rebuilt by the architect John Price in 1734-36, this church has a spired tower with octagonal upper stages. The galleried interior is watched over by Victorian carvings of cherubs affixed to the ceiling.

### St Giles Cripplegate
Fore Street, EC2
Central map: page 12, L7

Only the nave and tower of the original church built here in the 14th century survive. It was largely rebuilt in the 16th century, with further additions made to the tower a century later, and was badly damaged during World War II. It has now been restored. Among the many famous people buried here are Sir Martin Frobisher and the poet John Milton.

### St George Hanover Square
St George's Street, W1
Central map: page 9, G6

Many fashionable weddings have taken place in this church since it was built in the early part of the 18th century. It is an impressive Classical-style building with a galleried interior lit by 16th-century Flemish windows. Among those married here were Emma, Lady Hamilton and Benjamin Disraeli.

### St Giles-in-the-Field
St Giles High Street, WC2
Central map: page 10, I7

This church's fine 161ft Baroque steeple makes it a prominent landmark. A

ST HELEN, BISHOPSGATE

church was founded on this site by Matilda, the wife of Henry I, in the 12th century, but the present building dates from the 18th century. it was beautifully restored in 1952-3, and has superb interior fittings, many of which were made for the church in the 18th century.

### St Helen Bishopsgate
Great St Helen's, EC3 (off Bishopsgate)
Central map: page 12, M7

One of the largest churches in the City this magnificent structure was built in the 13th century and was originally two churches joined by an arcade of pillars. There are two naves, one of which served a monastery, and the other for the parish. The church is famous for its beautiful brasses, which are usually protected by carpets. Unfortunately brass rubbing is no longer allowed. There is much else of interest in the building, including several excellent monuments, two fine sword-rests (one dating from 1665 and very rare), and a Jacobean pulpit which is beautifully carved.

### St James-the-Less
Thorndyke Street, off
Vauxhall Bridge Road,
SW1
Central map: page 4, H3

G E Street, one of the
most accomplished of
Victorian architects,
designed this splendid
church in 1858. Its plain
exterior encases a
majestic vaulted interior
which is lit by windows
made by the famous firm
of Clayton and Bell.

### St James Garlickhythe
Upper Thames Street,
EC4
Central map: page 12, L6

Founded as long ago as
the 12th century, the
present church on this
site was built by Wren
after the Great Fire, and
is one of his more
elaborate designs. Its
most distinguishing
exterior feature is the
handsome spire. The
interior, which was
restored after bomb
damage, has excellent
woodwork, as well as
ironwork hat racks and
sword rests. The church
reputedly owes its name
to the fact that garlic
was once sold nearby.

### St James's
Piccadilly, W1
Central map: page 10, H6

This church, originally
built for the Earl of St
Albans by Wren in 1676
is said to be the one he
liked the best. It was
extensively damaged
during the Blitz, and was
restored to its former
glory in 1954. It has a
magnificent galleried
interior beneath a barrel-
vaulted ceiling. The font,
reredos, altarpiece and
organ case are all the
work of the master-
woodcarver, Grinling
Gibbons. The organ itself
was a gift from Mary II in
1690, and came from
Whitehall Palace.

### St John
Smith Square, SW1
Central map: page 4, I4

When the architect of
this church, Thomas
Archer, asked Queen
Anne what style she
would like it built in, she
is reputed to have kicked
over a stool, pointed at it
and said 'build me one
like that'. In fact the four
large towers at each
corner of the building
serve a strictly functional
purpose, in that they
were specially designed
to prevent the whole
structure sinking into the
marsh upon which it was
built. The church was
gutted during World War
II, and now serves as a
music and cultural
centre.

### St John's Church
Church Row, Hampstead
Not on map

St John's is the parish
church of Hampstead,
rebuilt 1745-7, and
subsequently added to
and altered in the 19th
century. The handsome
wrought-iron gates to the
churchyard date from
the 18th century, and
were brought from the
mansion of the Duke of
Chandos in Edgware
when it was demolished.
Many famous local
residents are buried in
the churchyard. In the
south-east corner lies the
painter John Constable
(1776-1837), in the newer
part north of the road
the actor-manager Sir
Herbert Beerbohm Tree
(1853-1917), the historian
of London, Sir Walter
Besant (1836-1901), and
George du Maurier.

### St Katherine Cree
Leadenhall Street, EC3
Central map: page 12, N7

This 16th-century church
is one of the few London
churches that escaped
damage both in the

Great Fire, and World
War II. It is built in the
Classical style, and is
now the headquarters of
the Industrial Christian
Fellowship.

### St Lawrence Jewry
Gresham Street, EC2
Central map: page 12, L7

Rebuilt by Wren on the
site of a medieval
church, this church
stands in the forecourt of
the Guildhall. The name
Jewry has survived from
the period between 1066
and 1290 when the
neighbourhood had a
large Jewish population.
The church was brilliantly
rebuilt after bomb
damage, and the present
steeple is actually a
fibreglass copy of the
original. It is the guild
church of the
Corporation of London,
and pews are set aside
for the lord mayor
other City dignitaries.

### St Leonard
Shoreditch High Street,
E1
Central

Restored by George
Dance the Younger
between 1736 and 1740,
this church has an
imposing portico and a
192ft steeple. There have
been subsequent
renovations following
bomb damage in World
War II, but the organ
console dates from 1756.
There are old stocks and
a whipping post in the
churchyard.

### St Magnus the Martyr
Lower Thames Street,
EC3
Central map: page 12,
M6

The church which
originally stood on this
site, dating from Saxon
times, overlooked the
northern approach to the
old London Bridge. It was
destroyed in the Great
Fire, and was rebuilt by

Sir Christopher Wren. A portion of timber from an 8th-century Roman wharf, and a stone from the first arch of old London Bridge, dating from 1176, are preserved in the churchyard near the main entrance. Today the church is hemmed in by tall buildings, but its fine tower is still prominent. Inside, much of the 17th-century woodwork and wrought ironwork has been preserved.

### St Margaret's Lothbury

Lothbury, EC2
Central map: page 12, M7

Rebuilt by Wren between 1686 and 1690, this church contains a good deal of ancient woodwork from other City churches, including the screen and pulpit from All Hallows the Great, Upper Thames Street, which was demolished in 1894. The Scientific Instrument Makers' Company hold their services here, and the church is also a venue for music recitals.

### St Margaret's Westminster

Parliament Square, SW1
Central map: page 4, I4

Dating from the late 15th century, St Margaret's has been the official church of the House of Commons since 1614. Although it is rather overshadowed by its mighty neighbour, Westminster Abbey, it is equally worthy of attention, and is especially notable for its wealth of monuments. Sir Walter Raleigh is buried in the chancel. The glass in the east window, 16th-century work from the Netherlands, is some of the finest in London. Chaucer and Caxton were famous early parishioners.

### St Margaret Pattens

Rood Lane, Eastcheap, EC3
Central map: page 12, M6

This church was redesigned by Wren, and contains much interesting woodwork, including the only 17th-century canopied churchwardens' pews in the City, and a beadles' pew complete with a low punishment bench where members of the congregation who misbehaved were made to sit for the remainder of the service. The name Pattens is thought to derive from the wooden soles, mounted on iron rings called pattens, designed to raise the wearer above the debris of London's streets, which were made and sold in a nearby lane.

### St Martin-within-Ludgate

Ludgate Hill, EC4
Central map: page 12, K7

It is thought that a church stood on this site some 13 centuries ago, but reliable records date only from the 12th century. It was rebuilt in 1437, destroyed in the Great Fire, and subsequently rebuilt by Wren in 1684. He incorporated the remains of the old tower into the fabric of the new church. The interior is magnificently decorated, and contains carved woodwork by Grinling Gibbons, and a double 17th-century church warden's chair, believed to be the only one of its kind in existence.

### St Martin-in-the-Fields

Trafalgar Square, WC2
Central map: page 10, I6

The medieval church on this site, once surrounded as its name suggests by open fields, was extensively rebuilt by

James Gibbs in the early 18th century. It has an imposing temple-like portico, and a spacious galleried interior. Buckingham Palace is within the parish boundaries, and there are royal boxes at the east end of the church. The vaulted crypt contains a 16th-century chest and an 18th-century whipping post, but is better known for the fact that it is opened each evening as a shelter for the homeless. This carries on the tradition of H R L Sheppard, a World War I army chaplain, who, on his return from the Front, always kept the church open for servicemen or others who were stranded.
Brass rubbing — see page 76.

### St Mary's

St Marychurch Street, SE16
Not on map

Rebuilt during the 18th century, this church has close connections with the sea and sailors. The altar table and sanctuary chairs were made from timber from the 18th-century warship *Fighting Temeraire*, and the nave columns are made from ships' masts enclosed in plaster.

### St Mary Abchurch

Abchurch Lane EC4 (off Cannon St)
Central map: page 12, L6

Wren rebuilt this church about 15 years after the Great Fire had destroyed the original, and subsequent renovations have done nothing to alter the late 17th-century appearance. It stands in a secluded courtyard, and is noted for its painted ceiling by William Stow, and rare Grinling Gibbons reredos. Most of the original fittings have survived, notably the pulpit, font, and finely carved pews.

### St Mary Aldermary

Queen Victoria Street, EC4
Central map: page 12, L6

One of the few churches that Wren rebuilt in the Gothic style after the Great Fire, this church was greatly altered during the 19th century. However, the beautiful fan-vaulted ceilings survive, as do Wren's pulpit and font.

### St Mary-le-Bow

Cheapside, EC2
Central map: page 12, L6

Restored by Wren after the Great Fire, this church was extensively fire-damaged during the Blitz. Wren's steeple survived, however, and its lofty spire, crowned by a 9ft weather vane in the form of a dragon, still towers over Cheapside. The famous Bow Bells originally rang as a curfew and it was their distinctive peal which is said to have recalled Dick Whittington from Highgate Hill. Those born within their sound are said to be true Cockneys. The bells were recast after severe damage in 1941, and rang out anew in 1961.

### St Mary-le-Strand

Strand, WC2
Central map: page 11, J6

The present building on this site, designed by James Gibbs in the early 18th century, is one of the best examples of Italian-influenced church architecture in London.

### St Mary Woolnoth

Lombard Street, EC3
Central map: page 12, M6

Partly damaged in the Great Fire, and subsequently restored by Wren, this church was completely rebuilt by Nicholas Hawksmoor between 1716 and 1727 in a highly original, almost fortified style. The interior has a tremendous feeling of sumptuous spaciousness which is heightened by the groups of Corinthian columns supporting the ceiling.

### St Michael-upon-Cornhill

Cornhill, EC3
Central map: page 12, M6

This church was built by Wren after the Great Fire, and its fine Gothic tower was added in 1721. Sir George Gilbert Scott restored and embellished it. The font and the altar-table date from the late 17th century, but the most unusual, and decorative, object is the carved wooden pelican by George Paterson, which dates from 1775.

### St Michael Paternoster Royal

College Hill, EC4 (off Queen St)
Central map: page 12, L6

Dick Whittington met the cost of rebuilding this church in 1409 and he was buried here in 1423, but his tomb was destroyed during the Great Fire. Wren rebuilt the church, but it was badly damaged by a flying bomb in 1944, and the restored building was not consecrated until 1968.

### St Nicholas Cole Abbey

Queen Victoria Street, EC4
Central map: page 12, L6

One of the first churches which Wren worked on after the Great Fire, St Nicholas was gutted by incendiary bombs in 1941. The architect Arthur Bailey undertook the rebuilding in 1962, adhering to Wren's design, and preserving the unusual spire, which has an inverted trumpet shape and is crowned by a weather vane in the shape of a ship.

### St Olave

Hart Street, EC3 (opposite Pepys St)
Central map: page 12, N6

Samuel Pepys and Admiral Sir William Penn saved this 15th-century church from the Great Fire by having the surrounding buildings torn down. No one, however, could prevent bomb damage in 1941. Access to the church from Seething Lane is via an unusual gateway decorated with skulls, which Dickens describes as belonging to the church of St Ghastly Grim in his *Uncommercial Traveller*. Pepys and his wife Elizabeth are buried here.

ST·MARY·LE·STRAND

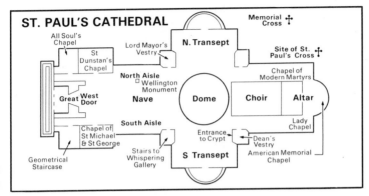

**ST. PAUL'S CATHEDRAL**

- Memorial Cross ✝
- All Soul's Chapel
- Lord Mayor's Vestry
- N. Transept
- Site of St. Paul's Cross ✝
- St Dunstan's Chapel
- Chapel of Modern Martyrs
- North Aisle
- Wellington Monument
- Great West Door
- Nave
- Dome
- Choir
- Altar
- South Aisle
- Chapel of St Michael & St George
- Entrance to Crypt
- Dean's Vestry
- Lady Chapel
- Geometrical Staircase
- Stairs to Whispering Gallery
- S Transept
- American Memorial Chapel

**St Paul's Cathedral**
EC4
Central map: page 12, L7
☎ 071-248 2705

This is Wren's masterpiece. It was built of Portland stone in 1675-1710 to replace the former Gothic cathedral of the 13th century, which was altered early in the 17th century by Inigo Jones and finally destroyed in 1666 by the Great Fire of London. The cathedral rises to a height of 365ft and in the south-west tower is 'Great Paul', a bell weighing some 17 tons. The west façade of the cathedral is 180ft wide and the famous dome, 112ft in diameter, is buttressed by twelve massive supports. Within the dome is the famous 'Whispering Gallery', where whispered words can be heard quite clearly 112ft away across the void. Carved woodwork by Grinling Gibbons and ironwork by Jean Tijou are features of the cathedral interior. The crypt contains the tombs of Wren, Nelson, Wellington, Reynolds and Turner. The Whispering Gallery and Golden Gallery may be visited for a small charge.
Open: daily 7.15am-6pm, subject to special services. Admission charged 9-4.

**St Paul's Church**
Covent Garden, WC2
Central map: page 10, I6

The first new Anglican church to be built in London after the Reformation, St Paul's was designed by Inigo Jones for the 4th Earl of Bedford, between 1631 and 1633. It has long associations with the theatre since both the Theatre Royal, Drury Lane and the Royal Opera House are in the parish. Amongst the famous buried here are Claude Duval the highwayman, Grinling Gibbons, Thomas Arne, composer of *Rule Britannia*, and the actress Vivien Leigh. J M W Turner was baptised here.

**St Paul**
Deptford High Street, SE8
Not on map

Built between 1712 and 1730 to a distinctive Baroque design by Thomas Archer, this church has a fine circular portico supported by Tuscan columns and surmounted by a slim tower. The square interior is galleried and has many Dutch oak fittings.

**St Peter-upon-Cornhill**
Cornhill, EC3
Central map: page 12, M6

This church, which stands on the highest ground in the City, is believed to occupy a site on which a church has stood since the 2nd century. This makes it by far the oldest church site in London. The present church was built by Wren after the Great Fire, and contains many fine fittings, including a 17th-century font and two Wren-type churchwardens' pews. However, the most outstanding feature is the chancel screen, designed by Wren and his 16-year-old daughter. Lunchtime recitals are held in the church.

**St Sepulchre**
Holborn Viaduct, EC1
Central map: page 11, K7

Wren assisted in the rebuilding of this church after the Great Fire. It is the largest of the City parish churches, and contains some 17th-century pews and a fine Renatus Harris organ, dating from 1677. The churchyard was so popular with body snatchers during the 18th century that a Watch House was erected so that the corpses could be guarded. This was restored following war damage. St Sepulchre's is known as the Musicians' Church, and the Musicians' Chapel contains the ashes of Sir Henry Wood, founder of the Promenade Concerts.

### St Stephen Walbrook

Walbrook, EC4
(next to Mansion House)
Central map: page 12, M6

This church is one of Wren's masterpieces. The magnificent dome was probably a prototype for the vast dome of St Paul's. It was badly damaged during World War II, and restored during the 1950s.

### St Vedast

Foster Lane, EC2
(off Cheapside)
Central map: page 12, L7

The most noteworthy feature of this Wren church is its elegant steeple. Inside there are a number of ancient fittings from defunct City churches.

### Southwark Cathedral

Borough High Street, SE1
Central map: page 6, M5

A church has stood on this site since the 7th century, but it was not until 1905 that the basically 16th-century parish church of St Saviour was elevated to cathedral status. Despite rebuilding, particularly during the 19th century, its medieval Gothic style has remained largely intact, and parts of the church date back to at least the 13th century. There are many monuments in the building, including an unusual one to a 17th-century quack doctor called Lyonell Lockyer. Ancient tombs include that of Edmund Shakespeare, William's younger brother.

### Westminster Abbey

Parliament Square, SW1
Central map: page 4, I4
☎071-222 5152

A church has stood on this site since at least as early as Saxon times. The church later built here was enlarged by Edward the Confessor and made the crowning place of English sovereigns. Henry III rebuilt the cathedral (1216-72) in tribute to Edward. Henry VII added the chapel at the eastern end (1503-19). The 225ft-high towers were added in the mid-18th century by Nicholas Hawksmoor. Many generations of English sovereigns are buried here in beautifully carved tombs. Elsewhere are memorials to the nation's great statesmen,

THOMAS CARLYLE

politicians, scientists, poets and others. (Brass rubbing — see page 76). Open: Nave and cloisters, daily 8am-6pm, admission free. Royal Chapels, Mon-Fri 9-4, Sat 9-2 and 3.45-5, admission charge. Wed 6-7.45, no charge and photography allowed. Sun services only.

### Westminster Cathedral

Ashley Place, SW1
Central map: page 4, H4
☎071-834 7452

The largest and most important Roman Catholic church in England. A Byzantine structure completed in 1903, of red brick with contrasting bands of Portland Stone, its interior is richly ornamented. You can take a lift to the top of the 273ft high campanile. Open: daily, 7am-8pm, admission free.

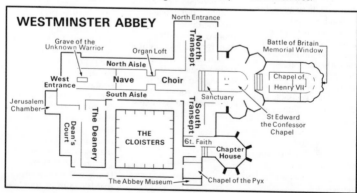

### WESTMINSTER ABBEY

North Entrance

Grave of the Unknown Warrior

Organ Loft

North Transept

Battle of Britain Memorial Window

North Aisle

West Entrance — Nave — Choir

Chapel of Henry VII

South Aisle

Jerusalem Chamber

Sanctuary

Dean's Court

The Deanery

South Transept

St Edward the Confessor Chapel

THE CLOISTERS

St. Faith

Chapter House

The Abbey Museum — Chapel of the Pyx

# Statues, Monuments and Plaques

London has more statues than any other city in the world, and there are hundreds of 'blue plaques' commemorating famous people's homes. Described on the following pages is a selection of London's more interesting monuments, statues and plaques.

### Achilles
Hyde Park, W1
Central map: page 3, F5

Sculpture by Sir Richard Westmacott, 1822. This statue of the Greek god was made from a cannon captured during the Peninsular Wars, and erected in 1822.

### Prince Albert
The Albert Memorial, Kensington Gore, SW7 (opposite Royal Albert Hall)
Central map: page 2, D4

Sculpture designed by Sir Gilbert Scott, 1872. This enormous and imposing memorial is a monument not only to Prince Albert, but also to the benevolent aspects of Victorian Imperialism. The memorial was commissioned by Queen Victoria in memory of her husband. The sculpture of the Prince, which was made by John Foley, sits under an ornate and intricately decorated canopy. The Prince is depicted reading a catalogue of the Great Exhibition of 1851, for which he was largely responsible.

### Alfred the Great
Trinity Church Square off Trinity Street, SE1
Central map: page 6, L4

Thought to date from 1395, this is the oldest statue in London.

### Queen Anne
EC4 (front of St Paul's Cathedral)
Central map: page 12, L7

Sculpture by Richard Belt, 1886.
This marble statue is a copy of the one by Francis Bird, 1712, and erected to commemorate the completion of St Paul's.

### Queen Boadicea
Westminster Bridge, SW1
Central map: page 4, I5

Sculpture by Thomas Thornycroft, 1902. Queen Boadicea (or Boudicca) is depicted in her war chariot, accompanied by her daughters.

### Robert Burns
Victoria Embankment Gardens, WC2
Central map: page 10, I6

Sculpture by Steeller, 1884.

### The Burghers of Calais
Victoria Tower Gardens, SW1 (off Millbank)
Central map: page 4, I4

Sculpture by Rodin. Rodin's superb group of figures represents the citizens of Calais who surrendered to Edward III in 1340 to save their town from destruction.

### Lord Byron
Hyde Park Corner, W1 (opposite Achilles)
Central map: page 3, F5

Sculpture by Richard Belt, 1880.

### George Canning
Parliament Square, SW1
Central map: page 4, I4

Sculpture by Richard Westmacott, 1832. This bronze statue of the statesman in a toga is chiefly notable for the fact that while it was still in the sculptor's studio it fell over and killed a man.

### Thomas Carlyle
Cheyne Walk, SW3
Central map: page 2, E2

Sculpture by Sir Edgar Boehm, 1900.
This statue shows the 'Sage of Chelsea' sitting in Cheyne Walk Gardens.

### Edith Cavell
WC2 (junction of St Martin's Lane and Charing Cross Rd)
Central map: page 10, I6

Sculpture by Sir George Frampton, 1920. Memorial to the First World War nurse who was shot in Belgium (1915) for helping prisoners to escape.

### The Cenotaph
Whitehall, SW1
Central map: page 4, I5

Monument by Sir Edwin Lutyens, 1919.
Set in the middle of Whitehall, the Cenotaph is a simple pillar of Portland stone unveiled in 1920 on the anniversary of Armistice Day. It was originally built to the memory of the men who lost their lives in World War I. Now memorial services for the dead of both world wars are held here every year on the second Sunday in November.

**Sir Charles Chaplin**
Leicester Square, WC2
Central map: page 10, I6

Sculpture by John Doubleday, 1981.

**Charles I**
Trafalgar Square, SW1
Central map: page 10, I6

Sculpture by Hubert le Sueur, 1633.
Cast in bronze, this statue was to have been melted down during the Commonwealth period but was hidden and re-erected in 1660. It was moved to Mentmore in Buckinghamshire during World War II and was refurbished in 1947 with a new sword. The old sword is said to have been dislodged by a photographer in 1867 and stolen while a procession was in progress.

**Sir Winston Churchill**
Parliament Square, SW1
Central map: page 4, I4

Sculpture by Ivor Roberts-Jones, 1973.
This bronze statue of the great statesman and war leader depicts Churchill in a typically pugnacious attitude.

**Cleopatra's Needle**
Victoria Embankment
Central map: page 11, J6

Mehemet Ali, a viceroy of Egypt, presented this famous landmark to Great Britain in 1819. It was not erected in its present position until 1879, after an eventful sea journey which cost the lives of six seamen. Originally the Needle stood in Heliopolis, where it was one of a pair erected 3,500 years ago. Its twin now stands in Central Park, New York, and neither of them has any connections with Cleopatra.

**Oliver Cromwell**
Old Palace Yard, SW1
(outside Westminster Hall)
Central map: page 4, I4

Sculpture by Sir William Thornycroft, 1899.

**Edward VII**
Waterloo Place, SW1
(junction of Pall Mall and Regent St)
Central map: page 4, H5

Sculpture by Sir Bertram Mackennal, 1921.

**Eros**
Piccadilly Circus, W1
Central map: page 10, H6

Sculpture by Sir Alfred Gilbert, 1833.
One of London's most famous landmarks, this figure of an archer was erected as a memorial to a Victorian reformer and philanthropist, the Earl of Shaftesbury. The archer actually represents the Angel of Christian Charity, not Eros.

**The Fat Boy**
Giltspur Street, EC1
Central map: page 12, K7

This peculiar little gilded figure marks the spot, originally known as Pie Corner, where the Great Fire was halted in 1666.

**Mahatma Gandhi**
Tavistock Square, WC1
Central map: page 10, I8

Sculpture by Fredda Brilliant, 1968.

**George III**
WC2 (corner of Haymarket/Trafalgar Square)
Central map: page 4, I5

Statue by Wyatt, 1836.
Fine equestrian statue.

**George IV**
Trafalgar Square, WC2
Central map: page 10, I6

Sculpture by Chantrey, 1834.

**George V**
Old Palace Yard, SW1
(outside Westminster Hall)
Central map: page 4, I4

Sculpture by Sir William Reid Dick, 1947.

**The Griffin**
Strand, EC4
Central map: page 11, J6

The Griffin, the unofficial badge of the City of London, stands at the point where the Strand ends and Fleet Street begins. Originally this was the site of the Old Temple Bar gateway, and the spot traditionally marks the western limit of the City.

**Sir Henry Irving**
St Martin's Place, WC2
(Trafalgar Square)
Central map: page 10, I6

Sculpture by Thomas Brock, 1910.
Irving is regarded as being one of the greatest actors who ever lived.

**James II**
Trafalgar Square, WC2
(outside National Gallery)
Central map: page 10, I6

Sculpture by Grinling Gibbons, 1686.
Usually regarded as the finest statue in London, this figure of the King is shown in Roman costume.

**Dr Edward Jenner**
Italian Gardens, Kensington Gardens, W2
Central map: page 8, D6

Sculpture by William Calder Marshall, 1858.
Pioneer of vaccination, notably discoverer of smallpox vaccine.

**Dr Samuel Johnson**
St Clement Danes, Strand, WC2
Central map: page 11, J6

Sculpture by Percy Fitzgerald, 1910.

**President John F Kennedy**
1 Park Crescent, W1
Central map: page 9, G8

Sculpture by Jacques
Lipchitz, 1965.
Bronze bust which was
paid for by readers of the
*Sunday Telegraph*.
Unveiled by his brothers
Edward and Robert
Kennedy.

**Abraham Lincoln**
Parliament Square, SW1
Central map: page 4, I4

Replica of a statue in
Chicago by Saint-
Gaudens, 1920, the
sculpture shows Lincoln
in a frock coat standing
in front of his Grecian
chair.

**Monument**
Monument Street, EC3
Central map: page 12,
M6

See page 104.

**Sir Thomas More**
Cheyne Walk, SW3
(corner of Old Church St)
Central map: page 2, E2

Sculpture by Cubitt Bevis,
1969.

**Lord Nelson**
Trafalgar Square, WC2
Central map: page 10, I6

Sculpture by E H Baily,
1843.
This 17ft 4in statue
stands on the top of the
famous column. Together
they reach a combined
height of almost 185ft.
Four identical lions, cast
from a single original by
Sir Edwin Landseer, guard
the base of the column.
This memorial to the
nation's greatest sailor
was set up between 1842
and 1867.

**Florence Nightingale**
Waterloo Place, SW1
(junction of Pall Mall and
Regent St)
Central map: page 4, H5

Sculpture by A Walker,
1915.

The statue of the 'Lady
with the Lamp',
immortalized for her
work to wounded
servicemen, stands
adjacent to the Guards
Crimean War memorial.

**Peter Pan**
Kensington Gardens, W2
Central map: page 2, D5

Sculpture by George
Frampton, 1911.
This statue of Sir James
Barrie's immortal
character has delighted
several generations of
children.

**Sir Walter Raleigh**
Banqueting House,
Whitehall, SW1
Central map: page 4, I5
Sculpture by William
Macmillan, 1959.
Raleigh was beheaded
near this spot in 1618.
The bronze statue, in
Elizabethan dress, is
extremely small,
reflecting Raleigh's
diminutive stature.

**Richard I**
Old Palace Yard, SW1
(outside Westminster
Hall)
Central map: page 4, I4

Sculpture by Baron Carlo
Marochetti, 1860.
This spirited equestrian
statue of Richard the
Lionheart was made for
the Great Exhibition.

**Franklin D Roosevelt**
Grosvenor Square, W1
Central map: page 9, F6

Sculpture by Sir William
Reid Dick, 1948.

**Royal Regiment of
Artillery Memorial**
Hyde Park Corner, SW1
Central map: page 3, G5

Sculpture by C Sargeant
Jagger, stone base by
Lionel Pearson, 1925.
Magnificent memorial of
stone field gun with over-
life size bronze gunners.
In remembrance of the

49,076 men of all ranks
who lost their lives in the
1914-18 war.

**Captain Robert Falcon
Scott**
Waterloo Place, SW1
(junction of Pall Mall and
Regent St)
Central map: page 4, H5

Sculpture by his widow
Lady Scott, 1915.

**William Shakespeare**
Leicester Square, WC2
Central map: page 10, I6

Sculpture by Giovanni
Fontana, a copy of one
by Scheemakers in
Westminster Abbey,
1874.

**Field Marshal Jan
Christian Smuts**
Parliament Square, SW1
Central map: page 4, I4

Sculpture by Jacob
Epstein, 1958.

**South Bank Lion**
Central map: page 5, J5

The lion standing on a
plinth on the east side of
Westminster Bridge
previously surmounted
the Lion Brewery, which
was demolished to build
the Royal Festival Hall. It
was made from Coade's
famous artificial stone
which had superb
weathering qualities.
Unfortunately the
formula — which was a
closely guarded secret —
was lost after the factory
was demolished.

**Queen Victoria**
Queen Victoria
Memorial, The Mall, SW1
Central map: page 4, H5

Sculptures by Sir Thomas
Brock, 1911.
This elegant group of
statuary stands in front
of Buckingham Palace. It
was designed by Sir
Aston Webb.

Kensington Gardens,
WC2
(near the Round Pound)
Central map: page 1, C5

Princess Louise, one of
Queen Victoria's
daughters, made this
statue in 1893.

**George Washington**
Trafalgar Square, WC2
(outside National Gallery)
Central map: page 10, I6

Sculpture, replica of
original in Richmond,
Virginia, USA by Jean-
Antoine Houdon.
Presented by Virginia in
1921.

**The 1st Duke of
Wellington**
Hyde Park Corner, W1
Central map: page 3, G5

Sculpture by J E Boehm,
1888.
The Duke is shown here
riding Copenhagen, the
horse he rode
throughout the Battle of
Waterloo.

**King William III**
St James's Square, SW1
Central map: page 4, H5

Sculpture by John Bacon
the Younger, 1808.
Portrayed as a Roman
General. Under the
horse's hoof is the
molehill which caused his
fatal accident while riding
at Hampton Court.

**Duke of York**
Carlton House Terrace,
SW1 (off The Mall)
Central map: page 4, I5

Sculpture by Sir Richard
Westmacott, 1833.
This 112ft granite pillar,
crowned by a statue of

DUKE OF WELLINGTON

the Grand Old Duke of
York, commemorates the
second son of George III
and was designed by
Benjamin Wyatt. The
cost of its erection is
supposed to have been
largely defrayed by
stopping a day's pay
from every man in the
army.

## BLUE PLAQUES — Famous People

Blue plaques to commemorate the residences of famous people have been erected
in London since 1866. Today the number exceeds 600. The first plaque
commemorated Byron's home at 24 Holles Street. It was made from deep-blue
terracotta with white lettering. Since then various designs have been used:

| | |
|---|---|
| 1867-1900 | The tablets were made by Minton in chocolate-brown terracotta with white lettering |
| 1907-1921 | Introduction of additional rectangular design in bronze, stone and lead |
| 1921 | Doulton glaze adopted as standard material for plaque. During the 1920s after various use of colours the 'blue' plaque was adopted as the standard colour |
| 1937 | Plain design (still used today) was adopted |
| 1939 | White edging was added to the plaques |
| 1955 | Plaques manufactured by Carter's at Poole, Dorset |
| 1982/83 | Plaques manufactured by Alan Dawson of Staffordshire |

Listed below are a few of the famous residences:

| NAME | ADDRESS | PLAQUE ERECTED |
|---|---|---|
| BADEN-POWELL, Robert (1857-1941) founder of the Scouting movement | 9 Hyde Park Gate Central map: page 2, D4 | 1972 |

| | | |
|---|---|---|
| BAIRD, John Logie (1888-1946)<br>In 1926 he demonstrated<br>television in this house | 22 Frith Street<br>Central map: page 10, H6 | 1951 |
| BLIGH, William (1754-1817)<br>Captain of the *Bounty* | 100 Lambeth Road<br>Central map: page 5, K4 | 1952 |
| CANAL, Antonio, (Canaletto) (1697-1768)<br>Venetian Painter | 41 Beak Street<br>Central map: page 10, H6 | 1925 |
| CARLYLE, Thomas (1795-1881)<br>Essayist and historian (see page<br>133) | 24 Cheyne Row<br>Central map: page 2, E2 | 1907 |
| CHURCHILL, Lord Randolph (1849-1895)<br>Statesman | 2 Connaught Place (off<br>Bayswater Road)<br>Central map: page 7, E6 | 1962 |
| CLIVE OF INDIA, Lord (1725-1774)<br>Soldier and<br>administrator | 45 Berkeley Square<br>Central map: page 9, G6 | 1953 |
| DICKENS, Charles (1812-1870)<br>Novelist (see page 82) | 48 Doughty Street<br>Central map: page 11, J8 | 1903 |
| DISRAELI, Benjamin, Earl of Beaconsfield<br>Statesman, born here 1804 | 22 Theobalds Road<br>Central map: page 11, J8 | 1948 |
| DISRAELI, Benjamin Earl of Beaconsfield<br>(1804-1881)<br>Statesman, died here | 19 Curzon Street<br>Central map: page 3, G5 | 1908 |
| ELGAR, Sir Edward (1857-1934)<br>Composer | 51 Avonmore Road<br>Central map: page 1, A3 | 1962 |
| ELIOT, George (Mary Ann Cross)<br>(1819-1880)<br>Novelist | 4 Cheyne Walk<br>Central map: page 2, E2 | 1949 |
| ELLIOT, T S (1888-1965)<br>Poet | 3 Kensington Court<br>Gardens<br>Central map: page 1, C4 | 1986 |
| FRANKLIN, Benjamin (1706-1790)<br>American Statesman | 36 Craven Street (off N<br>side of Northumberland<br>Ave)<br>Central map: page 4, I5 | 1914 |
| GLADSTONE, William (1809-1898)<br>Statesman | 11 Carlton House Terrace<br>(off N side of The Mall)<br>Central map: page 4, I5 | 1925 |
| GRIMALDI, Joseph (1778-1837)<br>Clown | 56 Exmouth Market<br>Central map: page 11, K8 | 1989 |
| HANDEL, George Friederic (1685-1795)<br>Musician | 25 Brook Street<br>Central map: page 9, G6 | 1952 |
| HILL, Sir Rowland (1795-1879)<br>Postal reformer | 1 Orme Square (off Orme<br>Lane)<br>Central map: page 7, C6 | 1907 |
| IRVING, Sir Henry (1838-1905)<br>Actor | 15a Grafton Street (N end<br>of Albemarle St)<br>Central map: page 9, G6 | 1950 |
| JOHNSON, Dr Samuel (1709-1784)<br>Writer | 17 Gough Square<br>Central map: page 11, K7 | 1957 |
| KIPLING, Rudyard (1865-1936)<br>Poet and writer | 43 Villiers Street (off John<br>Adams St)<br>Central map: page 10, I6 | 1957 |
| LAWRENCE, T E (1888-1935)<br>'Lawrence of Arabia' | 14 Barton Street (off Gt<br>Peter St)<br>Central map: page 4, I4 | 1966 |
| MARCONI, Guglielmo (1874-1937)<br>Inventor of wireless<br>communication | 71 Hereford Road<br>Central map: page 7, B6 | 1954 |
| MARX, Karl (1818-1883)<br>Philosopher | 28 Dean Street<br>Central map: page 10, H6 | 1967 |

| NAME | ADDRESS | PLAQUE ERECTED |
|---|---|---|
| MOZART, Wolfgang Amadeus (1756-1791) Composer | 180 Ebury Street Central map: page 3, G3 | 1939 |
| NEWTON, Sir Isaac (1642-1727) Scientist and philosopher | 87 Jermyn Street Central map: page 4, H5 | 1908 |
| NIGHTINGALE, Florence (1820-1910) Nurse and hospital reformer | 10 South Street Central map: page 3, F5 | 1955 |
| NOVELLO, Ivor (1893-1951) Actor, song writer and dramatist | 11 Aldwych Central map: page 11, J6 | 1973 |
| PEPYS, Samuel (1633-1703) Diarist, Secretary of the Admiralty          also at | 12 Buckingham Street 14 Buckingham Street (off John Adam St) Central map: page 10, I6 | 1947 |
| PITT, William, Earl of Chatham (1708-1778) Prime Minister also STANLEY, Edward, Earl of Derby (1799-1869) Prime Minister GLADSTONE, William (1809-1898) Prime Minister | 10 St James's Square Central map: page 4, H5 | 1910 |
| PITT, William (the Younger) (1759-1806) Prime Minister | 120 Baker Street Central map: page 9, F7 | 1949 |
| ROSSETTI, Dante (1828-1882) Artist and Poet | 110 Hallam Street Central map: page 9, G7 | 1906 |
| SCOTT, Captain Robert (1868-1912) Antarctic explorer | 56 Oakley Street Central map: page 2, E2 | 1935 |
| SHERATON, Thomas (1751-1806) Cabinet maker | 163 Wardour Street Central map: page 10, H6 | 1954 |
| STOKER, Bram (1847-1912) Novelist, creator of Dracula | 18 St Leonard's Terrace Central map: page 3, F3 | |
| TWAIN, Mark, (Samuel Langhorne Clemens) (1835-1910) Writer | 23 Tedworth Square Central map: page 3, F2 | 1960 |
| VAUGHAN WILLIAMS, Ralph (1872-1958) Composer | 10 Hanover Terrace (off Outer Circle) Central map: page 8, E8 | 1972 |
| WHISTLER, James (1834-1903) Artist | 96 Cheyne Walk Central map: page 2, E2 | 1925 |
| WILBERFORCE, William (1759-1833) Abolition of slavery | 44 Cadogan Place Central map: page 3, F4 | 1961 |
| WILDE, Oscar (1854-1900) Dramatist | 34 Tite Street Central map: page 3, F2 | 1954 |
| WREN, Sir Christopher (1632-1723) Architect | 49 Bankside Central map: page 12, L6 | — |

ST. PAUL'S CATHEDRAL

# Thames Bridges

The first bridge across the Thames was built in Roman times, and it was that bridge which helped London to grow into one of the most important cities in the world. It remained the lowest bridging point of the river for many centuries; most of the other bridges were built only in the 19th century. The bridges to be seen today are extremely varied in design, and some are of considerable beauty. Given below is a brief history of the bridges from Hampton to the Tower.

### Hampton Court Bridge
District map: page 168, B2

Built in 1933 to the designs of Sir Edwin Lutyens, this elegant bridge connects Hampton Court with East Molesey. The River Mole flows through East Molesey to enter the Thames just below the bridge. To the north of the bridge is Hampton Green, where there is a splendid group of mainly 18th-century buildings. Amongst these is Old Court House, which was the home of Sir Christopher Wren for a while, and the Royal Mews, which now houses the headquarters of the Horse Rangers Trust. On the other side of the Green is Hampton Court House, an imposing structure dating from the middle of the 18th century.

### Kingston Bridge
District map: page 168, B2

Kingston owes it origins to the fact that here was one of the two safe fords across the Thames above Westminster. It made Kingston an extremely important place. A bridge had been built here by the 12th century, and for centuries the only bridge below it was London Bridge. The present bridge was built between 1825 and 1828. An excellent tow path leads upstream from it to Hampton Court.

### Richmond Bridge
District map: page 168, B3

Excellent views up and down the Thames may be obtained from this majestic bridge. It was built in 1777 to the designs of James Paine in a pleasing Classical style.

### Chiswick Bridge
(on A316)
District map: page 168, C3

This concrete bridge was built in 1933 to the designs of the architect Sir Herbert Baker. Just downstream from it, opposite the Ship Inn, is the finishing point of the Oxford and Cambridge Boat Race. Between the bridge and the inn is an attractive group of houses of varying dates, and beyond them, on the south bank, is the huge Mortlake Brewery.

### Hammersmith Bridge
District map: page 168, C3

Sir Joseph Bazalgette, the architect who did so much to change the appearance of the Thames in central London, designed this fanciful suspension bridge in 1887. Just downstream from the bridge, on the north bank, is the converted warehouse used by Riverside Studios, a flourishing arts centre. On the opposite bank is the Harrods warehouse, an imposing building decorated in *art-nouveau* style. Below this is Barn Elms Park, which once comprised the grounds of a mansion that was demolished in 1954. The history of the mansion goes back to Tudor times, when it was the home of Sir Francis Walsingham, Secretary of State to Elizabeth I. The park is now used for recreational activities.

### Putney Bridge
District map: page 168, C3

Graceful Putney Bridge is a 19th-century replacement of an earlier wooden toll bridge. It marks the starting point of the Oxford and Cambridge boat race, and all along the riverside there are well-kept boathouses and clubhouses.

### Albert Bridge
Central map: page 2, E2

This combined cantilever and suspension structure resembles a gigantic iron cobweb and is one of the most distinctive of all London's bridges. It was designed by R M Ordish and opened in 1873.

### Chelsea Bridge
Central map: page 3, G2

This handsome suspension bridge was opened in 1937 and replaced a similar structure of 1858. The river here is the widest reach west of London Bridge and was once the scene of extravagant aquatic displays. During the reign of Charles II it was so popular that it became known as 'Hyde Park on the Thames' or 'Pall Mall afloat'.

Between Chelsea Bridge and Grosvenor Bridge the entry to the now disused Grosvenor Canal can be seen. A large pumping station dominates the scene here.

## Vauxhall Bridge
Central map: page 4, I3

Dating from 1906 this bridge is decorated with several enormous figures, one of them holding a model of St Paul's Cathedral.

## Westminster Bridge
Central map: page 4, I4

The present bridge was designed by Thomas Page and completed in 1862. It replaced a stone bridge of 1750 on which Wordsworth composed his famous sonnet in 1802. At the western end stands a statue of Queen Boadicea.

## Waterloo Bridge
Central map: page 11, J6

John Rennie's beautiful Waterloo Bridge, which had been built in the early part of the 19th century, began to show signs of structural weakness in 1923. In 1934 demolition work began, and the old bridge was replaced by

the present structure in 1939. It was designed by the architect Sir G G Scott and is considered to be the most graceful bridge in London.

## Blackfriars Bridge
Central map: page 11, K6

This bridge, designed by James Cubitt in 1899, replaced an 18th-century structure. Its name is derived from the Dominican Priory which once stood nearby. Beneath the bridge the Fleet River — which runs below the streets of London for almost its entire length — can be seen flowing from a culvert into the Thames.

## Southwark Bridge
Central map: page 12, L6

Sir Ernest George designed this undistinguished bridge in 1919. Many archaeological finds have been made on the north bank of the river here. They include Roman artifacts and the foundations of Baynard's Castle, a Norman fortress originally built by one of William the Conqueror's followers. It was demolished and rebuilt several times, and the site was not finally cleared until the 1880s.

## London Bridge
Central map: page 12, M6

London Bridge was first built in stone between 1176 and 1209. It became almost a town on its own, having houses, shops, a chapel, fortified gates, and even water mills built upon it. All the buildings were pulled down in 1760, and the bridge itself was replaced in 1832 as it was rapidly being eroded away. The present structure dates from 1968, at which time its predecessor was dismantled stone by stone and reassembled in Lake Havasu City in Arizona, USA.

## Tower Bridge
Central map: page 6, N5

This fairy-tale structure, with its Gothic towers, steel lattice-work footbridge and road drawbridge was designed by Sir John Barry and Isambard Kingdom Brunel in 1886-94. It was opened by the then Prince of Wales. The twin bascules, or drawbridges, weighing 1,100 tons each, were operated by four steam hydraulic engines until 1975, when these were replaced by electric motors as they had become uneconomical. The 142ft-high glass-covered walkway is open to the public (see page 105).

TOWER BRIDGE

# ROYAL AND PUBLIC PARKS

A touch of countryside in London

# The Royal Parks

### Bushy Park

*District map,*
*page 168, B2*
☏ *081-979 1586*

*Open: all year 7am —*
*½ hour before dusk*
*(vehicles 6.30 —*
*midnight)* 🚗♿

Hampton Court Road separates its namesake park from less formal acres of Bushy Park, an engagingly pastoral area that recreates the seeming randomness of the real countryside. With one notable exception, that is — Sir Christopher Wren's magnificent Chestnut Avenue. This superb double row of enormous trees is best seen in spring, when the candle-like blooms form a frothy pink and white line that bisects the park from north to south.

Close to the Hampton Court end of the avenue is the Diana Fountain, which once stood in the grounds of the great house, but now marks the junction of the chestnut way with an avenue of limes. The latter is a smooth, formal highway through an otherwise wild part of the park.

North of the limes is the Longford River. Although it looks entirely natural, it was in fact built on the order of Charles I to supply Hampton Court with water, and still feeds many of the park's water features. At one point it flows through the mature woodland and picturesque glades of Waterhouse Plantation, where it hurls itself over an artificial ledge in the heart of one of the most beautiful rural retreats in the country.

Most visitors to the park congregate near the cricket ground and children's playground — both well worth visiting, but not to the exclusion of all else. Bushy House, a handsome 18th-century building, contains the National Physical Laboratory.

### Green Park

*Central map,*
*page 3, G5*
☏ *071-930 1793*

*Open: 5am — midnight*

This is indeed a green park. Its close turf, graduating towards a more carefree rankness round the roots of lovely old trees, might have been borrowed from the sheep-cropped slopes of the Sussex Downs. There are no flower beds, though in springtime the grass is sprinkled with the flowers of daffodils and crocuses. There is no visible water in the park, but the Tyburn Stream flows just beneath the surface and is the reason for the park's verdancy.

Just across the thin tarmac boundary of The Mall is St James's Park, but even without the road the two

GREEN PARK.

areas would be distinct from one another. It is easy to forget their shared history in picturesque St James's, where the magical combination of water and flowers masks the memory of violent crimes that have been enacted on its lawns. In the slightly severe greenness of Green Park, however, stories of past events spring easily to mind.

The ghosts of duellists battle in the damp shadows of the trees at twilight, the slightest breeze entices an almost human sigh from the gnarled plane tree near Piccadilly, and occasionally the setting sun turns patches of grass an unsettling red.

The times of violence have gone from the park now, along with Charles II's constitutional stroll that gave its name to Constitution Hill, and the walls of the ice house that he built to keep his wines cool in summer.

## Greenwich Park, Greenwich

*District map,
page 169, 36 E3
☎081-858 2608*

*Open: Summer 7am —
dusk, winter 7am — 6pm*
🖥♿

It is difficult to consider Greenwich Park without involving the magnificent Wren buildings that rise from the foot of the valley. It is a matter of taste; those interested in architecture will find the park an apt foil to those masterly designs, while other might thank providence that they complement rather than spoil the Thames-side greenness lapping at their walls.

The park was enclosed in medieval times, used as a hunting chase by the Tudor monarchs, and formalised by the Stuarts. Several tumuli, traces of a Roman villa, and records of a castle demolished by Charles II show that the area now occupied by the park was inhabited fairly constantly from prehistoric times.

The most extensive changes were made by the great French landscaper Le Nôtre, who was commissioned by Charles II. His love of symmetry, and of the straight line opposed by the curve, is very much in keeping with another of the park's aspects — as a place of science. Here stood the old Royal Observatory, now pensioned off as a museum, and here also is the Meridian — a stone-set strip of brass that marks zero degrees longitude, the point on which such measurements all around the world are based.

Away from all this, in the park's eastern corner, is the Wilderness, 13 acres of bracken and wild flowers inhabited by a herd of red and fallow deer. Close by is a delightful flower garden. Everywhere there are trees, and the sense of not being far from running water. On the park's northern perimeter near the Ranger's House is the largest children's playground in any of the Royal Parks. Sports facilities include rugby, cricket, hockey, tennis and a putting green. In the centre of the park is the historic 20ft stump of Queen Elizabeth's Oak. (see also Old Royal Observatory, page 97)

### Hampton Court

*District map,*
*page 19, B2*
📞*081-977 1328*

*Open: Gardens and*
*grounds daily, summer*
*7am — 9pm (or dusk),*
*winter 9am — dusk.*
🖥 ♿ *shop*

Before Macadam made the biggest single revolution in road building since the Romans, the River Thames was the main access to London. That, and the sylvan beauty of its wild valley, must have been the deciding factors in Cardinal Wolsey's choice of site for Hampton Court, the most magnificent house of the Tudor age.

Nestling inside an elbow of Britain's premier river is an outstanding collection of formal gardens and little architectural conceits — stunning herbaceous borders and long, shaded walks lined by ancient trees. The combination of flowers, statues, and fountains in the Privy Garden is considered to show formal gardening at its very best, and the heady breath of the elaborate Herb Garden intoxicates the senses.

There is water here too. The magnificent Long Water was created by Charles II in French-canal style, and the very old Pond Garden demonstrates that strange, botanical no-man's land between dry and submerged habitats.

The Rose Garden grows in what was once the hoof-hammered lists of Henry VIII's Tiltyard, and the modern Knot Garden recreates the almost tortured complexity that was sought after by gardeners during the 16th century.

Above all Hampton Court is a place of opposites, contrasts that are summed up in just two of its features — the charming Wilderness dell which is surrounded by a carpet of daffodils in springtime and the geometric perfections of the famous Maze. (See also Hampton Court Palace, page 86)

### Hyde Park

*Central map, page 2,*
*E5, F5*
📞*071-262 5484*

*Open: 5am — midnight*

Hyde Park merges imperceptibly with Kensington Gardens, which makes it seem a lot larger than it is, but there is a marked character difference between the two parks.

Before Henry VIII enclosed the area as a hunting chase, the park was a wild tract of countryside that once formed part of a vast primeval forest. It was watered by the little River Westbourne, a tributary of the Thames. After it was dammed to form the enchanting Serpentine lake the Westbourne vanished underground.

LION GATE, HAMPTON COURT.

The Serpentine is undoubtedly the main feature of the park. It is the habitat of wild creatures that find scant sanctuary elsewhere in the city centre. It is also a source of pleasure to humankind, a large silvery flatness that rests easily on the eye and murmurs to the dip of oars or the swish of sailing dinghies. Its shrub-covered islands are the homes of breeding waterfowl, sanctuaries guarded from the tread of man. At the eastern end of the Serpentine is the Dell, often considered the park's most picturesque feature. At its centre is a large block of granite called the Standing Stone; it is in fact all that remains of a 19th-century drinking fountain.

Here the horse is still welcome, whether it be of the King's Troop of the Royal Horse Artillery come to fire a salute, or a civilian out for a casual canter along the *Route du Roi* — now known as Rotten Row. There was once an enclosure in the park called The Tour where courtiers drove a circular route in an ostentatious parade of fashion. Ever since the Stuart Kings threw open the gates, Hyde has been a people's park. Its history is one of gaiety, of racing and sports, folk dancing, and minor self indulgence. This spirit of relaxed tolerance, of democratic freedom, is nowhere more typified than at Speaker's Corner. Here, at the Marble Arch corner of the park, anyone can stand up and say just what they please, so long as they can tolerate the remarks of their audience.

## Kensington Gardens

*Central map, page 2, D5*

☎ *071-262 5484*

*Open: dawn — dusk*

The boundary between Kensington Gardens and Hyde Park which were one and the same place before William III enclosed his palace garden, runs north to south across the Serpentine Bridge. Both parks have the Serpentine waters in common, though in Kensington Gardens it is called The Long Water.

It is not until the walker has penetrated some distance into the gardens that the individual characteristics of the areas become apparent.

The gardens become more orderly. The manicured greenery of Hyde Park gives way to colourful regimentation. Avenues of trees shade the pathways, and sculpture adds excitement to the views. Kensington Palace is the focal point providing a dignity characterised by the unmistakable workmanship of Sir Christopher Wren, which can be glimpsed through a cloak of trees. The beautiful sunken gardens round the rectangular pond in front of the palace is the culmination.

There is fantasy here too. In the children's playground the pixies and other small creatures of Ivor Innes' imagination rampage over the Elphin Oak in the frozen motion of carved wood near playground swings donated by the writer J M Barrie. A statue of Barrie's eternal youth Peter Pan stands beside The Long Water, and serves as a reminder of his enchanting story, much of which is set in the gardens. The tranquillity of

Kensington Gardens is as deliberate as its formality; note the 'sail only' rule for model boats on the Round Pond. Monthly exhibitions of contemporary art are held in the Serpentine Gallery under the auspices of the Arts Council.

### Primrose Hill

*Central map, page 9, F9*
*℡071-486 7905*

*Open: at all times*

Once part of the same hunting forest as its neighbour Regent's Park, Primrose Hill retains in its name the rural character that it undoubtedly had in the past. It lost a great deal of charm during World War II, when it was cleared and used for allotments, but it is gradually recovering its attractiveness. The view from the summit is panoramic and encompasses virtually the whole of central London.

The hill's height made it prominent in the otherwise flat farmland that surrounded it, and it became an obvious place for the quenching of revenge by dark deed or duel.

In 1842 it gained gaslights, a gymnasium, and respectability as a Royal Park. It also gained a fence to keep the public out, but nowadays its 62 acres are open to anybody wishing to enjoy them.

### Regent's Park

*Central map, page 9, F9*
*℡071-486 7905*

*Open: 5am — dusk*

After the execution of Charles I, the great royal hunting ground of Marylebone Park fell into the hands of Oliver Cromwell, who sold its timber and deer to pay his war debts. Further erosion occurred when Charles II sold leases on the ground to various noblemen, and it was not until the early 19th century that any attempt was made to regain what had been lost. Then, however, it became part of the Prince Regent's grand design for a vast neo-classical redevelopment under the talented hand of John Nash — hence 'Regent's' Park. Nash's original plans were never completed. That would have meant building on the park itself, and the Prince Regent decided that the open space was preferable to more development. The focus of the overall design was the Inner Circle. This now encloses the lovely Queen Mary's Garden, which has an attractive little lake, cascades of delicate and many-hued rockery plants, and one of the most beautiful rose gardens in the capital.

The subterranean Tyburn River fills the lake and pours into the boating pond from the only visible stretch on its route to the Thames.

PRIMROSE HILL.

The park's other waterway, the Regent's Canal, makes a much more definite impact on the landscape. A pleasure-boat service carries passengers to Regent's Park Zoo from the terminal in Little Venice. The elegant charm of the park is enhanced by several Victorian garden ornaments, notably two large flower vases on the Broad Walk. Near the lake is a group of fossil tree trunks which are the only surviving reminders that the Royal Botanical Gardens were once situated here. The park has an open-air theatre (Shakespeare), and the public amenities include playing fields, swings, rowing boats and cafés.
(See also London Zoo, page 92, and canal trips, page 29).

### Richmond Park

*District map, page 168, B2*
*☎081-948 3209*

*Open: dawn — ½ hour before dusk*
🚻♿

This vast tract of virtually wild countryside on the very doorstep of London's urban sprawl remains from an ancient forest that once covered much of southern England.

Charles I enclosed the park area as part of a royal estate, and successive monarchs have shaped the land to suit their hunting needs. The deer that they so avidly sought no longer display the furtive timidness of the hunted. Instead they wander unharmed among copses and spinneys high above the Thames Valley, and are not averse to bullying the picnicking tourist into parting with a sandwich or two. In sharp contrast is King Henry VIII's Mound, built so that the monarch could watch the slaughter of the deer. This area has been fenced off and is an informal garden with a look-out area on the mound.

In the 18th century severe restrictions on public access to Richmond Park were imposed by the Crown, but — thanks to a brewer called John Lewis — today's public can wander there at will. Lewis fought to preserve a public right of way through the park, and won.

A formal garden can be seen at Pembroke Lodge, and the various plantations show a wealth of exotic shrubs and wild flowers. Model sail boats are allowed on Adam's Pond, where the deer drink, and 18-acre Pen Ponds have been specially made for angling (a fishing permit is required).

RICHMOND PARK

### St James's Park

*Central map, page 4,*
*H5*
*☎071-930 1793*

*Open: 5am — midnight*

Here, on the fringe of one of London's busiest shopping and entertainment centres, is a green oasis of peace.

St James's is a reminder of the countryside, a great contrast to the city greyness that surrounds it. In autumn it is one of the few places in the West End where the commuter can see the first frosts; in summer it is full of relaxing office workers, many of whom have made a habit of feeding the park's flourishing population of birds.

Medieval St James's was a vastly different place, a brooding, marshy waste where the morning breeze stirred mist round a hospital for female lepers. Things changed in the 16th century when Henry VIII swept away the hospital, built St James's Palace and converted the surrounding area into a deer park. The Stuart Kings drained the marsh and formed the lake, and Charles II transformed the land into a Versailles-type formal garden. At this time the lake was a featureless strip known as the Canal, but it was waterscaped in 1828 when the great architect John Nash was employed to remodel the park. Today pleasant walks and paths thread through a mixture of flower borders, shrubs and trees. The nucleus of the park is formed by the lake, which is almost oriental in flavour with its fringe of weeping willows and resident ornamental ducks floating serenely upon it. Duck Island in the centre provides a lush haven for water birds, the most famous being the pelicans which parade its banks with a proprietory air.

# The Public Parks

### Battersea Park, SW11

*Central map, page 3,*
*F1*
*☎081-871 7530*
*Open: 7.30am — dusk*

This Victorian park is set around a large lake, ideal for fishing and boating. Attractions include the London Peace Pagoda, an 'old English' garden, fountain displays and a deer park. There are many recreational facilities including for the children, a zoo, playground, 1 o'clock club and an adventure playground.

### Crystal Palace Park, SE19

*District map, page 169, E2*
*☎081-778 7148*

*Open: Park, summer 7.30am — dusk, winter 8am — dusk.*
*Sport facilities, boating, pony rides: admission charge. Children's zoo, adventure playground and park: admission free.*

This 200-acre park is named after the huge glass-and-iron structure that was built in 1851 for the Great Exhibition. It was moved here from Hyde Park in 1854, and destroyed by fire in 1936. Situated in the park, whose hillside site commands extensive views, is the National Sports Centre, housing Britain's premier athletics stadium. The only survivors of the Great Exhibition are the life-sized models of prehistoric creatures which are to be found on an island in the lake. These brightly-coloured denizens are perennial favourites with children and photographers.

PREHISTORIC ANIMALS, CRYSTAL PALACE PARK.

### Holland Park, W8

*Central map, page 1,A4*
☎*071-603 3498*

*Open: 7am — dusk*

Less than 30 years ago Holland Park was the garden of a private house, and even now it retains that air of intimacy that is so peculiar to the inviolate. Its flock of peacocks mount guard for long-gone inhabitants of the house, and visitors stroll on smooth lawns where open-air Kensington tea parties may have been held not too many summers ago.

In the 18th and 19th centuries the house here was a popular meeting place for the literary and political personalities of the day. Only part of it now faces across the elegant quadrangle that it once dominated, but it is easy to imagine the intellectuals of the time threading through lighted rooms at the end of a summer evening. Macauley called Holland Park the 'Favourite resort of wits and beauties, painters and poets, scholars, philosophers, and statesmen'. Such people, jaded by the effort of creation or wearied by their excursions into the labyrinthine politics of high social life, must have found the park easy on the eye and relaxing to the mind.

That feeling remains, though the sparkling company and locked gates have gone. In springtime the Dutch and Iris Gardens are a constant delight to the visitor — especially the person who has unexpectedly stumbled upon this strange little haven while lost in the masonry heart of Kensington. Also here is a *yucca* garden, where the Mexican *yucca* plant guards its delicate clusters of white flowers with bunches of spearlike leaves.

A new major attraction to Holland Park is the Japanese 'Kyoto' garden, constructed as part of the '1991 Japan Year' celebrations. The northern part of the park however has been left as a semi-natural woodland for the benefit of wildlife. Recreational facilities include an adventure playground for older children, a toddlers' playground, tennis courts and a football pitch.

### Kew Gardens, Kew (Royal Botanic Gardens)

*District map,
page 168, B3*
📞 *081-940 1171*

*Open: Gardens daily
9.30am to between 4 &
6.30pm on weekdays,
between 4 & 8pm Sun &
B H, depending on the
time of sunset. Some
buildings close lunchtime.
(Closed Xmas day & New
Year's day.)
Admission charge.*
🏪♿ *shop 🐕 (ex guide
dogs)*

London Zoo may be the showcase of the animal kingdom, but when it comes to plants there is nowhere to beat the Royal Botanic Gardens at Kew. Here, firmly established on 300 acres of Thames-side London, are exotics from all over the world — the mice and the mammoths of botany.

The garden's facilities for research are unrivalled, but it is not as a purely scientific establishment that Kew is known. The great beauty and strangeness of its charges are part of London legend, and its earthen 'laboratory' beds have been laid out to be pleasing to the eye.

The first nine acres of gardens were laid out by George III's mother, Princess Augusta, some 200 years ago, and they really began to flourish during the reign of her son. Their present-day success is largely due to the eminent 19th-century botanist Sir Joseph Banks, a close friend of the king, who worked with Head Gardener William Aiton to lay the basis for the superb collection that now exists. Royal patronage continued, even after the gardens came into public ownership in 1841. Today's visitors can be thankful for this as they enjoy the conserved wildness of the Queen's Cottage and grounds — a gift from Queen Victoria.

The largest living collection in the gardens is the

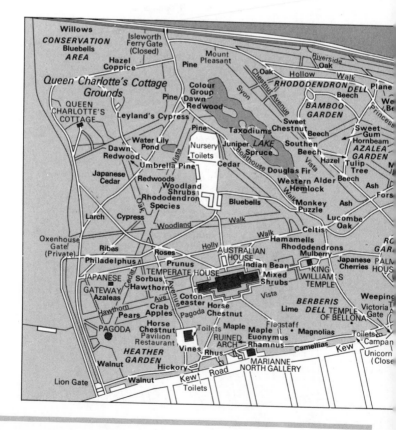

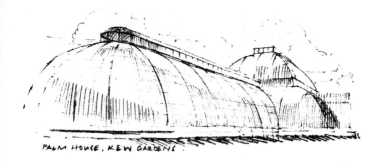

PALM HOUSE, KEW GARDENS

Arboretum, where many species of trees and shrubs grow harmoniously. The Palm House is the most elegant: an early example of glass and wrought iron. The most famous landmark is perhaps the Chinese Pagoda; it stands 163ft high in ten storeys. In 1987 The Princess of Wales Tropical Conservatory was opened, housing specimens from the wet and dry tropics. An all year round attraction is the Alpine House with over 3,000 mountain plants, including specimens from the Arctic to the Andes.
(See also Kew Palace and Queen Charlotte's Cottage, page 90).

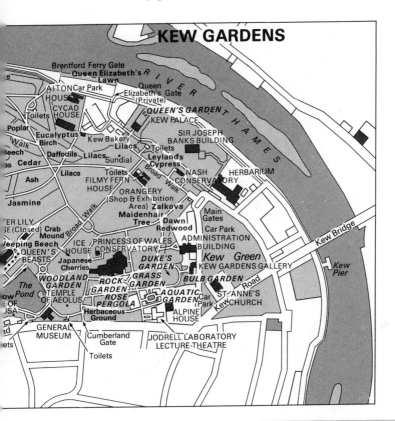

# KEW GARDENS

### Osterley Park, Osterley

District map,
page 168, 38, B3
☎081-560 3918

Open: daily 10am — 8pm
or sunset if earlier.

Osterley is indeed a 'green lung' for London, or at least for the city's heavily built-up western suburbs. Nearby the M4 motorway carries its never-ending metallic stream into the warrens of the capital, growling to itself in a constant monotone of labouring car and lorry engine. Yet nothing detracts from the park.

Its delightfully informal landscape preserves the character and tranquillity of the English countryside. The 120 acres of level ground that it covers have been cleverly and sympathetically landscaped so that the flatness is not apparent. Trees have been planted singly and in copses to break the lie of the land still further, and the whole is complemented by enchanting lakes.

Osterley House — the reason for all this carefully contrived rurality — stands amid smooth lawns and fragrant stands of old cedars (see page 97).

The house and park complement each other well. Adam's elegant lines rise grandly from the formal gardens laid out around the house, throwing the 'wild' parkland into a rugged relief that it might not have achieved on its own.

### Syon Park, Isleworth

District map,
page 168, 47, B3
☎081-560 0881

Open: Apr — Oct daily
10am-6pm; Nov — Mar
10am-dusk. (Closed
Xmas). Conservatory
closed during Winter
months.
Admission charge.
☐(licensed)
& (gardens only) shop
garden centre ✖

Close to Kew Gardens in spirit, but divided from it by the waters of the Thames, is Syon Park — the country's first national gardening centre.

Its horticultural reputation goes back to the 16th century, when the use of trees as purely decorative contributions to its layout was looked upon with amazement. The park that exists today, however, is the work of that master of landscape design — 'Capability' Brown. As such it is a valuable cultural record, as well as a beautiful retreat from the bustle of modern town life.

There is water in plenty. The capital's major artery flows sedately past the 16th-century exterior of Syon House, and the picturesque lake supports large colonies of water-loving plants.

The focal point of Syon, if not the house, must certainly be the Great Conservatory. This vast crescent of metal and glass, with small pavilions at either end and a lofty central dome, was the first construction of its type in the world. It was also the inspiration for the ill-fated Crystal Palace, but apart from all this it houses one of the finest private collections of tropical plants in the country. It is the only place in Britain where the coconut palm has reached full maturity.

A particularly beautiful — if somewhat overwhelming — feature of the park is the six-acre Rose Garden.

There is also a butterfly house and the largest garden centre in England. Admittance to the house and park is by separate entrances. (See also Syon House and Heritage Motor Museum, page 103).

# CENTRAL LONDON

## ey to map pages

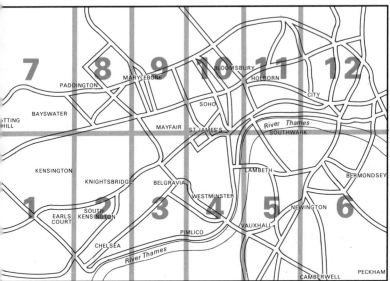

## egend

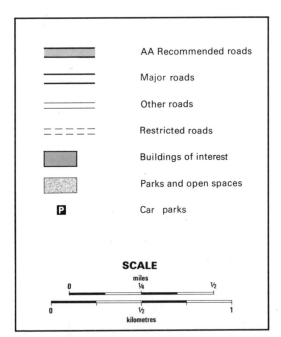

AA Recommended roads

Major roads

Other roads

Restricted roads

Buildings of interest

Parks and open spaces

P  Car parks

### SCALE
miles

kilometres

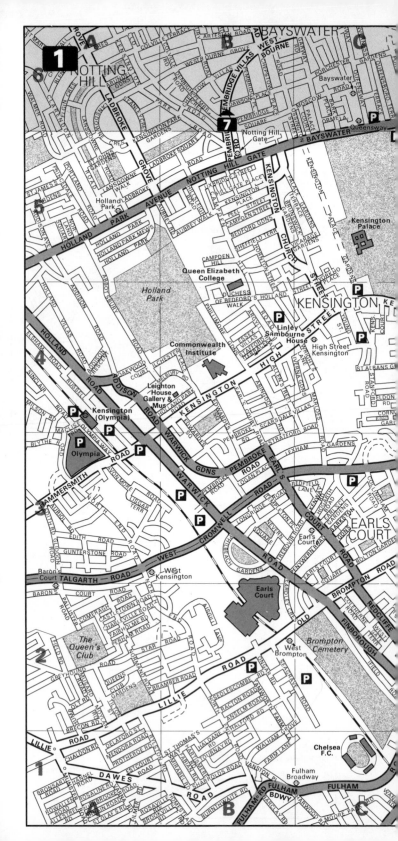

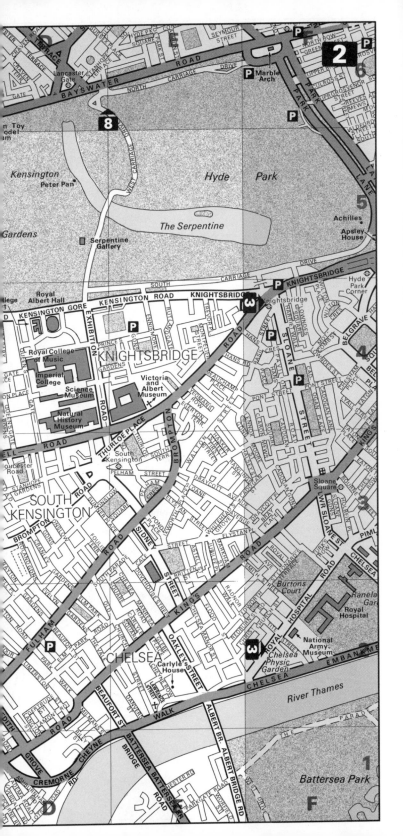

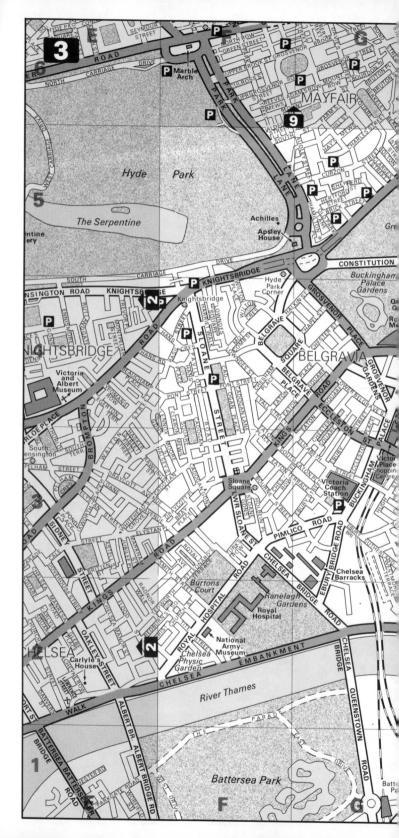

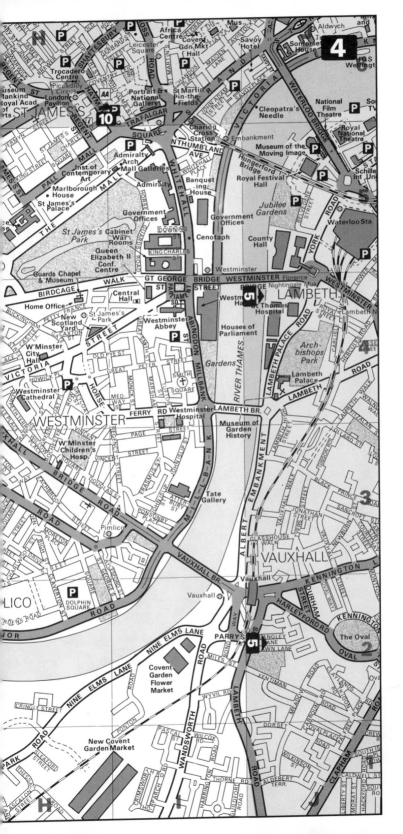

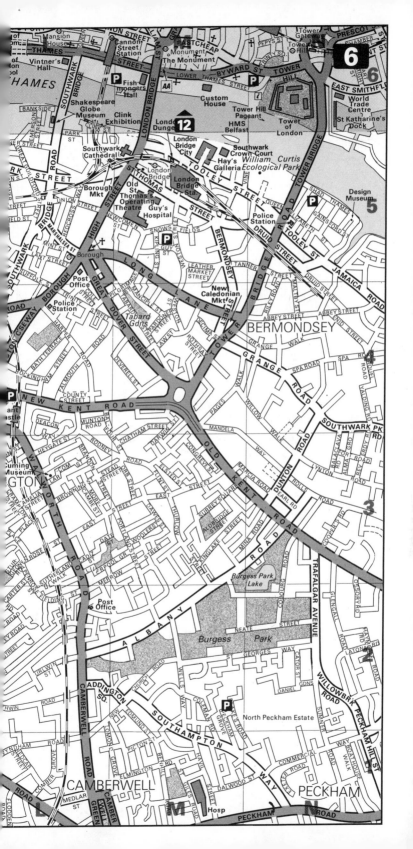

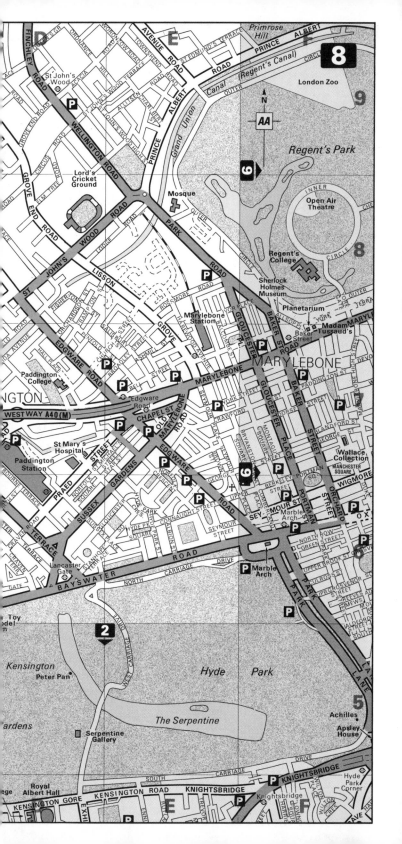

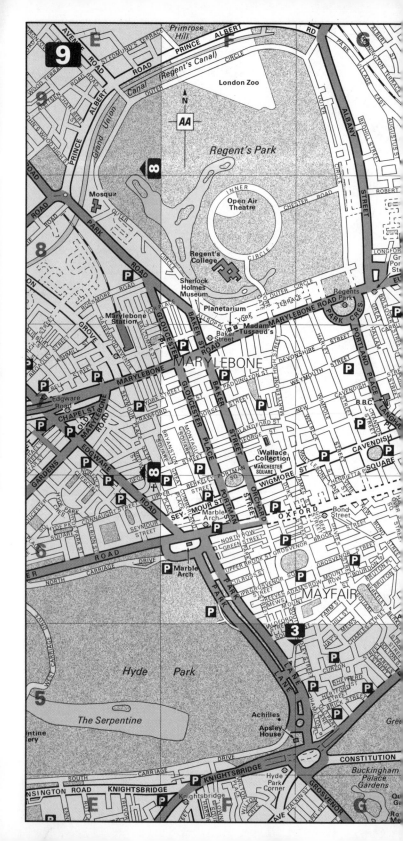

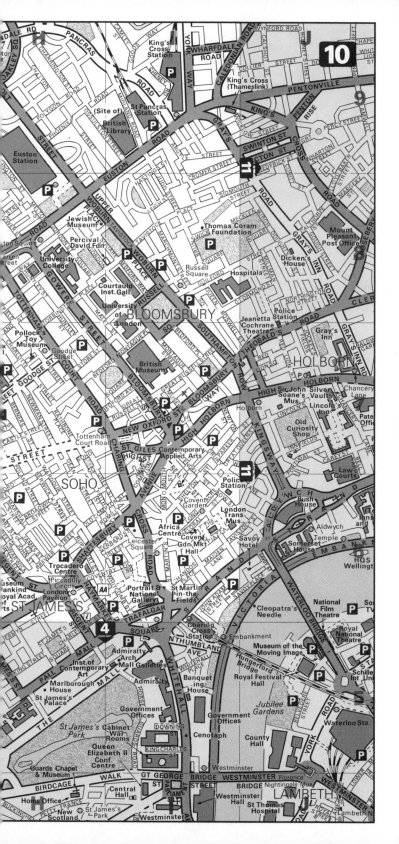

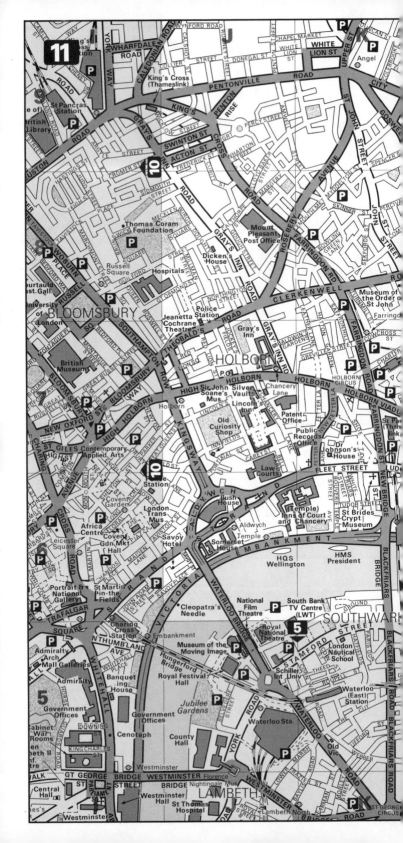

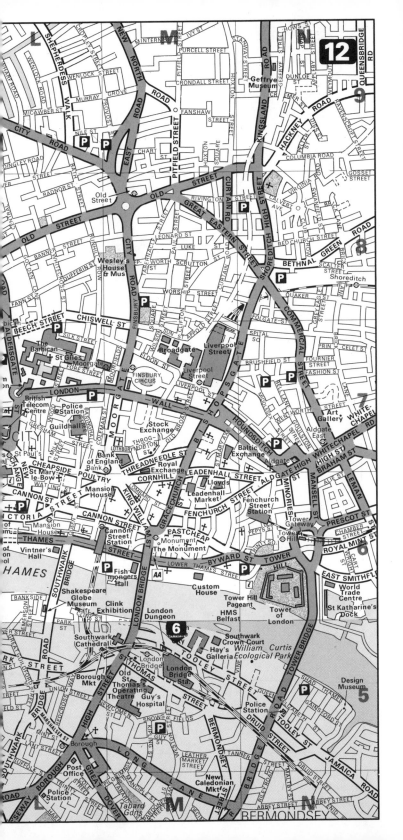

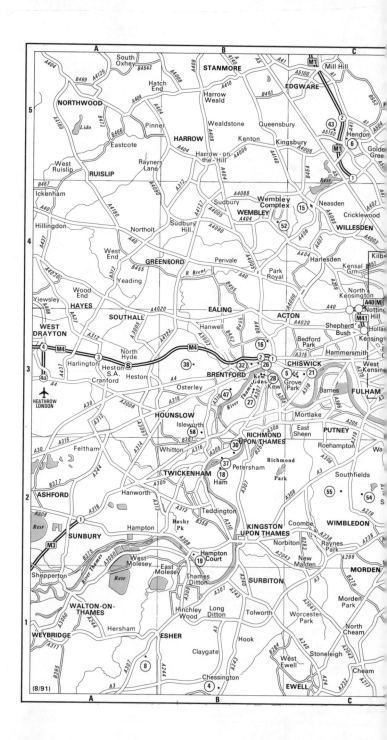

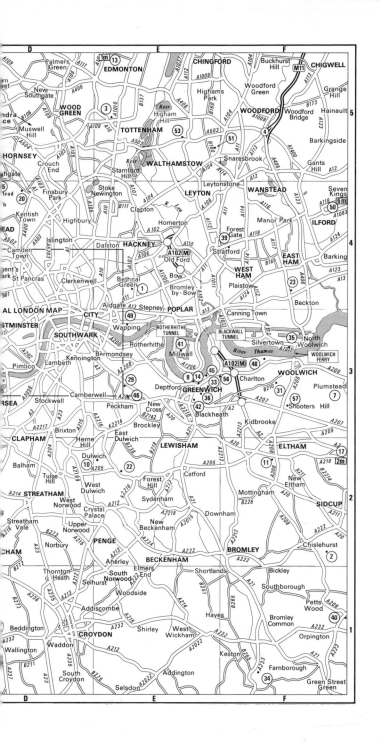

## STREET INDEX
## CENTRAL LONDON

### A

| | Map Ref. | Page |
|---|---|---|
| Abbey Road | C9-D9 | 7/8 |
| Abbey Street | N4 | 6 |
| Abbotsbury Road | A4 | 1 |
| Abercorn Place | C9-D9 | 7/8 |
| Abermarle Street | G6 | 9 |
| Abingdon Road | B4 | 1 |
| Abingdon Street | I4 | 4 |
| Acacia Road | D9-E9 | 8 |
| Acklam Road | A7 | 7 |
| Acton Street | J9 | 11 |
| Adam's Row | F6-G6 | 9 |
| Addington Square | L2 | 6 |
| Addison Avenue | A5 | 1 |
| Addison Crescent | A4 | 1 |
| Addison Road | A4 | 1 |
| Albany Road | M2-N3 | 6 |
| Albany Street | G8-G9 | 9 |
| Albert Bridge | E1-E2 | 2 |
| Albert Bridge Road | E1 | 2 |
| Albert Embankment | I3-J3 | 4/5 |
| Albert Road | A9-B9 | 7 |
| Albert Street | G9 | 9 |
| Alberta Street | K3 | 6 |
| Albion Street | E6 | 8 |
| Aldbridge Street | M3 | 6 |
| Aldebert Terrace | J1 | 5 |
| Alderney Street | G3-H3 | 3/4 |
| Aldersgate Street | L7 | 12 |
| Aldford Street | F6 | 9 |
| Aldgate High Street | N6-N7 | 12 |
| Aldwych | J6 | 11 |
| Alexander Street | B6-B7 | 7 |
| Alie Street | N6-N7 | 12 |
| Allen Street | B4 | 1 |
| Allestree Road | A1 | 1 |
| Allitsen Road | E9 | 8 |
| Alisop Place | F7-F8 | 9 |
| Alma Grove | N3 | 6 |
| Amelia Street | L3 | 6 |
| Amwell Street | J9 | 11 |
| Anselm Road | B2 | 1 |
| Appleby Street | N9 | 12 |
| Appold Street | M7-M8 | 12 |
| Argyle Street | I9 | 10 |
| Argyll Road | B4 | 1 |
| Argyll Street | H6 | 10 |
| Artesian Road | B6 | 7 |
| Arundel Gardens | A6 | 7 |
| Ascalon Street | H1 | 4 |
| Ash Mill Street | E7 | 8 |
| Ashmore Road | A8 | 7 |
| Ashworth Road | C8 | 7 |
| Astell Street | E3 | 2 |
| Atterbury Street | I3 | 4 |
| Aubrey Road | B5 | 1 |
| Aubrey Walk | B5 | 1 |
| Augustus Street | G9 | 9 |
| Avenue Road | E9 | 8 |
| Avonmore Road | A3 | 1 |
| Aylesford Street | H3-I2 | 4 |

### B

| | Map Ref. | Page |
|---|---|---|
| Baker Street | F7 | 9 |
| Balaclava Road | N3 | 6 |
| Balcombe Street | E7 | 8 |
| Baldwin's Gardens | J7-K7 | 11 |
| Balfour Street | L4-M3 | 6 |
| Bankside | L6 | 12 |
| Banner Street | L8 | 12 |
| Barclay Road | B1 | 1 |
| Bark Place | C6 | 7 |
| Barkston Gardens | C3 | 1 |
| Baron's Court Road | A2 | 1 |
| Basil Street | F4 | 3 |
| Basinghall Street | L7 | 12 |

| | Map Ref. | Page |
|---|---|---|
| Bath Street | L8-L9 | 12 |
| Bath Terrace | L4 | 6 |
| Battersea Bridge | E1 | 2 |
| Battersea Bridge Road | E1 | 2 |
| Battersea Park Road | G1-H1 | 3/4 |
| Baylis Road | K4 K5 | 5 |
| Bayswater Road | D6-E6 | 8 |
| Beak Street | H6 | 10 |
| Bear Lane | K5 | 6 |
| Beauchamp Place | E4 | 2 |
| Beaufort Street | D2-E2 | 2 |
| Bedford Avenue | I7 | 10 |
| Bedford Gardens | B5 | 1 |
| Bedford Place | I7 | 10 |
| Bedford Square | H7-I7 | 10 |
| Bedford Way | I8 | 10 |
| Beech Street | L7-L8 | 12 |
| Belgrave Place | F4-G4 | 3 |
| Belgrave Road | G3-H3 | 3/4 |
| Belgrave Square | F4 | 3 |
| Bell Lane | N7 | 12 |
| Bell Street | E7 | 8 |
| Bell Yard | J7 | 11 |
| Belvedere Road | J5 | 5 |
| Benhill Road | M1 | 6 |
| Berkeley Square | G6 | 9 |
| Berkeley Street | G5-G6 | 9 |
| Bermondsey Street | M4-M5 | 6 |
| Berners Street | H7 | 10 |
| Berwick Street | H6 | 10 |
| Bethnal Green | N8 | 12 |
| Bethwin Road | L2 | 6 |
| Bevington Road | A7 | 7 |
| Birdcage Walk | H4 | 4 |
| Bishop's Bridge Road | C6-C7-D7 | 7 |
| Bishopsgate | M7 | 12 |
| Black Prince Road | J3 | 5 |
| Blackfriars Bridge | K6 | 11 |
| Blackfriars Road | K4-K5 | 5 |
| Blake's Road | M2 | 6 |
| Blandford Street | F7 | 9 |
| Blenheim Crescent | A6 | 7 |
| Blomfield Road | C7-D7 | 7/8 |
| Bloomsbury Street | I7 | 10 |
| Bloomsbury Way | I7 | 10 |
| Blythe Road | A3 | 1 |
| Boathouse Walk | N1 | 6 |
| Bolsover Street | G7-G8 | 9 |
| Bolton Crescent | K2 | 5 |
| Bolton Gardens | G3 | 3 |
| Bolton Street | G5 | 3 |
| Bond Way | I2 | 4 |
| Borough High Street | L4-L5 | 6 |
| Borough Road | K4-L4 | 6 |
| Boswell Street | I8-I7 | 10 |
| Bourdon Street | G6 | 9 |
| Bourne Street | F3 | 3 |
| Bourne Terrace | C7 | 7 |
| Bouverie Street | K6 | 11 |
| Bow Street | I6 | 10 |
| Bowling Green Lane | K8 | 11 |
| Braganza Street | K3-L3 | 5/6 |
| Bramber Road | A2-B2 | 1 |
| Brandon Street | L3 | 6 |
| Bravington Road | A8 | 7 |
| Bray Place | F3 | 3 |
| Bressenden Place | G4-H4 | 3/4 |
| Brewer Street | H6 | 10 |
| Brick Lane | N7-N8 | 12 |
| Brick Street | G5 | 3 |
| Bridge Street | I4 | 4 |
| Britten Street | E3 | 2 |
| Brixton Road | K1 | 5 |
| Broadley Street | E7 | 8 |
| Broadwick Street | H6 | 10 |
| Brompton Road | E3-E4 | 2 |
| Brondesbury Road | A9-B9 | 7 |

| | Map Ref. | Page |
|---|---|---|
| Brondesbury Villas | B9 | 7 |
| Bronsart Road | A1 | 1 |
| Brook Drive | K4 | 5 |
| Brook Street | G6 | 9 |
| Brookville Road | A1 | 1 |
| Brown Street | E7 | 8 |
| Browning Street | L3 | 6 |
| Brunswick Gardens | B5-C5 | 1 |
| Brunswick Square | I8 | 10 |
| Brushfield Street | N7 | 12 |
| Bruton Place | G6 | 9 |
| Bruton Street | G6 | 9 |
| Bryanston Square | F7 | 9 |
| Buckingham Gate | G4-H4 | 3/4 |
| Buckingham Palace Road | G3-G4 | 3 |
| Bunhill Row | L8 | 12 |
| Burnthwaite Road | B1 | 1 |
| Byward Street | M6-N6 | 12 |

### C

| | Map Ref. | Page |
|---|---|---|
| Cadiz Street | L3 | 6 |
| Cadogan Gardens | F3 | 3 |
| Cadogan Lane | F4 | 3 |
| Cadogan Place | F4 | 3 |
| Cadogan Square | F3-F4 | 3 |
| Cadogan Street | F3 | 3 |
| Caldwell Street | J1-K1 | 5 |
| Cale Street | E3 | 2 |
| Caledonian Road | I9-J9 | 10/11 |
| Calshot Street | J9 | 11 |
| Calthorpe Street | J8 | 11 |
| Calvert Avenue | N8 | 12 |
| Cambridge Avenue | B9 | 7 |
| Cambridge Gardens | A6-A7 | 7 |
| Cambridge Street | G3-H3 | 3/4 |
| Camberwell Green | L1 | 6 |
| Camberwell Road | L1-L2 | 6 |
| Camberwell New Road | K2 | 5 |
| Camley Street | I9 | 10 |
| Cannon Street | L6-M6 | 12 |
| Carburton Street | G7-G8 | 9 |
| Cardigan Street | J3-K3 | 5 |
| Cardington Street | H8-H9 | 10 |
| Carey Street | J7 | 11 |
| Carlisle Lane | J4 | 5 |
| Carlisle Place | H4 | 4 |
| Carlton Hill | C9 | 7 |
| Carlton Vale | B9-C9 | 7 |
| Carlyle Square | E2 | 2 |
| Carnaby Street | H6 | 10 |
| Carroun Road | J1-J2 | 5 |
| Carter Lane | K6-L6 | 12 |
| Carter Street | L2-L3 | 6 |
| Cartwright Street | N6 | 12 |
| Castellain Road | C8 | 7 |
| Castle Lane | H4 | 4 |
| Castletown Road | A2 | 1 |
| Cathcart Road | C2 | 1 |
| Cator Street | N2 | 6 |
| Cavendish Square | G7 | 9 |
| Caxton Street | H4 | 4 |
| Central Street | L8-L9 | 12 |
| Chaldon Road | A1 | 1 |
| Chalton Street | H9 | 10 |
| Chamber Street | N6 | 12 |
| Chancery Lane | J7 | 11 |
| Chandos Place | I6 | 10 |
| Chandos Street | G7 | 9 |
| Chapel Market | J9-K9 | 11 |
| Chapel Street | G4 | 3 |
| Chapel Street | E7 | 8 |
| Chapter Road | L2 | 6 |
| Charing Cross Road | I6-I7 | 10 |
| Charlbert Street | E9 | 8 |
| Charles II Street | H5 | 4 |

| | Map Ref. | Page |
|---|---|---|
| Charles Street | G5 | 3 |
| Charleville Road | A2 | 1 |
| Charlotte Street | H7 | 10 |
| Charlwood Street | H3 | 4 |
| Charrington Street | H9 | 10 |
| Chart Street | M9 | 12 |
| Charterhouse Street | K7-L7 | 11/12 |
| Chatham Street | M3-M4 | 6 |
| Cheapside | L7 | 12 |
| Chelsea Bridge | G2 | 3 |
| Chelsea Bridge Road | F3-G2 | 3 |
| Chelsea Embankment | F2 | 3 |
| Chelsea Manor Street | E2 | 2 |
| Chelsea Square | E3-E2 | 2 |
| Chepstow Place | B6 | 7 |
| Chepstow Road | B6-B7 | 7 |
| Chepstow Villas | B6 | 7 |
| Chesham Place | F4 | 3 |
| Chester Road | F8-G8 | 9 |
| Chester Row | F3 | 3 |
| Chester Square | G3-G4 | 3 |
| Chester Street | G4 | 3 |
| Cheyne Row | E2 | 2 |
| Cheyne Walk | D1-E2 | 2 |
| Chilworth Street | D6 | 8 |
| Chippenham Road | B7-B8 | 7 |
| Chiswell Street | L8-M8 | 12 |
| Christchurch Street | F2 | 3 |
| Church Street | D7-E7 | 8 |
| Churchill Gardens Road | H2 | 4 |
| Circus Road | D9 | 8 |
| City Road | K9-L9 | 11/12 |
| Clabon Mews | F3-F4 | 3 |
| Clapham Road | J1-J2 | 5 |
| Clarendon Road | A5-A6 | 1/7 |
| Clarendon Street | G3-H3 | 3/4 |
| Clarges Street | G5 | 3 |
| Claverton Street | H2 | 4 |
| Claylands Road | J2 | 5 |
| Clayton Street | J2-K2 | 5 |
| Clerkenwell Road | J8-K8 | 11 |
| Cleveland Square | C6-D6 | 7 |
| Cleveland Street | G8-H7 | 9/10 |
| Cleveland Terrace | C6-D6-D7 | 7 |
| Clifford Street | G6-H6 | 9/10 |
| Clifton Gardens | C7-D8 | 7 |
| Clifton Hill | C9 | 7 |
| Clifton Street | M7-M8 | 12 |
| Clink Street | L6 | 12 |
| Clipstone Street | G7 | 9 |
| Club Row | N8 | 12 |
| Cobourg Road | N2-N3 | 6 |
| Cock Lane | K7 | 11 |
| Coin Street | K5 | 5 |
| Cole Street | L4 | 6 |
| Colebrooke Row | K9 | 11 |
| Coleherne Road | C2 | 1 |
| Coleman Road | M2 | 6 |
| Coleman Street | L7 | 12 |
| Collier Street | J9 | 11 |
| Collingham Road | C3 | 1 |
| Columbia Road | N9 | 12 |
| Colville Road | B6 | 7 |
| Colville Terrace | A6-B6 | 7 |
| Comber Grove | L1 | 6 |
| Comeragh Road | A2 | 1 |
| Commercial Street | N7-N8 | 12 |
| Commercial Way | N1 | 6 |
| Compton Street | K8 | 11 |
| Conduit Street | G6 | 9 |
| Congreve Street | M3 | 6 |
| Connaught Street | E6 | 8 |
| Constitution Hill | G5 | 3 |
| Conway Street | G8 H8 | 9/10 |
| Cooks Road | K2 L2 | 5/6 |
| Cooper's Road | N3 | 6 |
| Copperfield Street | L5 | 6 |

| | Map Ref. | Page |
|---|---|---|
| Cork Street | G6-H6 | 9/10 |
| Cornhill | M6 | 12 |
| Cornwall Crescent | A6 | 7 |
| Cornwall Gardens | C4 | 1 |
| Cornwall Road | K5 | 5 |
| Cosser Street | J4 | 5 |
| County Street | L5 | 6 |
| Courtenay Street | J3 | 5 |
| Courtfield Road | C3-D3 | 1 |
| Covent Garden | I6 | 10 |
| Coventry Street | H6-I6 | 10 |
| Cowan Street | M2 | 6 |
| Cowcross Street | K7 | 11 |
| Crampton Street | L3 | 6 |
| Cranley Gardens | D3 | 2 |
| Craven Hill | D6 | 8 |
| Craven Road | D6 | 8 |
| Craven Street | D6 | 8 |
| Craven Terrace | D6 | 8 |
| Crawford Street | E7-F7 | 8/9 |
| Cresswell Place | D2-D3 | 1/2 |
| Crewsdon Road | J1-K1 | 5 |
| Crimsworth Road | I1 | 4 |
| Cringle Street | H2 | 4 |
| Cromer Street | I8-I9 | 10 |
| Cromwell Road | B3-C3-D3 | 1/2 |
| Crondall Street | M9 | 12 |
| Cropley Street | L9 | 12 |
| Crowndale Road | H9 | 10 |
| Cubitt Street | J8-J9 | 11 |
| Culross Street | F6 | 9 |
| Cumberland Street | G3-H3 | 3/4 |
| Curtain Road | M8 | 12 |
| Curzon Street | G5 | 3 |

| | Map Ref. | Page |
|---|---|---|
| Dalwood Street | M1 | 6 |
| Danbury Street | K9-L9 | 12 |
| Dante Road | K3-K4 | 5/6 |
| Danvers Street | E2 | 2 |
| Dart Street | A8 | 7 |
| Darwin Street | M3-M4 | 6 |
| Dale Street | L3-M3 | 6 |
| Davies Street | G6 | 9 |
| Dawes Road | A1-B1 | 1 |
| Dawes Street | M3 | 6 |
| Dawson Place | B6 | 7 |
| De Laune Street | K2-K3 | 5 |
| De Vere Gardens | C4 | 1 |
| Deacon Way | L3-L4 | 6 |
| Dean Street | H6-H7 | 10 |
| Decima Street | M4 | 6 |
| Delaford Street | A1-A2 | 1 |
| Delamare Terrace | C7 | 7 |
| Delaware Road | C8 | 7 |
| Denbigh Road | B6 | 7 |
| Denbigh Street | H3 | 4 |
| Derry Street | C4 | 1 |
| Deverell Street | M4 | 6 |
| Devonshire Street | F7-G7 | 9 |
| Dingley Road | L9 | 12 |
| Diss Street | N9 | 12 |
| Doddington Grove | K2-K3 | 6 |
| Dolben Street | K5 | 5/6 |
| Dolphin Square | H2 | 4 |
| Donaldson Road | A9-B9 | 7 |
| Donegal Street | J9 | 11 |
| Dorset Road | J1 | 5 |
| Dorset Street | F7 | 9 |
| Doughty Street | J8 | 11 |
| Douglas Street | H3-I3 | 4 |
| Dovehouse Street | E2-E3 | 2 |
| Dover Street | G6 | 9 |
| Downing Street | I5 | 4 |
| Draycott Avenue | E3 | 2 |
| Draycott Place | F3 | 3 |
| Drayton Gardens | D2-D3 | 2 |
| Droop Street | A8 | 7 |
| Druid Street | N4-N5 | 6 |

| | Map Ref. | Page |
|---|---|---|
| Drummond Street | H8 | 10 |
| Drury Lane | I7-J6 | 10/11 |
| Dufferin Street | L8 | 12 |
| Duke Street | F6-G6 | 9 |
| Duncan Street | K9 | 11 |
| Dunton Road | N3 | 6 |
| Durham Street | J2 | 5 |

**E**

| | Map Ref. | Page |
|---|---|---|
| Eardley Crescent | B2 | 1 |
| Earl Road | N3 | 6 |
| Earls Court Road | B4-B3-C3 | 1 |
| Earls Court Square | C3 | 1 |
| Earls Court Gardens | C3 | 1 |
| East Drive | G1 | 3 |
| East Road | M8-M9 | 12 |
| East Row | A7-A8 | 7 |
| East Smithfield | N6 | 12 |
| East Street | L3-M3 | 6 |
| Eastbourne Terrace | D6-D7 | 8 |
| Eastcastle Street | H7 | 10 |
| Eastcheap | M6 | 12 |
| Eaton Place | F4-G4 | 3 |
| Eaton Place | F3 | 3 |
| Eaton Square | F4-G4 | 3 |
| Eaton Terrace | F3-G3 | 3 |
| Ebury Bridge Road | G2-G3 | 3 |
| Ebury Street | G3-G4 | 3 |
| Eccleston Place | G3-G4 | 3 |
| Eccleston Square | G3 | 3 |
| Eccleston Street | G3-G4 | 3 |
| Edgware Road | D7-E7 | 8 |
| Edith Grove | D1-D2 | 2 |
| Edith Road | A3 | 1 |
| Edmund Street | M2 | 6 |
| Egerton Terrace | E4 | 2 |
| Eldon Road | C4 | 1 |
| Eldon Street | M7 | 12 |
| Elgin Avenue | B8-C8 | 7 |
| Elgin Crescent | A6 | 7 |
| Elia Street | K9 | 11 |
| Elizabeth Street | G3 | 3 |
| Elkstone Road | A7 | 7 |
| Elliots Row | K4 | 6 |
| Elmington Road | M1 | 6 |
| Elm Park Gardens | D2 | 2 |
| Elm Park Road | D2-E2 | 2 |
| Elm Tree Road | D8-D9 | 8 |
| Elsham Road | A4 | 1 |
| Elsted Street | M3 | 6 |
| Elvaston Place | D4 | 1/2 |
| Elystan Place | E3 | 2 |
| Elystan Street | E3 | 2 |
| Emerson Street | L6 | 12 |
| Endell Street | I6-I7 | 10 |
| Enid Street | N4 | 6 |
| Ennismore Gardens | E4 | 2 |
| Epworth Street | M8 | 12 |
| Erasmus Street | I3 | 4 |
| Essendine Road | B8 | 7 |
| Essex Villas | B4 | 1 |
| Euston Road | G8-H8-I9 | 9/10 |
| Evelyn Gardens | D2 | 2 |
| Eversholt Street | H9 | 10 |
| Ewer Street | L5 | 6 |
| Exeter Street | N1 | 6 |
| Exhibition Road | C4 | 1 |
| Exmouth Market | K8 | 11 |

**F**

| | Map Ref. | Page |
|---|---|---|
| Fabian Road | B1 | 1 |
| Fairholme Road | A2 | 1 |
| Falmouth Road | L4 | 6 |
| Fann Street | L8 | 12 |
| Fanshaw Street | M9 | 12 |
| Farmer's Road | L1 | 6 |
| Farm Lane | B1 | 1 |
| Farm Street | G6 | 9 |
| Farringdon Road | K8-K7 | 11 |

| | Map Ref. | Page |
|---|---|---|
| Farringdon Street | K7 | 11 |
| Fashion Street | N7 | 12 |
| Fawcett Street | C2-D2 | 1 |
| Fenchurch Street | M6-N6 | 12 |
| Fentiman Road | J2 | 5 |
| Fernhead Road | A8 | 7 |
| Fernshaw Road | D1-D2 | 1/2 |
| Field Road | A2 | 1 |
| Fielding Street | L2 | 6 |
| Fifth Avenue | A8 | 7 |
| Finborough Road | C2 | 1 |
| Finchley Road | D9 | 8 |
| Finsbury Circus | M7 | 12 |
| Finsbury Square | M8 | 12 |
| First Avenue | A8 | 7 |
| First Street | E3 | 2 |
| Fisherton Street | D8 | 8 |
| Fitzalan Street | J4 | 5 |
| Fitzroy Street | H8 | 10 |
| Fleet Street | K7 | 11 |
| Fleming Road | K2 | 5 |
| Flint Street | M3 | 6 |
| Flodden Road | L1 | 6 |
| Flood Street | E2 | 2 |
| Floral Street | I6 | 10 |
| Foley Street | H7 | 10 |
| Folgate Street | N7-N8 | 12 |
| Fore Street | L7 | 12 |
| Formosa Street | C7 | 7 |
| Fort Road | N3 | 6 |
| Foulis Terrace | D3 | 2 |
| Fournier Street | N7 | 12 |
| Foxley Road | K1 | 5 |
| Frampton Street | D8 | 8 |
| Francis Street | H3-H4 | 4 |
| Frazier Street | J4-K4 | 5 |
| Frederick Street | J9 | 11 |
| Frith Street | H6 | 10 |
| Fulham Road | B1-C1-D2 | 1/2 |
| **G** | | |
| Gainsford Street | N5 | 12 |
| Garway Road | C6 | 7 |
| Gee Street | L8 | 12 |
| Geffrye Street | N9 | 12 |
| George Street | F7 | 9 |
| Gerrard Street | I6 | 10 |
| Gertrude Street | D2 | 2 |
| Gilbert Road | K3 | 5 |
| Gilbert Street | G6 | 9 |
| Gillingham Street | H3 | 4 |
| Gilston Road | D2 | 2 |
| Giltspur Street | K7 | 12 |
| Glasshouse Walk | J3 | 5 |
| Glebe Place | E2 | 2 |
| Glengall Road | N2 | 6 |
| Gliddon Road | A3 | 1 |
| Gloucester Place | F7 | 9 |
| Gloucester Road | D4-D3 | 1/2 |
| Gloucester Square | E6 | 8 |
| Gloucester Street | H3 | 4 |
| Gloucester Terrace | D6 | 7/8 |
| Gloucester Terrace | C7 | 7 |
| Golborne Road | A7 | 7 |
| Golden Lane | L8 | 12 |
| Goldney Road | B7 | 7 |
| Goodge Street | H7 | 10 |
| Goods Way | I9 | 10 |
| Gordon Square | H8 | 10 |
| Gordon Street | H8 | 10 |
| Gosfield Street | G7 | 9 |
| Gosling Way | K1 | 5 |
| Gossett Street | N8 | 12 |
| Goswell Road | K9-L8 | 12 |
| Gough Street | J8 | 11 |
| Goulston Street | N7 | 12 |
| Gower Street | H8 | 10 |
| Gracechurch Street | M6 | 12 |

| | Map Ref. | Page |
|---|---|---|
| Grafton Way | H8 | 10 |
| Graham Street | L9 | 12 |
| Grange Road | N4 | 6 |
| Grange Walk | N4 | 6 |
| Grantully Road | C8 | 7 |
| Gray's Inn Road | J8-J7 | 11 |
| Great Castle Street | G7 | 9 |
| Great Cumberland Place | F6 | 9 |
| Great Dover Street | L4-M4 | 6 |
| Great Eastern Street | M8-N8 | 12 |
| Great George Street | I4 | 4 |
| Great Guildford Street | L5 | 6 |
| Great Marlborough Street | H6 | 10 |
| Great Ormond Street | J8 | 11 |
| Great Percy Street | J9 | 11 |
| Great Peter Street | I4 | 4 |
| Great Portland Street | G7-G8 | 9 |
| Great Queen Street | I7-J7 | 10/11 |
| Great Russell Street | I7 | 10 |
| Great Smith Street | I4 | 4 |
| Great Suffolk Street | K5-L5 | 6 |
| Great Titchfield Street | G7-H7 | 9/10 |
| Great Western Road | B7 | 7 |
| Greek Street | H6-I6 | 10 |
| Green Street | F6 | 9 |
| Greencoat Place | H3-H4 | 4 |
| Grenville Place | C3-C4 | 1 |
| Gresham Street | L7 | 12 |
| Greville Place | C9 | 7 |
| Greville Road | C9 | 9 |
| Greville Street | K7 | 11 |
| Grey Eagle Street | N8 | 12 |
| Greycoat Street | H4 | 4 |
| Greyhound Road | A2 | 1 |
| Grosvenor Gardens | G4 | 3 |
| Grosvenor Place | G4 | 3 |
| Grosvenor Road | H2 | 4 |
| Grosvenor Square | F6-G6 | 9 |
| Grosvenor Street | G6 | 9 |
| Grosvenor Terrace | L2 | 6 |
| Grove End Road | D8 | 8 |
| Guildford Road | I1 | 4 |
| Guildford Street | I8-J8 | 10/11 |
| Gunter Grove | C2-D1 | 1 |
| Gunterstone Road | A3 | 1 |
| Guy Street | M5 | 6 |
| **H** | | |
| Hackford Road | J1 | 5 |
| Hackney Road | N9 | 12 |
| Haldane Road | B1 | 1 |
| Halford Road | B2 | 1 |
| Halkin Street | F4-G4 | 3 |
| Hall Place | D7 | 8 |
| Hall Road | D8 | 7/8 |
| Hallam Street | G7 | 9 |
| Halsey Street | F3 | 3 |
| Hamilton Place | G5 | 3 |
| Hamilton Terrace | C9-D8 | 7/8 |
| Hammersmith Road | A3 | 1 |
| Hampstead Road | H9-H8 | 10 |
| Hannel Road | A1 | 1 |
| Hanover Square | G6 | 9 |
| Hans Crescent | F4 | 3 |
| Hans Place | F4 | 3 |
| Hans Road | E4 | 2 |
| Harcourt Terrace | C2 | 1 |
| Harewood Avenue | E7 | 8 |
| Harley Street | G7 | 9 |
| Harleyford Road | J2 | 5 |
| Harleyford Street | J2-K2 | 5 |
| Harper Road | L4 | 6 |
| Harriet Walk | F4 | 3 |
| Harrington Gardens | C3-D3 | 1 |
| Harrington Road | I1 | 4 |
| Harrow Road | A8-B7 | 7 |
| Hartismere Road | B1 | 1 |
| Hartland Road | A9 | 7 |

| | Map Ref. | Page |
|---|---|---|
| Harvist Road | A9 | 7 |
| Harwood Road | C1 | 1 |
| Hasker Street | E3 | 2 |
| Hastings Street | I8-I9 | 10 |
| Hatfields | K5 | 5 |
| Hatton Garden | K7 | 11 |
| Havil Street | M1 | 6 |
| Hay's Mews | G5 | 3 |
| Hayles Street | K4 | 5 |
| Haymarket | H6 | 10 |
| Haymerle Road | N2 | 5 |
| Henrietta Place | G6-G7 | 9 |
| Hercules Road | J4 | 5 |
| Hereford Road | B6 | 7 |
| Hertford Street | G5 | 3 |
| Hester Road | E1 | 2 |
| Heygate Street | L3 | 6 |
| High Holborn | I1-J7 | 10/11 |
| Hill Gate Place | B5 | 1 |
| Hillingdon Street | K2 | 5 |
| Hill Road | D9 | 7 |
| Hill Street | G6 | 9 |
| Hillsleigh Road | B5 | 1 |
| Hogarth Road | C3 | 1 |
| Holbein Place | F3 | 3 |
| Holborn | J7-K7 | 11 |
| Holborn Viaduct | K7 | 11 |
| Holland Park | A5 | 1 |
| Holland Park Avenue | A5 | 1 |
| Holland Park Mews | A5 | 1 |
| Holland Park Road | B4 | 1 |
| Holland Road | A4 | 1 |
| Holland Street | K6-L5 | 12 |
| Holland Street | B4-C4 | 1 |
| Holland Villas Road | A4 | 1 |
| Holland Walk | B4 | 1 |
| Hollywood Road | C2-D2 | 1 |
| Holyoake Road | K3 | 5 |
| Homestead Road | B1 | 1 |
| Hopton Street | K5-K6 | 5/6 |
| Hornton Street | B4-B5 | 1 |
| Horse Guards Road | I5 | 4 |
| Horseferry Road | H4-I4 | 4 |
| Houndsditch | M7-N7 | 12 |
| Howick Place | H4 | 4 |
| Howland Street | H7 | 10 |
| Hows Street | N9 | 12 |
| Hoxton Square | M9 | 12 |
| Hoxton Street | M9 | 12 |
| Hugh Street | G3 | 3 |
| Humbolt Road | A2 | 1 |
| Huntley Street | H7-H8 | 10 |
| Hyde Park Crescent | E6 | 8 |
| Hyde Park Gate | D4 | 2 |
| Hyde Park Square | E6 | 8 |
| Hyde Park Street | E6 | 8 |
| **I** | | |
| Ifield Road | C2 | 1 |
| Ilbert Street | A8 | 7 |
| Ilchester Place | B4 | 1 |
| Ilton Street | A2 | 1 |
| Inner Circle | F8 | 9 |
| Inverna Gardens | C4 | 1 |
| Inverness Terrace | C6 | 7 |
| Ivor Place | E8-F8 | 8/9 |
| Ivy Street | M9 | 12 |
| Ixworth Place | E3 | 2 |
| **J** | | |
| James Street | G6 | 9 |
| James Street | H6 | 10 |
| Jermyn Street | H5 | 4 |
| Jockey's Fields | J7 | 11 |
| John Adam Street | I6 | 10 |
| John Islip Street | I3 | 4 |
| John Ruskin Street | K2 | 5 |
| John Street | H6 | 10 |
| Jonathan Street | J3 | 5 |

| | Map Ref. | Page |
|---|---|---|
| Jubilee Place | E3 | 2 |
| Judd Street | I8 | 10 |

**K**

| | Map Ref. | Page |
|---|---|---|
| Kempsford Road | K3 | 5 |
| Kennington Lane | J3-K3 | 5 |
| Kennington Oval | J2 | 5 |
| Kennington Park Place | K2 | 5 |
| Kennington Park Road | K2-K3 | 5 |
| Kennington Road | K4-K3 | 5 |
| Kensal Road | A8 | 7 |
| Kensington Church Street | B5-C5 | 1 |
| Kensington High Street | B4-C4 | 1 |
| Kensington Palace Gardens | C5 | 1 |
| Kensington Park Gardens | A5 | 1 |
| Kensington Park Road | A6-B6 | 7 |
| Kensington Place | B5 | 1 |
| Kensington Road | D4 | 1 |
| Kilburn High Road | B9 | 7 |
| Kilburn Lane | A9 | 7 |
| Kilburn Park Road | B8-B9 | 7 |
| Kilburn Priory | C9 | 7 |
| King Charles Street | I5 | 4 |
| King James Street | K4-L4 | 6 |
| King Street | H5 | 4 |
| King William Street | M6 | 12 |
| King's Cross Road | J8-J9 | 11 |
| Kinglake Street | M3 | 6 |
| Kingly Street | H6 | 9 |
| Kings Road | C1-D2- | |
| | E2-F3 | 2/3 |
| Kingsland Road | N9 | 12 |
| Kingsway | J7 | 11 |
| Kingswood Avenue | A9 | 7 |
| Kipling Street | M5 | 6 |
| Knightsbridge | E4-F4 | 2/3 |

**L**

| | Map Ref. | Page |
|---|---|---|
| Ladbroke Grove | A7-A6 | 7 |
| Ladbroke Road | A5-B5 | 1 |
| Ladbroke Square | B5 | 1 |
| Lambeth Bridge | I4 | 4 |
| Lambeth High Street | J3-J4 | 5 |
| Lambeth Palace Road | J4 | 5 |
| Lambeth Road | J4-K4 | 5 |
| Lambeth Walk | J4 | 5 |
| Lamont Road | D2 | 2 |
| Lanark Road | C8 | 7 |
| Lancaster Gate | D6 | 7/8 |
| Lancaster Road | A6 | 7 |
| Langham Place | G7 | 9 |
| Langley Lane | J2 | 5 |
| Langton Road | K1 | 5 |
| Langton Street | D2 | 2 |
| Lansdowne Crescent | A5-A6 | 1/7 |
| Lansdowne Road | A5 | 1 |
| Lansdowne Walk | A5 | 1 |
| Lant Street | L5 | 6 |
| Larcom Street | L3 | 6 |
| Latona Road | N2 | 6 |
| Lauderdale Road | C8 | 7 |
| Lawrence Street | E2 | 2 |
| Launceston Place | C4 | 1 |
| Lavington Street | L5 | 6 |
| Law Street | M4 | 6 |
| Lawn Lane | J2 | 5 |
| Leadenhall Street | M6-N6 | 12 |
| Leather Lane | K7-K8 | 11 |
| Leather Market Street | M5 | 6 |
| Ledbury Road | B6 | 7 |
| Leicester Square | I6 | 10 |
| Leigh Street | I8 | 10 |
| Leinster Gardens | C6 | 7 |
| Leman Street | N6-N7 | 12 |
| Lennox Gardens | F3-F4 | 3 |
| Leonard Street | M8 | 12 |
| Lever Street | L8 | 12 |
| Lexham Gardens | B3-C3 | 1 |
| Liberty Street | J1 | 5 |

| | Map Ref. | Page |
|---|---|---|
| Lillie Road | A1-B2 | 1 |
| Limerston Street | D2 | 2 |
| Lincoln's Inn Fields | J7 | 11 |
| Lisgar Terrace | A3 | 1 |
| Lisle Street | I6 | 10 |
| Lisson Grove | D8-E8 | 8 |
| Liverpool Grove | L3-M3 | 6 |
| Liverpool Street | M7 | 12 |
| Lloyd Baker Street | J8-J9 | 11 |
| Lodge Road | D8-E8 | 8 |
| Logan Place | B3 | 1 |
| Lollard Street | J3 | 5 |
| Lombard Street | M6 | 12 |
| Lomond Grove | L1-M1 | 6 |
| London Bridge | M6 | 12 |
| London Road | K4-L4 | 5/6 |
| London Wall | L7-M7 | 12 |
| Long Acre | I6 | 10 |
| Long Lane | L7 | 12 |
| Long Lane | M5-M4 | 6 |
| Longford Street | G8 | 9 |
| Longridge Road | B3 | 1 |
| Lorrimore Road | L2 | 6 |
| Lothbury | M7 | 12 |
| Lothian Road | K1 | 5 |
| Lots Road | D1 | 2 |
| Loudon Road | D9 | 7/8 |
| Lower Belgrave Street | G4 | 3 |
| Lower Marsh | J4-J5-K5 | 5 |
| Lower Sloane Street | F3 | 3 |
| Lower Thames Street | M6 | 12 |
| Lowndes Square | F4 | 3 |
| Lowndes Street | F4 | 3 |
| Ludgate Hill | K7-K6 | 11/12 |
| Luke Street | M8 | 12 |
| Lupus Street | H2-H3 | 4 |
| Lyall Street | F4 | 3 |
| Lynton Road | N3 | 6 |

**M**

| | Map Ref. | Page |
|---|---|---|
| Maclise Road | A4 | 1 |
| Maddox Street | G6 | 3 |
| Maida Avenue | D7 | 8 |
| Maida Vale | C9-C8 | 7 |
| Maiden Lane | I6 | 10 |
| Malet Street | H8-I7 | 10 |
| Maltby Street | N4-N5 | 6 |
| Malvern Road | B8 | 7 |
| Manciple Street | M4 | 6 |
| Manor Place | L3 | 6 |
| Manresa Road | E2 | 2 |
| Mansell Street | N6-N7 | 12 |
| Marban Road | A8 | 7 |
| Marchmont Street | I8 | 10 |
| Marcia Road | M3-N3 | 6 |
| Margaret Street | G7-H7 | 9/10 |
| Margery Street | J8 | 11 |
| Markham Street | E3 | 2 |
| Marlborough Place | C9 D9 | 7/8 |
| Marloes Road | C3-C4 | 1 |
| Marne Street | A8 | 7 |
| Marshall Street | H6 | 10 |
| Marshalsea Street | L5 | 6 |
| Marsham Street | I3-I4 | 4 |
| Marylands Road | B7-B8 | 7 |
| Marylebone High Street | F7 | 9 |
| Marylebone Lane | G6-G7 | 9 |
| Marylebone Road | E7-F7-G8 | 9/10 |
| Meadow Road | J2 | 5 |
| Mecklenburgh Square | J8 | 11 |
| Medway Street | I4 | 4 |
| Melbury Road | A4-B4 | 1 |
| Melton Street | H8 | 10 |
| Mendora Road | A1 | 1 |
| Merrow Street | L3-M3 | 6 |
| Methley Street | K3 | 5 |
| Micawber Street | L9 | 12 |
| Middlesex Street | N7 | 12 |

| | Map Ref. | Page |
|---|---|---|
| Midland Road | I9 | 10 |
| Miles Street | I2 | 4 |
| Milk Street | L7 | 12 |
| Millbank | I3-I4 | 4 |
| Millman Street | J8 | 11 |
| Milmans Street | D1-D2 | 2 |
| Milson Road | A4 | 1 |
| Mina Road | M3-N3 | 6 |
| Minories | N6 | 12 |
| Mint Street | L5 | 6 |
| Mintern Street | M9 | 12 |
| Mirabel Road | B1 | 1 |
| Monck Street | I4 | 4 |
| Monmouth Street | I6-I7 | 10 |
| Montagu Square | F7 | 9 |
| Montagu Place | I7 | 10 |
| Montague Street | I7 | 10 |
| Montford Place | J2-K2 | 5 |
| Montpelier Street | E4 | 2 |
| Moore Park Road | C1 | 1 |
| Moore Street | F3 | 3 |
| Moorfields | M7 | 12 |
| Moorgate | M7 | 12 |
| Moorhouse Road | B6 | 7 |
| Morat Street | J1 | 5 |
| Morecambe Street | L3 | 6 |
| Moreland Street | K9-L9 | 12 |
| Moreton Place | H3 | 4 |
| Morley Street | K4 | 5 |
| Mornington Crescent | G9 | 9 |
| Mornington Terrace | G9 | 9 |
| Morpeth Terrace | H4 | 4 |
| Morshead Road | B8-C8 | 7 |
| Mortimer Street | G7-H7 | 9/10 |
| Moscow Road | C6 | 7 |
| Motcomb Street | F4 | 3 |
| Mount Row | G6 | 9 |
| Mount Street | F6-G6 | 9 |
| Mowll Street | J1-K1 | 5 |
| Moylan Road | A2 | 1 |
| Munster Road | A1 | 1 |
| Munton Road | L4 | 6 |
| Murray Grove | L9-M9 | 12 |
| Musard Road | A2 | 1 |
| Museum Street | I7 | 10 |
| Myddleton Street | K8-K9 | 11 |

**N**

| | Map Ref. | Page |
|---|---|---|
| Neal Street | I6-I7 | 10 |
| Neate Street | M2-N2 | 6 |
| Nevern Square | B3 | 1 |
| New Bond Street | G6 | 9 |
| New Bridge Street | K6 | 11 |
| New Cavendish Street | G7 | 9 |
| New Change | L6-L7 | 12 |
| New Church Road | L2-M2 | 6 |
| New Compton Street | I6-I7 | 10 |
| New Kent Road | L4-M4 | 6 |
| New North Road | M9 | 12 |
| New Oxford Street | I7 | 10 |
| Newburn Street | J3 | 5 |
| Newcomen Street | L5-M5 | 6 |
| Newgate Street | K7-L7 | 12 |
| Newington Butts | K3-L3 | 6 |
| Newington Causeway | L4 | 6 |
| Newman Street | H7 | 10 |
| Newton Road | B6-C6 | 7 |
| Newton Street | I7 | 10 |
| Nile Street | L9-M9 | 12 |
| Nine Elms Lane | H2-I2 | 4 |
| Noel Road | K9-L9 | 12 |
| Norfolk Crescent | E6-E7 | 8 |
| Norfolk Square | D6 | 8 |
| Norland Square | A5 | 1 |
| Normand Road | A2 | 1 |
| North Carriage Drive | E6 | 8 |
| North End Road | A3-A2-B1 | 1 |
| North Gower Street | H8 | 10 |

| | Map Ref. | Page |
|---|---|---|
| North Row | F6 | 9 |
| Northington Street | J8 | 11 |
| Northumberland Avenue | I5 | 4 |
| Notting Hill Gate | B5 | 1 |
| **O** | | |
| Oakley Street | E2 | 2 |
| Oakwood Court | A4 | 1 |
| Old Bailey | K7 | 11/12 |
| Old Bond Street | H6 | 10 |
| Old Broad Street | M7 | 12 |
| Old Brompton Road | C3-D3 | 1/2 |
| Old Church Street | D2-E2 | 2 |
| Old Compton Street | H6-I6 | 10 |
| Old Kent Road | M3-N3 | 6 |
| Old Marylebone Road | E7 | 8 |
| Old Park Lane | G5 | 3 |
| Old Pye Street | H4-I4 | 4 |
| Old Street | L8-M8 | 12 |
| Olney Road | L2 | 6 |
| Olympia Way | A3-A4 | 1 |
| Ongar Road | B2 | 1 |
| Onslow Gardens | D3 | 2 |
| Onslow Square | D3-E3 | 2 |
| Ontario Street | L4 | 6 |
| Orb Street | M3 | 6 |
| Orbain Road | A1 | 1 |
| Orchard Street | F6 | 9 |
| Orchardson Street | D7-D8 | 8 |
| Ordnance Hill | D9 | 8 |
| Orme Lane | C6 | 7 |
| Orsell Terrace | C6-C7 | 7 |
| Ossington Street | B6-C6 | 7 |
| Ossory Road | N2-N3 | 6 |
| Ossulston Street | H9-I9 | 10 |
| Oswin Street | K4 | 6 |
| Outer Circle | F9-G9-G8-F8 | 9 |
| Oval Place | J1 | 5 |
| Oval Way | J2 | 5 |
| Oxford Gardens | A7 | 7 |
| Oxford Road | B9 | 7 |
| Oxford Street | F6-G6-H7 | 9/10 |
| **P** | | |
| Paddington Street | F7 | 9 |
| Page Street | I3 | 4 |
| Pages Walk | M4 | 6 |
| Palace Court | C6 | 7 |
| Palace Gardens Terrace | B5-C5 | 1 |
| Palace Gate | C4 | 1 |
| Palace Street | H4 | 4 |
| Palfrey Place | J1-J2 | 5 |
| Pall Mall | H5 | 4 |
| Pancras Road | H9-I9 | 10 |
| Pardoner Street | M4 | 6 |
| Paris Garden | K5 | 5 |
| Park Crescent | G8 | 9 |
| Park Lane | F6-F5 | 3/9 |
| Park Road | E8 | 8 |
| Park Street | F6 | 9 |
| Park Street | L5-L6 | 6/12 |
| Park Village East | G9 | 9 |
| Park Walk | D2 | 2 |
| Parker Street | I7-J7 | 10/11 |
| Parkgate Road | E1 | 2 |
| Parliament Square | I4 | 4 |
| Parry Street | I2 | 4 |
| Pascal Street | I1 | 4 |
| Patmos Road | K1 | 5 |
| Paul Street | M8 | 12 |
| Pavillion Road | F3-F4 | 3 |
| Pearman Street | K4 | 5 |
| Peckham Grove | M2 | 6 |
| Peckham Hill Street | N1-N2 | 6 |
| Peckham Road | N | 6 |
| Peel Street | B5 | 1 |
| Pelham Crescent | E3 | 2 |
| Pelham Street | E3 | 2 |

| | Map Ref. | Page |
|---|---|---|
| Pembridge Crescent | B6 | 7 |
| Pembridge Place | B6 | 7 |
| Pembridge Road | B5-B6 | 1/7 |
| Pembridge Square | B6 | 7 |
| Pembridge Villas | B6 | 7 |
| Pembroke Road | B3 | 1 |
| Penfold Street | D7-E7 | 8 |
| Penrose Street | L3 | 6 |
| Penton Place | K3-L3 | 6 |
| Penton Rise | J9 | 11 |
| Penton Street | J9 | 11 |
| Pentonville Road | J9 | 11 |
| Penywern Road | B3-C3 | 1 |
| Pepys Street | N6 | 12 |
| Percival Street | K8 | 11 |
| Perham Road | A2 | 1 |
| Petty France | H4 | 4 |
| Philbeach Gardens | B3 | 1 |
| Phoenix Road | H9 | 10 |
| Piccadilly | G5-H5 | 3/4 |
| Picton Street | M1 | 6 |
| Pilgrimage Street | L4-M4-M5 | 6 |
| Pimlico Road | F3-G3 | 3 |
| Pitfield Street | M8-M9 | 12 |
| Pocock Street | K5-L5 | 6 |
| Poland Street | H6-H7 | 10 |
| Polygon Road | H9 | 10 |
| Pond Place | E3 | 2 |
| Ponsonby Place | I3 | 4 |
| Pont Street | F4 | 3 |
| Ponton Road | I2 | 4 |
| Porchester Gardens | C6 | 7 |
| Porchester Terrace | C6 | 7 |
| Portland Place | G7 | 9 |
| Portland Road | A5 | 1 |
| Portland Street | M3 | 6 |
| Portman Square | F6-F7 | 9 |
| Portman Street | F6 | 9 |
| Portnall Road | A8 | 7 |
| Portobello Road | A7-A6-B6 | 7 |
| Portugal Street | J7 | 11 |
| Poultry | L7-L6 | 12 |
| Praed Street | D6-D7 | 8 |
| Prince Albert Road | E9-F9 | 8/9 |
| Prince's Gardens | D4-E4 | 2 |
| Princedale Road | A5 | 1 |
| Princelet Street | N7 | 12 |
| Princess Road | B9 | 7 |
| Protheroe Road | A1 | 1 |
| Provost Street | M9 | 12 |
| Purcell Street | M9 | 12 |
| **Q** | | |
| Quaker Street | N8 | 12 |
| Queen Elizabeth Street | N5 | 6 |
| Queen Square | I8 | 10 |
| Queen Street | L6 | 12 |
| Queen Victoria Street | L6 | 12 |
| Queen's Gate | D4 | 2 |
| Queen's Gate Terrace | D4 | 2 |
| Queen's Grove | D9 | 8 |
| Queens Club Gardens | A2 | 1 |
| Queens Gate Gardens | C6-D6 | 7 |
| Queens Gate Gardens | D3-D4 | 2 |
| Queensborough Terrace | C6 | 7 |
| Queensbridge Road | N6 | 12 |
| Queenstown Road | G1-G2 | 3 |
| Queensway | C6 | 7 |
| **R** | | |
| Racton Road | B2 | 1 |
| Radnor Street | L8 | 12 |
| Radnor Walk | E2 | 2 |
| Randolph Avenue | C9-C8 | 7 |
| Rathbone Place | H7 | 10 |
| Ravenscroft Street | N9 | 12 |
| Rawlings Street | E3-F3 | 2/3 |
| Red Church Street | N8 | 12 |
| Red Lion Square | J7 | 11 |

| | Map Ref. | Page |
|---|---|---|
| Red Lion Street | J7 | 11 |
| Redburn Street | E2-F2 | 2/3 |
| Redcar Street | L1 | 6 |
| Redcliffe Gardens | C2 | 1 |
| Redcross Way | L5 | 6 |
| Redfield Lane | B3-C3 | 1 |
| Redhill Street | G9 | 9 |
| Reeves Mews | F6 | 9 |
| Regency Street | I3 | 4 |
| Regent Street | G7-H6 | 9/10 |
| Renfrew Road | K3 | 5 |
| Reverdy Road | N3 | 6 |
| Riding House Street | G7-H7 | 9/10 |
| Riley Road | N4 | 6 |
| Riley Street | D1 | 2 |
| Rivington Street | M8-N8 | 12 |
| Robert Street | G8 | 9 |
| Rochester Row | H3-H4 | 4 |
| Rockingham Street | L4 | 6 |
| Rodney Road | L3-M3 | 6 |
| Rodney Street | J9 | 11 |
| Roland Gardens | D3 | 2 |
| Rolls Road | N3 | 6 |
| Romilly Street | H6-I6 | 10 |
| Rosaline Road | A1 | 1 |
| Rosaville Road | A1 | 1 |
| Roseberry Avenue | J8-K8 | 11 |
| Rossmore Road | E8 | 8 |
| Rothsay Street | M4 | 6 |
| Rouel Road | N4 | 6 |
| Roupell Street | K5 | 5 |
| Rowallen Road | A1 | 1 |
| Royal Avenue | F3 | 3 |
| Royal Hospital Road | F2-F3 | 3 |
| Royal Mint Street | N6 | 12 |
| Royal Street | J4 | 5 |
| Rupert Street | H6 | 10 |
| Russell Road | A4 | 1 |
| Russell Square | I7-I8 | 10 |
| Rutland Gate | E4 | 2 |
| Rylstone Road | A1-B1 | 1 |
| **S** | | |
| St Agnes Place | K2 | 5 |
| St Albans Grove | C4 | 1 |
| St Edmund's Terrace | E9 | 7 |
| St George Street | G6 | 9 |
| St George's Circus | K4 | 5 |
| St George's Drive | G3-H3 | 3/4 |
| St George's Road | K4 | 5 |
| St George's Square | H3-H2 | 4 |
| St George's Way | M2-N2 | 6 |
| St Giles High Street | I7 | 10 |
| St Giles Road | M1 | 6 |
| St James's Gardens | A5 | 1 |
| St James's Square | H5 | 4 |
| St James's Street | H5 | 4 |
| St John Street | K7-K8-K9 | 11 |
| St John's Wood High Street | D9-E9 | 8 |
| St John's Wood Road | D8-E8 | 8 |
| St John's Wood Terrace | D9-E9 | 8 |
| St John's Gardens | A5 | 1 |
| St Leonard's Terrace | F3 | 3 |
| St Luke's Road | A7-B7 | 7 |
| St Mark's Road | A6 | 7 |
| St Martins Lane | I6 | 10 |
| St Mary Axe | M7 | 12 |
| St Michael's Street | D7-E7 | 8 |
| St Olaf's Road | A1 | 1 |
| St Thomas Street | M5 | 6 |
| Saffron Hill | K7-K8 | 11 |
| Salisbury Road | A9 | 7 |
| Salisbury Street | E7 | 8 |
| Saltram Crescent | B8 | 7 |
| Sancroft Street | J3-K3 | 5 |
| Savile Row | G6-H6 | 9/10 |
| Savoy Place | I6-J6 | 10/11 |
| Savoy Street | J6 | 11 |

| | Map Ref. | Page |
|---|---|---|
| Scalter Street | N8 | 12 |
| Scarsdale Villas | B4-C4 | 1 |
| Scrutton Street | M8 | 12 |
| Seagrave Road | B2-C2 | 1 |
| Sedlescombe Road | B2 | 1 |
| Sekforde Street | K8 | 11 |
| Seymour Place | E7 | 8 |
| Seymour Street | E6 | 8 |
| Seymour Walk | D2 | 1/2 |
| Shad Thames | N5 | 6 |
| Shaftesbury Avenue | H6-I6 | 10 |
| Sharrolds Road | B1 | 1 |
| Sheffield Terrace | B5 | 1 |
| Shelton Street | I6-I7 | 10 |
| Shepherd Street | G5 | 3 |
| Shepherdess Walk | L9 | 12 |
| Sherbrooke Road | A1 | 1 |
| Shirland Road | B8-C8 | 7 |
| Shoe Lane | K7 | 11 |
| Shoreditch High Street | N8 | 12 |
| Sidmouth Street | I8-J8 | 10/11 |
| Sidney Street | E2-E3 | 2 |
| Silk Street | L7 | 12 |
| Skinner Street | K8 | 11 |
| Sleaford Street | H1 | 4 |
| Sloane Avenue | E3 | 2 |
| Sloane Gardens | F3 | 3 |
| Sloane Street | F3-F4 | 3 |
| Smith Square | I4 | 4 |
| Smith Street | F3-F2 | 3 |
| Snowsfields | M5 | 6 |
| Soho Square | H7 | 10 |
| South Audley Street | F5-F6 | 3/9 |
| South Carriage Drive | E4-F5 | 2/3 |
| South Eaton Place | F3-G3 | 3 |
| South Island Place | J1-K1 | 5 |
| South Lambeth Road | J2-I2-J1 | 4/5 |
| South Parade | D3-E3 | 2 |
| South Street | F5-G5 | 3 |
| South Terrace | E3 | 2 |
| Southampton Row | I7-J7 | 10 |
| Southampton Way | M1-M2-N1 | 6 |
| Southern Row | A7 | 7 |
| Southey Road | J1-K1 | 5 |
| Southwark Bridge | L6 | 12 |
| Southwark Bridge Road | L5 | 6 |
| Southwark Street | L5 | 6 |
| Spa Road | N4 | 6 |
| Spencer Street | K9 | 11 |
| Spital Square | N7 | 12 |
| Stafford Road | B8-B9 | 7 |
| Stafford Terrace | B4 | 1 |
| Stag Place | H4 | 4 |
| Stamford Street | J5-K5 | 5 |
| Stanford Road | C4 | 1 |
| Stanhope Gardens | D3 | 2 |
| Stanhope Street | G8-G9 | 9 |
| Stanhope Terrace | D6 | 8 |
| Stanley Crescent | A6 | 7 |
| Stannary Street | K2 | 5 |
| Stanway Street | N9 | 12 |
| Star Road | A2-B2 | 1 |
| Star Street | E7 | 8 |
| Stead Street | L3-M3 | 6 |
| Stewart's Lane | H1 | 4 |
| Store Street | H7 | 10 |
| Strand | I6-J6 | 10 |
| Stratford Road | B4-C4 | 1 |
| Stratton Street | G5 | 3 |
| Sturgeon Road | L3 | 6 |
| Sumner Place | D3-E3 | 2 |
| Sumner Road | N1-N2 | 6 |
| Sumner Street | L5 | 6 |
| Sun Street | M7 | 12 |
| Surrey Square | M3 | 6 |
| Sussex Gardens | D6-E6 | 8 |
| Sussex Place | D6-E6 | 8 |
| Sussex Street | H3 | 4 |
| Sutherland Avenue | B7-C7-C8 | 7 |
| Sutherland Street | G3 | 3 |
| Sutherland Walk | 6 | |
| Swanfield Street | N8 | 12 |
| Swinton Street | J9 | 11 |
| **T** | | |
| Tabard Street | M4 | 6 |
| Tabernacle Street | M8 | 12 |
| Tachbrook Street | H3 | 4 |
| Tadema Road | D1 | 2 |
| Talbot Road | B6 | 7 |
| Talgarth Road | A2-A3 | 1 |
| Tanner Street | M5-N5 | 6 |
| Tavistock Place | I8 | 10 |
| Tavistock Road | A7 | 7 |
| Tavistock Square | H8-I8 | 10 |
| Tavistock Street | I6-J6 | 10 |
| Tedworth Square | F2 | 3 |
| Temple Avenue | K6 | 11 |
| Templton Place | B3 | 1 |
| Telcott Road | D1 | 1/2 |
| The Boltons | C3-D3-C2-D2 | 1 |
| The Cut | K5 | 5 |
| The Littleboltons | C2 | 1 |
| The Mall | H5-I5 | 4 |
| The Parade | F1-F2 | 3 |
| The Vale | D2 | 2 |
| Theed Street | K5 | 5 |
| Theobald's Road | J7-J8 | 10 |
| Thessaly Road | H1 | 4 |
| Third Avenue | A8 | 7 |
| Thorne Road | I1 | 4 |
| Thorparch Road | I1 | 4 |
| Threadneedle Street | M7 | 12 |
| Throgmorton Street | M7 | 12 |
| Thurloe Place | D3-E3-E4 | 2 |
| Thurloe Square | E3-E4 | 2 |
| Thurlow Street | M3 | 6 |
| Tite Street | F2 | 3 |
| Tooley Street | M5-N5 | 6 |
| Torrington Place | H8 | 10 |
| Tottenham Court Road | H8-H7 | 10 |
| Tournay Road | B1 | 1 |
| Tower Bridge | N5 | 6 |
| Tower Bridge Road | M4-N4-N5 | 6 |
| Tower Hill | N6 | 6 |
| Townshend Road | E9 | 8 |
| Trafalgar Avenue | N2-N3 | 6 |
| Trafalgar Square | I5-I6 | 4/10 |
| Trebovir Road | B3-C3 | 1 |
| Tregunter Road | C2-D2 | 1 |
| Trevor Place | E4 | 2 |
| Trigon Road | J2 | 5 |
| Trinity Square | N6 | 12 |
| Trinity Street | L4 | 6 |
| Tudor Street | K6 | 11 |
| Tufton Street | I4 | 4 |
| Turk's Row | F3 | 3 |
| Turnmill Street | K7-K8 | 11 |
| Tyers Street | J3 | 5 |
| **U** | | |
| Ulford Street | K5 | 5 |
| Urlwin Street | L2 | 6 |
| Union Street | K5-L5 | 6 |
| Upcerne Road | D1 | 1/2 |
| Upper Berkeley Street | F6 | 9 |
| Upper Brook Street | F6 | 9 |
| Upper Grosvenor Street | F6 | 9 |
| Upper Ground | J5-K5-K6 | 5/11 |
| Upper Street | K4 | 5 |
| Upper Thames Street | K6-L6-M6 | 12 |
| Upper Woburn Place | H8-I8 | 10 |
| Uverdale Road | D1 | 2 |
| Uxbridge Street | B5 | 1 |
| **V** | | |
| Vassal Road | K1 | 5 |
| Vauxhall Bridge | I3 | 4 |
| Vauxhall Bridge Road | H4-H3 | 4 |
| Vauxhall Street | J2-J3 | 5 |
| Vauxhall Walk | J3 | 5 |
| Vere Street | G6 | 9 |
| Vicarage Gardens | C5 | 1 |
| Victoria Embankment | J6 | 11 |
| Victoria Road | A9-B9 | 7 |
| Victoria Road | C4 | 1 |
| Victoria Street | H4 | 4 |
| Vincent Square | H3-H4 | 4 |
| Vincent Street | H3-I3 | 4 |
| Vine Lane | M5-N5 | 6 |
| Virginia Road | N8-N9 | 12 |
| **W** | | |
| Walham Grove | B1-B2 | 1 |
| Walmer Road | A6 | 7 |
| Walnut Tree Walk | J4-K4 | 5 |
| Walterton Road | B8 | 7 |
| Walton Street | E3-E4 | 2 |
| Walworth Road | L3 | 6 |
| Wandon Road | C1 | 1 |
| Wandsworth Road | I1-I2 | 4 |
| Wardour Street | H6-H7 | 10 |
| Warren Street | G8-H8 | 9/10 |
| Warrington Crescent | C7-C8 | 7 |
| Warwick Avenue | C7-C8 | 7 |
| Warwick Gardens | B3 | 1 |
| Warwick Road | B3 | 1 |
| Warwick Square | H3 | 4 |
| Warwick Street | H6 | 10 |
| Warwick Way | G3-H3 | 3/4 |
| Waterloo Bridge | J6 | 11 |
| Waterloo Road | K5-K4 | 5 |
| Watling Street | L6 | 12 |
| Webber Street | K5-L5 | 5/6 |
| Welbeck Street | G7 | 9 |
| Wellington Road | D9-E9 | 8 |
| Wells Street | H7 | 10 |
| Wells Way | M2 | 6 |
| Wenlock Road | L9 | 12 |
| Wenlock Street | L9-M9 | 12 |
| Wentworth Street | N7 | 12 |
| Wescott Road | K2 | 6 |
| West Carriage Drive | E5-E6 | 2/8 |
| West Cromwell Road | A3-B3 | 1 |
| West Drive | F1 | 3 |
| West Square | K4 | 5 |
| Westbourne Grove | B6-C6 | 7 |
| Westbourne Park Road | A6-B7 | 7 |
| Westbourne Park Road | B7-C7 | 7 |
| Westbourne Park Villas | B7-C7 | 7 |
| Westbourne Terrace | C7-D6 | 7/8 |
| Westgate Terrace | C2 | 1 |
| Westminster Bridge | I4-J4 | 4/5 |
| Westminster Bridge Road | J4-K4 | 5 |
| Westmoreland Road | L2-M2 | 6 |
| Westmoreland Terrace | G2-G3 | 3 |
| Weston Street | M4-M5 | 6 |
| Westway | D7 | 8 |
| Wetherby Gardens | C3 | 1 |
| Weymouth Street | G7 | 9 |
| Weymouth Terrace | N9 | 12 |
| Wharf Road | L9 | 12 |
| Whardale Road | I9 | 10 |
| Wharton Street | J9 | 11 |
| Whitcomb Street | I6 | 10 |
| White Lion Street | J9-K9 | 11 |
| Whitechapel Road | N7 | 12 |
| Whitecross Street | L8 | 12 |
| Whitefriars Street | K6 | 11 |
| Whitehall | I5 | 4 |
| Whitehall Place | I5 | 4 |
| Whitehead's Grove | E3 | 2 |
| Whitfield Street | H7-H8 | 10 |

| | Map Ref. | Page |
|---|---|---|
| Wicklow Street | I9-J9 | 10/11 |
| Widley Road | B8 | 7 |
| Wigmore Street | F6-F7-G7 | 9 |
| Wilcox Road | I1 | 4 |
| Wild Street | I7-J7 | 10/11 |
| Wilkinson Street | J1 | 5 |
| Willowbrick Road | N2 | 6 |
| Willow Place | H3 | 4 |
| Willow Walk | N4-N3 | 6 |
| Wilson Street | M7-M8 | 12 |
| Wilton Crescent | F4 | 3 |
| Wilton Place | F4 | 3 |
| Wilton Road | H3-H4 | 4 |

| | Map Ref. | Page |
|---|---|---|
| Wimpole Street | G7 | 9 |
| Winchester Street | G3-H3 | 3/4 |
| Wincott Street | K3 | 5 |
| Woburn Place | I8 | 10 |
| Wood Street | L7 | 12 |
| Wooller Street | M3 | 6 |
| Worfield Street | E1 | 2 |
| Wornington Road | A7 | 7 |
| Woronzow Road | A7 | 7 |
| Worship Street | M8 | 12 |
| Wright's Lane | C4 | 1 |
| Wyndham Road | L1 | 6 |
| Wynford Road | J9 | 11 |

| | Map Ref. | Page |
|---|---|---|
| Wyvil Road | I2 | 4 |

**Y**

| | Map Ref. | Page |
|---|---|---|
| Yalding Road | N4 | 6 |
| Yeoman's Row | E4 | 2 |
| York Gate | F8 | 9 |
| York House Place | C5 | 1 |
| York Road | J5 | 5 |
| York Street | E7-F7 | 9 |
| York Terrace | F8 | 9 |
| York Way | I9 | 10 |
| Young Street | C4 | 1 |